LOCA

BIG CYRIL

BIG CYRIL

Cyril Smith MBE, MP

W. H. ALLEN · London
A Howard & Wyndham Company
1977

Copyright © by Cyril Smith MBE, MP, 1977

This book or parts thereof may not be
reproduced without permission in writing

Printed and bound in Great Britain by
Butler & Tanner Ltd, Frome and London,
for the Publishers, W. H. Allen & Co. Ltd,
44 Hill Street, London W1X 8LB
ISBN 0 491 02261 1

46530531

Dedication

To my mother, without whom none of this would have been possible.

Acknowledgements

I wish to pay a very special tribute to, and say a special 'thank you' to my good friend John Sheard. Without his real help and literary expertise, this book would not have been possible. I am most grateful to him and I place on record not only my appreciation, but my deep respect for his writing ability, and his help in that direction.

I would also like to give my thanks to Carole Anne for her excellent typing of the manuscript.

Contents

		Page
CHAPTER ONE:	Arrival	1
CHAPTER TWO:	Thru'penny Wrap-ups	15
CHAPTER THREE:	Religion and Politics	33
CHAPTER FOUR:	Breakfasts	46
CHAPTER FIVE:	Gas-lamps and Grammar Schools	64
CHAPTER SIX:	The Mayor Walks Out	84
CHAPTER SEVEN:	'The Cart-horse will Win this Race'	102
CHAPTER EIGHT:	'The Longest Running Farce in the West End'	123
CHAPTER NINE:	Gains and Losses	144
CHAPTER TEN:	Coalition...and Bribery	159
CHAPTER ELEVEN:	Scandal	177
CHAPTER TWELVE:	Where Now, Land Without Leaders?	213
Index		237

CHAPTER ONE

Arrival

It was one of the most curious nights in recent years in the Palace of Westminster, a place not unknown for curious happenings.

In the Chamber of the House of Commons, MPs were discussing Denis Healey's 1976 Finance Bill, which would allow the electorate of the United Kingdom tax reductions if people they had not voted for – the leaders of the Trades Union Congress – agreed to another year of pay restraint.

From the point of view of practical politics, it was not a bad idea. For democracy, it seemed to be sowing the seeds of disaster. Never before in history had the Chancellor of the Exchequer delegated the right to fix the nation's Budget to a powerful *minority* of men whose right to influence had never been tested at a ballot box open to the public at large.

The move had inflamed large sections of the public, Parliament and the press and, of course, the small group of Liberal MPs were equally concerned. Sadly, we had other worries. The so-called Jeremy Thorpe 'affair' had broken round our ears, with allegations of homosexuality, blackmail and cover-up. In Fleet Street, papers were acting as though they had uncovered the British Watergate, a totally absurd parallel.

It was not a happy night as I perched uncomfortably on a straight-backed wooden chair in Emlyn Hooson's room. Like many members' rooms at Westminster, it is half-panelled, cramped and dark – you need a table lamp on your desk even to write a letter. In the dismal hours of the early morning, Emlyn, a brilliant QC and Liberal member for Montgomeryshire, and I had been reminiscing fretfully.

A few months previously, Emlyn had turned down a Judgeship to continue his work as MP. He looked at me sadly and said, with just the trace of a sob in his voice: 'Do you know, Cyril, if you look round the Liberal members here, we are not a bad lot really. We have our personal faults, of course, and our Parliamentary failings, but it would be difficult to find another small group of people as dedicated and idealistic as us. We didn't ask to happen what has happened. I'm sure we don't really deserve it.'

I looked away and, for once, said nothing. There was nothing to be said. Emlyn had touched a raw nerve, an unspoken thought that had been lying just below the surface of my consciousness for some time. The truth was, I had never asked for anything to happen, at least in a Parliamentary way. In a lifetime which had been carefully planned, and in which I had achieved most of my major ambitions, I had never set out my stall to become a Member of Parliament.

As an illegitimate baby born in the back streets of Rochdale, I started life as a total 'nobody'. As a small boy – so small that I can no longer remember making the decision – I decided I wanted to be 'somebody'. When I stood for the first time in the Town Hall Square in Rochdale and saw the Mayor stride down the steps, complete with gown and chain of office, I decided that was the 'somebody' I wanted to be. And I did become the Mayor of Rochdale.

As a ragged-arsed kid, dressed in secondhand clothes, I knew the grinding poverty of a cotton town in the thirties. I decided I wanted to be prosperous, if not actually wealthy. I did that too. I am the principal shareholder in a spring factory, and am one of those people the Labour party has decided to 'soak'; in 1975 I paid twenty times more in income tax alone than I earned in the year after I left school.

But at no time – at least not until six years ago – did I ever think I would become an MP. That came virtually by accident, by submitting to pressures from friends and colleagues, including the very persuasive Jeremy Thorpe.

I suppose the thought of going to Westminster never really convinced me. Perhaps, with my background, I subconsciously felt that this was an objective beyond my reach. I now know if that *were* the case, I had deluded myself for the first forty years of my life. In all truth, it is much more difficult to become Mayor of Rochdale than an MP. With my present knowledge of the political system, I could take any promising eighteen year old with Parliamentary ambitions and, by playing the right game, could guarantee to have him or her in the Commons within twenty years.

I just could not make that claim for someone who wanted to be Mayor of Rochdale, or any other town for that matter.

My political career began as a teenager with the Liberals. At the age of seventeen, I was a national executive member of the Young Liberals, and became the party's youngest full-time agent. It wasn't to last. After policy disagreements during the 1950 General Election, I quit and joined the Labour party. I had plans then and for many years Labour was the party to help me carry them through.

In twenty-two years as a Councillor and Alderman in Rochdale, fourteen of them as Labour, I helped along the building of houses, the reorganisation of schools, and pushed for better welfare services for the old folk. In 1966, I became Mayor — and quit the Labour party after internecine rows which left the people of Rochdale astonished. The decision to quit was, frankly, rash and impetuous. But there are times when I am a rash and impetuous man, something which is no longer Britain's best-kept secret.

For two years, I soldiered on in local government as an independent. I had, in many ways, decided that my political career was more or less over. My spring business was thriving, and council houses and new schools which had sprung up around Rochdale were at least bricks and mortar monuments to the work I had done. It was time, I thought, to concentrate on business, to take things a little easier.

It was in 1968 that I decided to rejoin the Liberal party. It was a difficult decision, for it meant a new commitment. It would also mean more echoes of the cry 'turncoat', shouted after every public man in history who has changed parties. I didn't see it in the way that I had changed. For me, it was the *party* which had changed. In any case, the man who changes his mind admits that he is wiser today than he was yesterday.

For some years the alarm bells within me had been sounding louder and louder at the direction the Labour party was taking. It had ceased to be representative of the ordinary man. The desire to serve had been replaced by the lust for power. Like the Tories, whom I have always opposed, Labour was building a monolith to protect the entrenched interests of a tiny minority of its supporters – in this case, the extreme Left. A party which wins votes on the promise that it will protect the interests of the ordinary man, when it in fact is organising the ordinary man in the interests of the party, is, to me, downright fraudulent.

This appears to have become obvious to many millions of traditional Labour supporters in recent years. After all, the present Labour government rules on a minority of support from the country. Ten years ago, however, the drift to the Left was more secretive, more underhand. But to the insider, the signposts were there to read.

So I went back to the Liberals in 1968, not quite sure of the welcome I would receive, hesitant to think of what future – if any – I had within the party.

I was sure of only one thing. That the Liberals, with their freedom from vested interests, were blowing fresh air into the cobwebbed corners of the British political mind. Their attitudes towards industrial relations, welfare and Europe, were based on good sense and an optimistic view of the future.

They were, thank God, engaged in disentangling politics from the curse of the class system. It would be difficult to find three more diverse areas in Britain than Orpington, Roxburgh and Rochdale. What do the well-heeled commuters of Orpington, the farmers of Roxburgh and the cotton workers of Rochdale hold in common? Very little in wealth, lifestyle or religion. But as voters, they had taken part in – or were about to take part in – a great resurgence in Liberalism. That in itself must give the Liberal party great strength.

So I rejoined this party, offering to serve but in no way anticipating any honours. In 1970, I reluctantly agreed to stand as Parliamentary candidate in the General Election. My reluctance, I admit, was partly due to the knowledge that I was sure I would lose. My main opponent, Labour's Jack McCann, was an old friend and a popular sitting member. I knew just how popular he was. In one of the twists of fate which seem to pepper my life, I had been chairman of Rochdale Labour party in 1958 when Jack won the seat for the first time.

In 1970, I knew he would win – and I was right. He polled

ARRIVAL

19,247 votes to my 14,076 – a Labour majority of 5,171. I went back to Liberal party HQ in Rochdale that night an unhappy man. There were just eight people in the committee rooms!

It was the first time I had ever lost an election, and the eight faithful helpers who stayed behind to say, 'Hard luck, Cyril, better luck next time,' were little consolation. There wouldn't be a next time, I was sure of that.

I hated losing, and I always have hated it. I don't think it is because I am a bad loser – I don't envy the winner his success. But deep down in me, there is a stubbornness, a determination that I must win. I imagine it stems from those early days when every obstacle seemed so big. It was apparent very early that to make anything of my life, I had to try harder than most people.

It is difficult to remember in these permissive days the slur that illegitimacy once carried. The very week I was born, Rochdale Corporation had decided against allowing mixed bathing in its public baths. My local newspaper, the *Rochdale Observer*, carried an angry letter under the headline 'Mixed Bathing and Morals'.

Added to this, I was poor, at a time when poverty was looked upon as a self-indulgent vice rather than a sorry condition worthy of welfare and assistance. Although I managed to win a place at the local grammar school, I never had a circle of prosperous and well-connected friends to discreetly help my career along.

Thirdly, I was fat, an accident resulting from a childhood illness which could not be overcome by either diet or exercise. I began to grow fat in my early teens, and I remained fat for the rest of my life. Everyone can quote examples of attractive women whose lives and careers have been notably advanced by their beauty. But there is also a type of man, slender, quietly spoken and well dressed, who carries about with him a natural authority which is quite contrary to his intellectual or organisational abilities. Not by the wildest stretch of imagination of the world's greatest flatterer could I be called slim. I am not quietly spoken – I like to say my piece and I like it to be heard. And I have never been well dressed: in the days when I wanted to be, I couldn't afford it. Even now, an ordinary suit costs me a hundred and fifty pounds and, anyway, I decided a long time ago that any thought of dandyism would be a ludicrous waste of time and effort. Self-deception is not one of my traits.

I had, however, managed to overcome all these disadvantages to become, in Rochdale and the North-West at least, a man of some reputation. The 1970 General Election was the first major defeat I had ever suffered, either politically or personally, and I didn't like the feeling one little bit. I decided that it was to be my first and last attempt to enter Parliament.

It is curious now, in view of the events of the spring and summer of 1976, that the man who changed my mind was Jeremy Thorpe.

My old friend and, latterly, bitter critic, Jack McCann – one of many men life seems to have set me in conflict with – died after an illness in 1972, and Rochdale was set for a by-election. My suggestion for the candidate was Dr Michael Winstanley, the Cheshire GP and former MP, a television personality who argued the Liberal cause with wit and wisdom. The party had other ideas. Jeremy Thorpe phoned me from his home in Barnstaple and said: 'Cyril, we think you are the man. If you agree to stand, I will personally throw the whole weight of the Liberal party behind you. You can have our best agent, our best workers. I'll gamble my reputation that you will win.'

Jeremy, as I have already said, is a very persuasive man. And perhaps he could be right, I thought. There would be a new Labour man, Ted Heath's government was going through a period of unpopularity, and I would have a virtual army of supporters from all over the country. I accepted the nomination.

So in the early hours of 27 October 1972, I stood in Rochdale Town Hall, architecturally a minor Victorian Gothic masterpiece which has so often been compared in style to the Houses of Parliament, and heard the results read out. Two years earlier, I had lost by 5,171 votes. Now I had neatly reversed that result, winning by 5,093.

It was time to swap the Victorian Gothic of Rochdale for the bigger model in the City of Westminster.

My life, like most, has several high spots. Winning my scholarship to grammar school was one, being elected a Councillor for the first time another. I have already made clear that being made Mayor of my home town was a day of great pride and self-satisfaction. But these occasions no longer compare with the day that I took the train for London and my seat in the House of Commons.

We hired an entire carriage for the trip, for I had decided to take sixty of my most loyal supporters along with me. Many people took this for some sort of publicity gimmick, for the television crews and pressmen aboard the train almost outnumbered my many helpers. It is true that I liked the publicity of it: what victor doesn't wish others to share his triumph? But there were two other reasons – political good sense and a natural desire to say a civilised Thank You.

I have seen too many politicians rise to prominence by the efforts of good party workers, only to turn a haughty back when the desired success has been achieved. Few people realise how important party workers are in an election, the hours they put in, without pay and for little thanks, knocking on doors, addressing envelopes, licking stamps... and driving the cars to get the old and infirm voters to the polls on election day. They can, and do, win elections. It is obviously good sense for any candidate to woo his workers, but more than that, it is a proper thing to do.

I do not believe in political foolhardiness in the serious business of winning – and keeping – electoral seats. But I sincerely think that I am a grateful man, and I am sure that I have as good a personal relationship – friendship is a better word – with my party workers as any MP in the country. The success of the by-election was their triumph as well as mine. I wanted them to go along to Parliament with me to share the sweetness of victory.

So the Rochdale hordes descended on London, to a welcome which took even me by surprise. As the train pulled into Euston, the platform was blockaded by a solid phalanx of pressmen – I have never, before or since, seen so many cameramen in one place.

On the train with me were my mother, Eva, Norman, my brother, and sister Eunice. There was Hilda Wild, my one-time Sunday school superintendent who had been such a help to me as a child. There were workers from Smith's Springs, my company, who had helped me build up a prosperous business. Ex-Labour man John Holden was there, who had sworn he would support Jack McCann as long as he lived and had loyally kept his promise. Then he came to work for me after Jack's death.

All these people, family, old friends, hold strong emotional bonds for me, but I could see, on that Euston platform, that they really couldn't believe what was happening. 'Eh up, our Cyril,' said one of them in paralysed astonishment, 'this lot can't be 'ere for us. The Queen must be coming in on the next train or summat.'

I, too, was getting a little concerned. I had been promised an official Liberal welcoming party, but I couldn't make out any familiar face in the crush. It took several anxious minutes to spot them – Jeremy Thorpe, David Steel, then Chief Whip, and gently beaming Jo Grimond. The entire Liberal leadership, past, present... and future.

We managed to pack everyone into the coach that was waiting and set off for Westminster, my supporters singing happily and pointing out the sights as we passed. It was for all the world like a happy works' outing.

The coach pulled into Parliament Square. Outside the St Stephen's entrance to the Palace – the public entrance I had used myself on many previous visits to the House – waited even more pressmen and television crews. To my surprise, there was also a huge crowd of schoolchildren, shouting, laughing and waving. 'Well done, Cyril,' the youngsters called. 'You'll show them, Cyril.'

By now, I was at least half-accustomed to the press and television men. But I couldn't believe that one by-election victory, however well publicised, could have made me an idol to a bunch of schoolchildren, and London schoolchildren at that. Then a woman with a familiar face pressed through the crowd. I shook my head – and remembered. She was a teacher at Shawfield school at Norden, Rochdale, a new middle school which was establishing itself quickly as one of the best educational centres in the North.

And then it was explained. By the sheerest coincidence, Shawfield pupils were on a day-trip to London. Hearing that I was due to arrive to take up my seat they had – quite naturally – come along to give me a welcome.

It was a moment of the purest magic, the kindliest twist that fate had ever played on me. I had spent much of my public life up to that point arguing, skirmishing, battling for better educational and welfare facilities for the children of Rochdale. And here some of them were to share my hour of triumph. They queued up, holding out their sandwich bags for my autograph.

It was only with the greatest effort that I didn't enter the Palace of Westminster in tears. Can anyone imagine what the press would have made of that ... a twenty-eight stone, six feet two inches, forty-four-year-old MP entering Parliament blubbering like a babe in arms? On television, too?

The swearing in of a new MP is a solemn, some would say superfluous, ceremony. I might as well admit, now, that I had come to Parliament with the avowed intention not to be over-awed. After all, wasn't I now one of the landlords, not a tenant?

I walked to the Bar of the house, which is in fact a white line painted on the floor. John Pardoe, whom I had chosen as my sponsor – I was the first new Liberal he had had the chance to sponsor – stood on my right. David Steel, as Chief Whip, was on my left – a portentous trio in view of events to come.

The ritual cry went out, 'Is there any person desirous of taking his seat?'

I was acutely aware that, as the latest Parliamentary curiosity, all eyes were on me. As protocol demands, I bowed to the Speaker, Mr Selwyn Lloyd, formerly of Stop-Go fame, well knowing that my figure is not given to bowing with elegance.

I then proceeded to the Mace, and bowed again, grudgingly.

It was time to take the oath of allegiance. There was a buzz from the House as I chose to affirm, rather than 'Swear by Almighty God...' The affirmation is normally taken by atheists, which I most certainly am not. The church has played an important part in my life, but it is the Unitarian Church, which does not accept that the Bible is the word of God. We do not, therefore, swear on the Bible, which is treated merely as the work of mortal man.

There are probably still many members of the House of Commons who to this day think I am an atheist, but I haven't gone out of my way to disillusion them. They will believe what they will believe.

After signing the Book of Acceptance, I was IN – a full member of an assembly to whom every free man and woman in this country and the Western World owes the greatest of debts. It seemed a long way from the back streets of Rochdale.

It would be pleasant to record that the ceremony left me with a feeling of a life's ambition achieved. I felt an immense pride, a relief that I was finally there. As I walked to the second bench before the gangway – the same Liberal bench occupied by Gladstone and John Bright, the great Rochdale Liberal who did as much for the ordinary man as any politician in history – I certainly felt a strong sense of history. And, I confess, surprise that I had ever got there at all.

There was, however, little feeling of anything achieved. Achievements, if there were to be any, were in the future. This was the beginning of the first act of a new play, not a grand finale. Already, I had been given the first hint of the dramas to come.

In many years as an active Labour party worker in the North-West, I had come to know Harold Wilson quite well. I had chaired many meetings at which he spoke – indeed, I have a photograph of myself as chairman of one meeting sitting between Harold and Clement Attlee.

During the swearing-in ceremony, I had looked over to the Leader of the Opposition sitting only seven or eight feet away and smiled. He studiously looked straight through me, and indeed was to go on ignoring me for several months. There was obviously to be no fatherly guidance there. I hadn't expected him to welcome me with open arms, of course. After all, I had just captured one of his so-called safe seats. But I was still carrying that naïve expectation that political differences did not automatically kill off old friendships. It was a small, but significant lesson.

I was mulling this over as I sat, keeping an anxious eye on the public gallery. I had only been able to get six tickets for the Distinguished Strangers' gallery, where my family now sat. Outside, somewhere in the maze of corridors, other supporters were queueing to get into the public gallery. There was one other promise I had made to them, and I was impatient to keep it.

Once I had accused Jack McCann, my predecessor in the Rochdale seat, of being the 'silent member'. For some years he had not spoken in the House although, I admit, he had been busy with his work as a Labour Whip. I had sworn that I was going to Westminster to make my voice... the voice of the people of Rochdale... heard and, perhaps arrogantly, I wanted to get on with it.

Slowly, some of my friends began to filter into vacated seats in the gallery. Some of them managed nervous waves, others slightly bewildered smiles. As luck would have it, the debate under way was on the Queen's Speech, in fact a summary of the government's plans for the coming session. Although an absolute infant in Parliamentary procedure – if, in fact, I had even been born at all – I knew that the Queen's Speech gives the Chamber one of its very rare chances to discuss absolutely anything. One can debate either what has been in the Speech or, alternatively, what has been left out. In other words, you can discuss anything under the sun.

Most of my supporters were now in the gallery, so I rose to my feet, held my breath, and dived in. First I lambasted the Government for its total failure to stop the dumping of foreign cotton goods in Britain, and its refusal to give positive aid to the Lancashire textile industry. All my working life, MPs in the North-West have been demanding help for the sorely beset cotton industry. Never in my life can I remember those fiercely spoken demands being turned into actual votes – if a vote meant crossing party lines, that is.

Then I turned to another subject which greatly distresses many of the older voters in Rochdale, the question of television licence fees for pensioners. Few people realise that, because of one of the stranger legal anomalies, old folk who live in warden-supervised communities – not necessarily old folk's homes, but also bungalow estates with a resident warden, pay only five new pence a year for their television licences. Pensioners living alone in rented or owner-occupied property, without warden control, have to pay the full rate. This can cause genuine hardship, and often takes away the one source of comfort for people tormented by the scourge of old age, loneliness. It was, I said, quite indefensible, and sat down.

I had shot out of the starting gate firmly saddled to two of my hobby-horses. I had been a member of the House of Commons for one hour and forty minutes, I had made my Maiden

Speech and, perhaps significantly, I had already broken one of the House's unwritten laws.

By tradition, Maiden Speeches are expected to be non-controversial. It was a tradition I had no intention of keeping. I was duly complimented on my speech, but that is another Westminster formality which did not impress me. When one of the Rochdale party said later, 'You had a right good go there, Cyril', I felt a little more grateful, but that remark, too, was biased of course.

Tradition plays a very large part in the life of Parliament, and much of it is good. Tradition made Parliament the first and greatest centre of democracy of modern times. But whereas many of those traditions were laid down at a time when Britain was maturing politically, the people have gone on growing up and Parliament has remained adolescent. The protocol, the etiquette, were well suited to the style of the eighteenth-century gentry, but not to a modern industrial state.

I do not wish to be regarded as an enemy of Parliament. If plans were ever made for its abolition, I would be the first to chain myself to the railings in protest. But there are standards of behaviour, ways of thinking, which will have to be changed unless Parliament itself is to become the destroyer, rather than the champion, of democracy.

In the trivial way, Parliamentary protocol can be tiresome and irritating. It is thought necessary, for instance, for one MP visiting another's constituency to write a note asking for permission. Years ago, I founded a children's charity called Rochdale Childer. The idea was copied in a neighbouring town, which I visited regularly to give what advice and assistance I could. Soon after my election, I visited the town once again to serve at a 'Bring-and-Buy' stall to help raise urgently needed funds. I made no speech, but I was photographed in the local newspaper turning the handle of a hurdy-gurdy organ.

The local member wrote me a shrewish letter, complaining that I had appeared in his constituency without the customary letter announcing my intentions. I replied that I had been visiting the town for some years, and would continue to do so in future without seeking permission from anyone.

He then wrote to Jeremy Thorpe, accusing me of 'gross impertinence'. Jeremy, wisely, decided to take no further action in the matter and the incident was forgotten. It was only a pinprick, and my irritation quickly subsided. By this time, more important deficiencies – even abuses – of the system were attracting my attention.

How many electors know, for example, that many important Parliamentary debates take place with as few as ten, sometimes only half a dozen, members present in the House? How much valuable time is wasted by the system of night sittings, when members are told to report to the lobby at, say, eleven pm for the division? I have seen Government Whips pleading with members to make unplanned, unwanted speeches in debates which do not interest them just to keep the talking going until the 'appointed hour'. If a debate folds up suddenly, there is a danger that members will not be back from the restaurants, the theatres, their television appointments in time to vote. In other words, invaluable Parliamentary time must be squandered so that members can linger over the coffee and cigars. It is a scandal at a time when, session after session, important Bills which could improve the quality of life in Britain, or ease the burden on the needy, never reach fruition due to lack of Parliamentary time.

This is a serious fault in Parliament, and should be quickly rectified, but it is not the most serious. The most serious fault – one which, in my opinion, could reach the point of being fatal in the not too distant future – is the two-party system operated as it is today. I believe that unless the two-party system is blown to pieces – and soon – the future for real democracy in this country is very, very bleak.

My final disenchantment came after hours spent listening to speakers arguing vividly and passionately against certain measures – and then going into the lobby to vote in favour.

This is not an exception. This is approaching the level of being a general rule. Hypocrisy is an ugly trait in everyday life, but when the future of a nation is being decided in a welter of hypocrisy, the situation has become extremely serious, if not dangerous.

When a voter reads in his newspaper that his Member of Parliament had attacked a particularly unpopular piece of legislation, he nods his head and says, 'Good man, that – I'll vote for him again.' What that elector should realise is that the MP may well have attacked the particular piece of legislation in his speech but, if the matter was to be decided along party lines, and he was a member of the ruling party, the MP had also voted FOR the bill. MPs are judged by what they SAY, and not by what they DO. Frequently, their declared intentions and their actions are diametrical opposites.

We no longer have a Parliamentary democracy in this country, a statement which gives me cause for great pain. Because of the rigidity of the Whip system, because of the 'lobby-fodder' mentality of many members who simply toe the party line, we have a virtual dictatorship by the Cabinet. If there is a weak Cabinet, the situation is worse: the Prime Minister of the day can carry through any of his own legislation, however insane or unpopular, virtually without democratic checks.

When I had been a member of the Commons for only a few weeks, I caused some outrage – and earned a considerable weight of personal unpopularity – by declaring: 'Parliament is the longest running farce in the West End.'

The remark was dismissed as the loudmouthed sounding-off of a newly arrived nobody searching for attention. I know now that the remark was mistaken. What I should have said was: 'Parliament is the longest running *tragedy* in the West End.'

CHAPTER TWO

Thru'penny Wrap-ups

They call Rochdale the town with the clean face and the dirty neck. The clean face is W. H. Crossland's magnificent Victorian Gothic town hall, standing like a fortress over the Esplanade, which itself could claim to be the broadest main street in any English town. The dirty neck is the surrounding ring of slums, now, thankfully, being cleared.

They first planned that Town Hall a century and a quarter ago, a time of towering civic pride. The cotton trade – King Cotton, they called it then – had made British working towns the new wonders of the world, industrial showpieces which you now have to travel to Germany or Japan to see. It was a time when Trade – I am sure the word was always spoken with a capital 'T' – was tearing down the country's bastions of privilege, built and jealously defended over the centuries by Tory landowners.

From Rochdale came men like John Bright, a mill-owner, avid Temperance worker, and a true Radical. As a Liberal MP for first Durham and then Birmingham, he fought the Corn Laws, which allowed the great landowners to smother the import of cheap grain and charge greatly inflated prices for their own produce. It was the politics of the price of bread, a new thought then. The repeal of the Corn Laws in 1846 made Bright, a very wealthy man, a hero to the working classes. He spent much of his brilliant Parliamentary career fighting for votes for the workers.

From Rochdale, too, came another movement pledged to improving the lot of the hard-pressed industrial workers, the Co-op. Sadly, this is now simply a trading organisation. For a hundred years, it carried great social obligations to its members, not merely by freeing them from the grasp of profiteering shopkeepers, but also by supplying educational and leisure facilities and, eventually, its own MPs. In 1844, the Rochdale Society of Equitable Pioneers opened a tiny shop in Toad Lane, the first ever Co-op. The shop still stands, and the big department stores and supermarkets it spawned in the area are to this day known, not as the Co-op, but as the Pioneers.

When I see people walking through the streets of Germany and France, carrying those plastic carrier-bags with the distinctive Co-op symbol in blue letters, I can't resist a smile as I think of that crumbling little shop in Toad Lane.

The unavoidable truth of the matter is, however, that at the time when rich men like Bright and poor men like the Pioneers were working for the benefit of the ordinary man, Rochdale, and a score of towns like it, were already past their peak. King Cotton was already losing its grip on the world market. The textile industry is a cheap industry to put into production. The economic unreality of shipping raw cotton from India, to be sent back in the form of inexpensive loin-cloths, was soon apparent. King Cotton was never to recover fully from the dire wound of the American Civil War, when the flow of slave-produced raw material from the Deep South stopped gorging the gaping maws of the Lancashire mills.

Rochdale Town Hall is in itself a sort of historical bookmark. It was conceived and planned at a time when cotton and the British Empire would never see the setting sun. But even on opening day in 1871, when thousands crammed in to see the magnificent hammer-beam roof and stained glass, the sun was already past High Noon, for cotton at least. Perhaps Crossland, the architect, understood this better than most. He was to die in poverty and obscurity in Liverpool years later. As a Rochdale guidebook notes with unsentimental Northern humour, he had come to derive more pleasure from the bottle than from the practice of his art.

The decline which was started by the American Civil War in the 1860s never stopped. Many mills closed and became derelict. The mill cottages, which unbelievably had been considered the acme of workers' accommodation, became slums. Even by Lancashire standards, the future of Rochdale and the future of cotton were irretrievably linked. By the turn of the century and the Great War, Rochdale had become one of industrial England's forgotten towns, neglected by the politicians far away in Westminster, and treated as a bit of a joke even by the 'city-folk' of Manchester, all of twelve miles away.

The *Rochdale Observer* is published twice a week, on Wednesdays and Saturdays. The issues of the last week of June 1928 make interesting reading today – wistfully nostalgic or horrifying, depending on your mood or your social conscience.

That week, *Ben Hur* was showing at the New Coliseum, with Ramon Novarro, Carmel Myers 'and a cast of ten thousand'. You could buy a full-size oak bedstead for thirty-two and sixpence, and five and elevenpence would secure a pair of Bamford's 'famous trousers'. A man employed by the coal company had been taken to hospital with a broken arm after being kicked by his horse.

More seriously, for high-minded ratepayers, was the case of a man who had abandoned his four children. He was dragged before the local magistrates, charged with leaving his family chargeable to the Common Fund of the Rochdale Poor Law Union, at a cost of ninety-three pounds and ten shillings to the rates. The case was adjourned to give the man time to improve his behaviour.

Four of the town's larger mills were not working, and others – 'as appears to be the custom these days', notes the *Observer* – had machinery standing idle. There was some room for enthusiasm as the India Office had placed a substantial part of an order for two hundred and seventy thousand yards of silver-grey flannel in the town. Did Indians wear silver-grey flannels?

A meeting had been held in Bradford between owners and six textile unions to seek a solution to a lengthy strike. The matter had been thankfully resolved – to the satisfaction of five of the unions, anyway – by rises of between two and three shillings a week for male adults, to be offset by substantial reductions for female and junior workers!

The *Observer* of Saturday, 30 June 1928, has two points of interest for me, one of them a point of *omission*. The issue does carry a letter condemning Rochdale Corporation for refusing to permit mixed bathing at the public baths. 'As most of our Councillors are past the 50 mark, and some past the 60 mark, how can we possibly expect them to view favourably a proposal that is backed by youthful views and enthusiasm?' demanded a presumably youthful and enthusiastic correspondent, signing himself with the stirring pen-name of 'Attaboy'.

The point of omission is in the *Births* column. Three local families had that week been blessed with new arrivals, as the column proudly proclaims. There is no mention, however, of the entry into this world of one Cyril Smith, son of Eva Smith, at Birch Hill Hospital, Rochdale, on 28 June 1928. The reason for the omission is no mystery: at a time when to suggest mixed bathing was advanced to the point of being revolutionary, young housemaids did not make a habit of advertising the arrival of their fatherless children.

My mother, Eva, one of the great strengths of my life, had taken a couple of days off. After a couple more days, during which she took her first son back to her own mother's cottage, she returned to work as housemaid for the cotton family who lived at 8 Kilnerdyne Terrace, Rochdale, one of several addresses which has stayed in my memory all my life.

The people at Number Eight were kind and understanding, by the standards of the day. My mother arrived there at six am to light the fires, humping heavy coal scuttles up and down many flights of steps, before starting her other duties. She was allowed home for a couple of hours at tea-time and this was the only time I was sure of seeing her for many years. Then she returned to Number Eight until ten pm, where she helped nurse a bedridden daughter of the family. She liked the brief evenings of high summer in those days, because she could walk home in daylight.

These were her duties, seven days a week, fifty-two weeks a year – apart from five days' holiday – for some twenty years. She was paid a pound a week, and was occasionally allowed to take home some food for her family. The two hours at tea-time were valuable to her, for they allowed her to do the washing she took in to help supplement her income.

Yet I still say that the people at number eight were kind. They paid the going rate – Eva was as well off as anyone in service at the time. But the real depth of the family's kindness was that they employed her at all, for she had children – not only me, but my sister Eunice, four years older, and Norman, born four years after me. She was working, and working hard, for perhaps threepence an hour, but she was lucky to be working at all.

I have been asked, 'Do you know who your father was?' The answer is, no – I don't. My mother never chose to tell me, and I have never chosen to ask her. It is a matter of little importance to me. At grammar school, later on, boys would be pointed out as so-and-so, son of the magistrate, or so-and-so, son of the doctor. Mothers didn't seem to be particularly important in those days to most of the boys – although mine was the centre of my universe – so it was not necessary to be pointed out as 'Eva Smith's son'. I did not grow up as someone's son, I grew up as *me*, Cyril Smith, individual. It was one of the first lessons of life, perhaps one of the most painful, but I have no doubt that learning it has had an important and beneficial effect in moulding me.

The outstanding factor of my early life was my mother's total devotion to me, my brother and my sister. She can hold her peace, when she wishes. She can be totally withering when her patience is exhausted. She taught me to respect myself, and to work, work, work.

I suppose I must have been four or five years old when I gradually began to understand the struggles she underwent to keep the family together. In one mistily recalled episode, a neighbour was in the house and my mother was in an angry mood. Perhaps there was no money for food or coal, or perhaps I had been naughty, for I was no angel as a child. I heard the neighbour say, 'If you had taken my advice and put him in an orphanage, all this would never have happened.'

My mother hustled the neighbour out of the house, rudely, almost violently. It puzzled me, because I had never seen her act this way with a grown-up. The phrase stuck in my mind. I didn't really know what an orphanage was, but I believed it to be a place of terror, a place where wicked people sent bad children. It never occurred to me that I could be a candidate for such an institution.

No doubt my mother could have had a much easier life if she had decided to send her three children away. As a live-in maid she would have enjoyed better food, a warmer home – shortage of coal haunts the memory of my childhood – and perhaps she would have been able to save a few shillings from her paltry wage to buy the small fripperies which seem so important to a young woman's morale. I am sure the thought never crossed her mind. She had the determination and the courage to insist on her independent, and the pain that this single-min-mindedness caused her must have been great. In the moral climate of those days, it was not considered proper for a woman to be independent, particularly a woman blessed with a family of children and no man to keep them.

Because of the long hours my mother was forced to work, much of the burden of bringing up the family fell on her mother, my grandmother, Sarah. She too was a remarkable woman, daughter of the only man of public distinction I know of in my immediate forebears. He was James Standring, one of the founders of the trade union movement in the textile industry. A committed Liberal with an acute political mind, he opened the first Rochdale headquarters of the Operative Spinners. We used to have the gold key he used in the opening ceremony. Hundreds of mourners lined the streets at his funeral in 1915, and the Mayor walked behind his coffin. I tend to think that the trade unionists of those days, before general public acceptance and the advent of the welfare state, were men of real stature.

My grandmother was also a woman of stature who, I suppose, took the place of a father in my early days. She gave us a surfeit of love, but not in an overbearing, suffocating way. She adjudicated in our children's squabbles, and handed out most of the discipline in a stern, Victorian way. She, too, worked and worked. I remember her darting backwards and forwards between the sink and the fireplace, cooking, cleaning, sewing. Cleanliness was, as she reminded us almost hourly, next to Godliness. Our cottage may have had a stone flag floor, but it shone with a dull gleam. We would have eaten our meals off it without a second's hesitation. I think too little honour is given to the role of grannies in family life. They can be a major influence in the vital years of childhood. In 'one-parent families' – to use the current sociologist's phrase – the grandmother can be the balancing force between a future juvenile delinquent or solid citizen.

We lived with Grandma in a tiny cottage at 6 Falinge Road, Rochdale, all five of us – Grandma, Mother and the three children – all sleeping in the same room. In most people's minds, the average Industrial Revolution house would be a two-up, two-down. To me as a child, that would have been luxury beyond reach. We had a one-up, one-down, and the lavatory was three hundred yards away. We kept it locked, like all the more particular families, and the key hung on a hook by the sink in the house.

We slept upstairs, and all the other activities of life went on in the one ground-floor room. It was kitchen, washroom, dining room, sitting room, study and workshop combined. In one small way, our house was posher than some: we did have a curtain drawn round the sink, so that people could wash in proper privacy. It was usually a head-to-toe wash, anyway, because bath-night was a once-a-week ceremony. Water was heated slowly in a copper built into the fireplace. The tin bath, which was kept under the stairs, was dragged in and filled laboriously with saucepans used as ladles. Taking a bath was a bit of a bore, so the curtain round the sink was more necessity than luxury.

My grandmother cooked on the open fire in the grate, so meal times were the warmest times of the day. We managed to have coal most of the time, but there was always the fear that it would run out. To do so meant cold food as well as cold feet. One of my first jobs, shared by Eunice and Norman also, was to watch the coal drays as they made their deliveries. Bits of coal dropped on the road or pavement were surreptitiously pocketed and taken home and proudly presented to Grandma as though they were nuggets of gold. In winter, when things were very bleak, we would collect wood from derelict mill sites. It was in some ways a game, in others a real war, for other children were out on the same quest. A good log may have been spotted days before, and carefully hidden away until it was needed. Getting it home meant an anxious, anguished trot, with short breaks whilst we panted our wind back. We were wary of meeting bigger children, also looking for fuel, who might be tempted to steal ours although, in all honesty, I cannot remember this actually happening. The fear of it was real enough.

Occasionally, when things were very bad, we had to burn bits of furniture to cook a simple meal, but this had to be a matter of total desperation. The house was so sparsely furnished that we could have burned the lot, chairs, tables and beds, doors and floorboards, in a week.

Looking back now, it all seems so pitiful. At the time it was both unremarkable and unremarked: that is simply how life was. Other families in the street were living in the same way, and, I daresay, so were many thousands more in hundreds of other towns. It wasn't until my early teens that I began to realise that this way of life could possibly be changed.

Food has always been a bugbear of my life. By the time I could afford to eat what I wanted to eat I was medically disbarred from doing so. In those early days, however, family life revolved around the meal table. A meal was something to worry about before it arrived, linger over as long as possible during the actual eating, and remember happily for some hours afterwards.

We were never ever short of food; my mother worked herself to a standstill to avoid that. But the diet was plain and often boring. There was dripping on bread, and margarine on bread, but never butter on bread. A single egg was divided between the three children, lightly boiled, mashed and spread on – of course – bread. There were sometimes cakes as a special treat – stale cakes, mind you. If you went to the bread shop and asked for a pennyworth of stale cakes, you were given a whole bag of the previous day's leftovers. There were huge pans of potato hash, mostly potatoes boiled with scraps of meat. In the winning of those bits of meat, I made my first contribution to family welfare.

My first major errand was to go down to Sam Hoyle's butcher's shop at 14 St Mary's Gate, to buy the thru'penny wrap-ups. A kindly butcher, if he had the time and the patience, would throw as many spare bits of meat as he chose into a sheet of paper and wrap them up. The charge was threepence – just over one new penny – which even then was not a great deal of money. To be honest, the bits and pieces in the wrap-up were really waste: trimmings from the joints being taken off by the cotton-families' maids, scraps left over in such small quantities as to be unsaleable to housewives with a shilling in their purse. To the poor, the generosity of the butcher could mean the difference between a good feed or an empty belly. In the long run I imagine, children with mean butchers succumbed to rickets and the other diseases of poverty. We never had rickets in our house, and for that Sam Hoyle must take the credit.

Sam, a kindly, laughing man, had been doing our wrap-ups before I arrived on the scene. When I was finally old enough to tackle this vital errand, I was warned to be very polite to him. I remember resenting this at the time, for the suggestion seemed to be very close to actual begging. As it turned out, I grew to like the man so much that the trips to his stall became the highlights of my week.

He did, of course, know all about my family background. As a prosperous trader, he could, if he had wished, have shunned us – there were some who did. Sam took a kindly interest, and even went so far as to teach me the skills of my first 'proper' job – skinning sheep's heads. Today, these are boiled up as pet food: then, they were an important part of many a family's diet. Sam gave me an apron, honed a very sharp knife, and I became one of the best skinners in the town.

It sounds a gruesome job, but I cannot remember that thought ever occurring to me. It was a real job, a man's job in fact. It was important! Outside my family, Sam was the first adult I ever grew to know. What is more, our thru'penny wrap-ups were the best in town. In would go a bit of shin beef, perhaps some neck of lamb. There would be a slice of liver, perhaps, or a kidney and a lamb chop. This was the goodness in the family potato hash. Mother, Grandma, Eunice and Norman reaped the benefits as well as me, and I was proud of my efforts.

I never bought meat from anyone else until the day Sam Hoyle stopped trading.

So the family grew up in Falinge Road, certainly underprivileged, but never desperately unhappy. We were among people suffering the same tribulations, and the folk of the North-West had long since made up their minds: if you don't laugh, you cry. We laughed a lot, and everyone in the neighbourhood did too. There was a shoulder-to-shoulder spirit, born out of simple human need, which still exists in Rochdale but seems to have disappeared in many industrial towns in the South and Midlands which I now visit. Perhaps it was because the people in the cotton towns have had longer to grow accustomed to economic vicissitude. The golden days of King Cotton are now so far away that the oldest of old men are too young to remember.

Schooldays came to me as a sweet surprise. Older children, already at school, had regaled me with horrifying gossip. The lessons were boring and hard. The teachers were wicked witches, cruel and sneering, forever shouting and slapping. It was like a prison, really, they said, and I must admit that the tiled walls of Spotland Primary School did not induce a mood of immediate cheer. Yet it was a great school – and I know now that buildings do NOT make a school – people do.

In fact, I revelled in the place. I liked the books, and because I liked them the teachers took time to encourage me. I loved reading, and found to my surprise that I was very good at sums. This will probably come as a shock to some of my contemporaries, as mathematics is supposed to be the process of pure logic!

I was soon a monitor, and that gave me the right to keep classes quiet until the teacher arrived, or organise them into lines in the playground before they trooped into school. It gave me, in short, power. It was a feeling I enjoyed. I organised my own gangs in the playground, and was as good as anyone at football or cricket (both played with a tennis ball).

There were incidents, of course. I told one girl that the Headmistress wanted to see her, which caused the girl a good deal of distress and the Headmistress some share of puzzlement, because it was not true. I got the cane. I also suffered some disappointments, like the time when a promise that I could teach the class on the last day of term was withdrawn because of my bad behaviour. To this day, I do not recall why the promise was made, or what particular piece of misbehaviour caused it to be withdrawn. I do remember, however, being bitterly disappointed. I had wanted to teach the class and I can only imagine that my eagerness was due to a burgeoning desire to be in control, to be at the centre of attention. Alas, it wasn't to be.

Discipline was strict, with a sound slap being the normal mode of correction. The teachers, all women, kept a very proper distance between themselves and their pupils, but they were far from being the witches I had been led to expect. They were closer to angels, but would have been horrified to show it.

Christmas in Falinge Road was a cheerful affair, with a real Christmas tree, a little extra food, and a lot of carol singing.

Presents, though, were scarce and by necessity, cheap. One Christmas I received a Meccano set, an exceptionally lavish present, and was told that it came from someone who liked me, but who didn't want to be known. I smiled and said aloud, 'I wonder just who that could be?' It was, of course, no secret. I was upstairs when my Headmistress – Miss Sutcliffe – called at the house to give my mother the Meccano, and say, 'Please don't tell Cyril who it's from, Mrs Smith. He will tell the other pupils, and they will be jealous... but I just can't afford to buy everyone in the school a present.'

I didn't see her face, but I heard the conversation, and a teacher's voice is unmistakable to a child. I never did tell the other children in the class, or even the Headmistress. That would have embarrassed her and I suppose, even at that age, I was beginning to show some political acumen.

There was another teacher, too, who was more of a fairy godmother than a witch: Mrs Halstead, who also had a son at the school. It was the great age of the Hollywood tear-jerkers, and that masterpiece called *Boys' Town* with Spencer Tracy and Mickey Rooney was doing the rounds. As almost everyone must know, the film tells the story of a kindly priest who takes a young hoodlum under his wing and makes a fine man of him.

Our teachers decided that this film would provide their pupils from the poorer side of town with a rare opportunity to combine education with entertainment, but the admission fee was twopence and the Smith family could not afford twopence. I had heard about the film, of course, for in those days the cinema was a major topic of conversation, most of it lost on me because I had never been. I was determined I would not upset my mother by asking for the twopence, and I resigned myself to missing this much anticipated event.

It so happened that Mrs Halstead's son was celebrating his birthday that week. To my great surprise, I received an invitation to his party – we didn't have birthday parties in our street and anyway, to be invited to the teacher's house was quite out of the ordinary. It was held at another address I remember, even after some forty years, 17 Turf Hill Road.

We had fancy hats and games, jellies and cream and cakes, and a bagful of toffees each, typical party fare for most children, I suppose, but to me luxury beyond dreams. They saved the biggest surprise for the end, however: the announcement that we were all off to the cinema to see *Boys' Town*. I looked at Mrs Halstead, but she turned her eyes away. I knew immediately that this was the reason for my invitation to the party. It was her way of making sure I saw that film without having to accept a gift of twopence given as an out-and-out act of charity.

I didn't weep then. Some thirty years later, when I was to speak at a school speech day, I knew that Mrs Halstead was a member of the staff and that she was due to retire. I ordered a bouquet of flowers which was delivered to the school in secret. When I rose to speak, I began: 'I want to tell you all about a real-life fairy story. Once upon a time, there was a poor boy who couldn't go to the pictures to see a very special film because his family couldn't afford the tu'pence for the seat ...'

In the audience, I saw Mrs Halstead begin to squirm with embarrassment. I invited her onto the stage, and one of the pupils came on with my bouquet of flowers. I finished the story of *Boys' Town*, and presented her with the flowers. Then I began to weep, and so did she. We stood on the stage, tears pouring down, before an audience of several hundred children.

It gives me great pleasure to say 'thank you' to people who have shown me kindness, and the visit to that film had made a far deeper impression on me than I cared to reveal at the time. In the picture, Mickey Rooney, the boy from the slums, grows up to be Mayor. I wanted to know what a Mayor was. So whenever I had some spare time, I went to stand outside Rochdale Town Hall. I waited there for hours, but one day the Mayor came out, resplendent in robes and chain of office. If Mickey Rooney could do it, why not Cyril Smith?

If it was that incident at Spotland Primary School that sparked off my ambition, there was another which nearly took away any hope of its final achievement. One day when I was nine, I took a bad fall while playing football in the school yard. My knee was badly cut but, as boys were supposed to do then, I ignored it, eagerly flaunting the courage with which I withstood pain.

A few days later, I collapsed and was taken home from school. A piece of gravel had somehow entered the cut on my knee and had worked its way through my bloodstream to lodge in my kidney. I had nephritis, a disease regarded with such dread by the doctors that one of them, with alarming bluntness, told my mother: 'If he gets through the present crisis, he will never live to see forty.'

The one room downstairs took on yet a new role, as sick bay. The old iron bed was brought downstairs and I lay for eight months in the kitchen, next to the curtain round the sink. For six weeks, I lived on barley water. For the following six months, they fed me rice puddings and other milk dishes, which must have placed a heavy strain on the family budget. I read book after book – sentimental ones, full of tears, like *Black Beauty* – but I survived. Much of the credit for this should go to Dr Scarr, the family GP. In those pre-Health Service days, the medical treatment available to the poor depended almost entirely on the goodwill of their practitioner. Dr Scarr employed a man who went round collecting a penny a week from each of the four or five hundred families on his panel. One penny a week – and for that, five members of the Smith family received unstinted, uncomplaining medical care. I don't know how Dr Scarr managed to live. He must have had some prosperous patients, but very few in our part of Rochdale. In his case, you can really say that medicine was a vocation, more than a career.

Before the days of expensive drugs and antibiotics, the medical profession held a powerful tenet in the healing qualities of the cheapest medicine of all: good, wholesome fresh air – as much as could be forced into a patient's lungs. To this end, Rochdale boasted an Open Air School for what was euphemistically described as 'the delicate child'. It was to become a second home to me for the next nine months.

It differed from ordinary schools in one rather dramatic way: its classrooms had walls on only three sides. The fourth side looked out over a verandah, but was completely open to the elements. There were, I believe, emergency screens which could be pulled across if the weather became impossible, but I don't remember their being used, yet I had lessons there for a complete Pennines winter. It may seem a sort of 'kill-or-cure' solution, but I don't think I was ever particularly cold.

The other pupils were suffering from a variety of complaints.

There were weak hearts and a few mild TB cases, and several physically disabled. Some of them accepted their conditions philosophically, others mooned around condemning nature and God for picking on them.

I think my attitude on arrival must have shocked the teachers. Like the word 'orphanage', Open Air School was a phrase of doom to some ears. I was overjoyed to learn that the rules laid down two diet-controlled meals a day for each pupil – lunch and tea – plus a compulsory two-hour sleep every afternoon on camp beds. We had good meat at lunchtime, and a pudding; there was butter on our bread, not marge, and for tea we were sometimes given buns with real currants in them! To me, this was no retreat for physical freaks. It was a holiday camp!

I remained cheery, took an even greater interest in my lessons, and learned for perhaps the first time in my life that there were children in the world considerably worse off than myself. I spent many hours with the crippled pupils, talking to them, trying to make them laugh. Strangely – or is this in fact human nature? – the most miserable among my fellow pupils tended to be the ones who were physically nearest to normal.

Perhaps I enjoyed the Open Air School too much (I don't think you were actually supposed to *enjoy* school in those days), or perhaps because I was working hard, my stay there was cut from the anticipated two years to nine months. I went back to Spotland Primary in time for a few months of study for the scholarship exams to the grammar school.

I was so certain of passing the eleven-plus that my confidence must have merged into arrogance. A few days after the examination, my mother was offered a nice sports jacket for me, secondhand but in very good condition. I told her to save her money, for she would have to get me a High School blazer in a few weeks' time. She gave me a very old-fashioned look; I think she was beginning to wonder just what sort of child she had brought into the world.

I did pass, and the news was 'leaked' to the family by a kindly town hall official on a very opportune day. My mother was off at one of the large jumble sales which were major and regular events in our district. They were then, as they are today, valuable fund-raising efforts for local charities. They were also, in those days, the only opportunity for the poor of Rochdale to buy any item approaching the luxury-goods bracket. We would pick up a book, perhaps a hat for Mother, or a cheap little ornament to brighten up the house. The sales attracted great crowds, and were occasions of chatter and laughter as well as serious shopping expeditions.

Armed with the news from the town hall man who had called in as he passed the house, I ran round to the sale to tell my mother. I found her staring at a secondhand clothing stall. Lying there, right on the top, was the green blazer with the red badge of Rochdale Municipal High School for Boys.

'You can buy that now, Mam,' I said.

'Are you really sure, Cyril?' she asked with great seriousness.

I told her about the man from the town hall. She pretended to take it all calmly. After all, hadn't it been a foregone conclusion? The blazer fitted quite well, but her casual air couldn't stop her hands trembling with excitement as she fumbled to get the money from her purse.

The blazer cost sixpence and was the first of a series from jumble sales. I never did get a 'shop-bought' blazer. My only new one came when I was fifteen, and my mother made it for me herself, for by that time I was too big to fit normal school clothes. I did start at the grammar school, however, with a brand-new cap. It cost two and sixpence, enough to buy the family's thru'penny wrap-ups for ten weeks.

Many times in my life, I have been lucky enough to be in the right place at the right time. This did not happen the day I walked nervously into the forbidding Victorian pile of Rochdale High School. It was 5 September 1939, just two days after war broke out, and I was sent home within the hour!

Like the rest of the country, the school system was totally unprepared for war. We were supposed to have air-raid shelters, but we hadn't, of course. After giving our names, being shown our rooms, and meeting our teachers on that first day, we were sent home until the shelters could be built.

In my new-old blazer and my new-new cap, I walked back through the door of Falinge Road not much more than an hour after I had left. I was greeted with an intense scream from my grandmother.

'What have you been up to?' she demanded. 'Oh, the disgrace of it, to be sent home on your very first day. Have you been expelled? Oh, God, no – your mother will kill you.'

I was lucky to escape a beating there and then, because my grandmother could hand out a fair clout when she had the mind, but slowly she began to accept my garbled explanations. 'It won't be long before they blame everything that goes wrong on the war,' she muttered with a final suspicious glower. Grandma could remember 1914–18, of course.

They built the shelters in just one week, and my career there began in earnest. I was mixing for the first time with boys from 'good' homes, with fathers who were among the solid burghers of the town, but I was to suffer very little hostility because of my background.

The pain I had, and it wasn't unbearable, was to come when I grew fat.

One of the more unpleasant factors of obesity is that other people, slim people, naturally assume that fat people get fat through their own sloth and greed. The fat boy is forever Billy Bunter, stuffing himself with cakes and sweets, refusing to share his tuck with his friends, constantly scheming to cram more goodies down his ever-open throat.

In my case, and there are so many people like me, obesity was thrust on me unwelcomed and unsought. There were literally no steps I could take to avoid it. It was caused by three factors quite outside my control.

Firstly, the kidney damage of my illness had thrown my glandular system out of balance so that my body was unable to burn up the excess calories I consumed. On top of this was the diet forced on me by economic necessity: bread, boiled potatoes or chips, dripping, these were staples of my life. The sugar in my tea was not a luxury, but a source of energy I could not replace with other, more expensive, foods.

Finally, and this was particularly distressing in those days of the 'healthy mind, healthy body' approach to education, I was medically unable to take part in the more active sports. There was no way I could stop getting fat, no way I could exercise away the fat when it arrived.

I was twelve stones when I arrived at High School at the age of eleven, but I was tall and at first I was just a very big lad. But the weight continued to go on, and by the time

I was fifteen I weighed fourteen stones. Medically excused from the football and cricket teams – although I did play a fair game of table-tennis – I was the obvious butt for schoolboy jokes.

Children are known for their cruelty to each other. There were boys at school with spectacles who were known, automatically, as 'speckie-four-eyes'. Big ears, big feet, bow-legs were all legitimate targets for attacks often launched with great wit and cunning.

I was just huge, so there was no need for clever ways of deriding me. I was simply called Fatty, or Fatso, or Jumbo by boys both older and younger than me. As I progressed up the school, younger boys often literally half my weight, had a 'dare' game; they would dare someone to run up behind me, punch me, and run off knowing full well I was incapable of giving chase. It seemed to be a game to test their nerve, like the native boys out on a hunt with their fathers who run up at the end and shoot their toy arrows into the dying carcass of the elephant.

There is no point in my saying that I did not resent this, or that it did not upset me. Some evenings, I would go home and sit alone in the bedroom, brooding. To the best of my knowledge, I never cried – tears of happiness were allowed in our house, but tears of bitterness were very unwelcome. On the very rare occasions I found my mother in tears – and God knows, she had enough to cry about – the stock answer to my question was: 'I'm crying for my money back.' It is a sentence which doesn't mean much in words, but says a lot in the emotions of poverty.

I must not give the impression that my grammar school days were one long torment. That is far from the truth. I was happy with my books, and made many good friends and became a good debater and amateur actor. When I was chosen to play table-tennis for Rochdale, I became a bit of a 'character'.

The periods of my tauntings had always lasted for just a few days, to be forgotten in favour of another game. Gradually, the periods between episodes grew longer and longer until they virtually disappeared, and 'Hello, Fatty' and the rhyming nickname 'Squirrel' became a term of gentle affection rather than abuse.

Like many other things in my childhood, I learned to accept that fact that I was fat, and put that acceptance to good use. Obesity as a child can have considerable value. It builds armour for the resistance of ridicule in later life.

CHAPTER THREE

Religion and Politics

Political awareness came to me with an unexpected jolt as I hurried through the blacked-out streets of Rochdale on a winter night in 1941. I was bustling along, collar turned up, hands deep in pockets, with the iron studs in my boots skating and singing on the cobbles. It was approaching ten o'clock, and I was on my way to meet my mother when she finished her duties at Number Eight.

I didn't like the twenty-minute walk on the way there, alone in the darkness. Although I wouldn't admit it, I was frightened as I skirted the empty wastes of a big park, just as I had been frightened a few years earlier of the blackness of the unused cellar under our house. In my schoolboy imagination, there was always a lone Luftwaffe bomb-aimer somewhere up there in the clouds, his gloved thumb hovering over the button which would unleash the bomb manufactured by Herr Krupp just for me. Some people had taken to carrying candles in jam-jars, carefully lidded to stop the light shining upwards. The lids had to be punctured to allow the oxygen in, of course, so I reasoned that the escaping pinpricks were potentially fatal guides to hawk-like Teutonic eyes. And anyway, people carrying these jars would appear suddenly round corners like horrific wraiths similar to those grave-robbers in the Burke and Hare horror stories. I never took a candle.

It was a strange mixture of emotions that I carried with me that night – a night which I remember so clearly to this day. The simple fear of night, of a thirteen-year-old schoolboy, plus a combination of horror and excitement stirred by the remote possibility of being caught in an air-raid. I also questioned, in my half-comprehending way, the very need for my mission: was it *really* necessary for a young boy to stay up this late at night, to give a little company and comfort to a woman facing a long, cold walk home after a fourteen-hour working day?

For some months, if not years, this thought had been nagging at me. All my life, I had seen my mother in states varying from a quiet tiredness to occasional total exhaustion. Like all the men and women in my neighbourhood, my mother worked every hour she could. They grasped every penny that was available to them. Yet the rewards were so meagre. Did life always have to be this hard?

On the way to Number Eight that night, I found myself asking for the first time: what is it in the natural order of things that allows one woman to *be* a maid and another woman to *employ* a maid? Why can one family keep fires blazing in unused rooms day and night, when others have to worry about having sufficient coal to boil a kettle? What gives one family the right to waste enough food at breakfast time to feed another family for the whole day?

Please remember that I am talking about a Lancashire cotton town, not of Belgravia or the country estates of the leisured classes. There were no families that I knew of in Rochdale living the lives of society gadflies, dreaming up expensive frivolities with which to pass the day. The rich cotton people in Rochdale worked hard, and, given the state of the industry, must have had their own highly individual set of worries. Yet one fact remained unanswerable: hard work did not appear to be bringing in its own rewards, at least not for the Smith family and thousands like us. Somewhere, somehow, the spoils were being unequally divided. The system had gone wrong. It was then that the thought that had long been with me, but just out of grasp, finally broke through: *can the system be changed?*

I doubt that anyone younger than my generation can accept just how revolutionary that idea seemed to me at the time. I was tempted to push it away from me, forget about it, because what right had a boy not long out of short-trousers to question a set of circumstances accepted without comment by most of the adults he knew? The houses were bad, the work was hard and underpaid, food and fuel were short and clothing was shoddy – but it had always been that way and the people still survived. No schoolboy – even one who had won a place at the grammar school – could raise a question like that without receiving the cursory reply, 'Th's still wet behind the ears, pal. The likes of us don't change things, just make the best of them.'

Walking home with my mother that night, I asked her, 'Do you like being a maid, Mam?'

She said simply, 'It's my job.'

We arrived home in an unaccustomed silence.

My first dissatisfaction with 'the system' had grown from the everyday observation of how my family, and the neighbouring families, lived. The feeling was soon to be strengthened by two other prime influences in my life, Church and Rochdale Municipal High School.

The Unitarians are a small and much misunderstood sect. They have, if you can use the phrase, a Left wing religion, and one that deliberately fosters the use of independent thought amongst its followers. Unlike so many of the other Christian churches, the Unitarians welcome rigorous questioning. This seems to give a grave affront to the established churches, and for many years the Unitarians, along with the Quakers, another sect I admire, were refused admission to the British Council of Churches.

We believe in a God-father, but we do not accept that Christ was the son of God, although we rejoice in his work as a gifted prophet. We do not accept the existence of the Holy Trinity and we look upon the Bible, although a fine book, as the work of man and not the word of God. We try to make our church play an active part in everyday life, in providing leisure and study facilities. I would much rather see a church used for a weekly tea-party for a hundred pensioners than solely as a place of worship for fifty Sunday hymn-singers.

My family had been staunch Unitarians for several generations, and it was natural that I too should participate actively in its affairs. I went to Sunday school, and became first a teacher, then School Superintendent, a headmaster-like role. I sang in the choir and the marvellous Christmas pantomimes. I was taught to question established thinking, and eventually this fuelled my growing rebelliousness in a way which was to worry even the officers of the Church.

My first-ever clash with authority came when I was leader of the Unitarian youth club, which met weekly in the church hall in Clover Street. It is regrettable, I suppose, but perhaps inevitable that all societies of people, however open-minded, suffer the traumas of the 'generation-gap'. If anything went wrong in the church hall it was the youth club's fault. If a chair was broken, or some litter left behind, it was the youth club's fault. Our weekly meetings ended with a pot of tea and, to my growing annoyance, we were allowed to use only the old, cracked crockery. I complained, and nothing was done. I complained again, and still nothing was done. One week in a cold controlled temper, I smashed every cracked cup.

It was my first confrontation. I would have to go, they said. In riposte, I threatened to lead the entire youth club out of the church, and even wrote to the local education authority for the hire of another room. Tempers cooled, and the club was allowed to stay – with new crockery!

A few years later, I was asked to preach the Sunday sermon from the pulpit of the Blackwater Street chapel. I was seventeen, and fire and brimstone were my staffs of life. I accused the elders of hypocrisy, of condemning drinking and gambling from their chapel pews, only to go home to bring out the cards and uncap the bottles. Several old ladies were actually led out on the verge of fainting, and the chapel council met in uproar. A motion was passed, and it still lies in the minutes, that Cyril Smith was never again to be allowed access to the chapel pulpit!

Yes, I had been encouraged to question the order of things, and perhaps I went too far! On the other hand, perhaps I had prodded the truth into some uncomfortable niches. What is certain is that I was soon forgiven. Although the motion exiling me from the pulpit is still technically in force, I have in fact preached there many times. Twenty-five years after that first sermon, I am chairman of the Chapel Trustees and when I finally quit public life it is there that I will expend my remaining energies.

It was the Unitarians' love of singing, their lusty pounding out of hymns in chapel or carols in the Christmas streets, that first made me aware of an important gift. I had always had a strong belief that every human being, however humble, has been blessed with at least one talent, to be nurtured, cherished and, when necessary, exploited. Some people are given the eye of a painter, the ear of a musician, the nimble fingers of the born mechanic or needlewoman.

As a youth, growing uncontrollably bigger and singularly lacking in the accepted graces of the football field or cricket pitch, I discovered I had a voice to which people would listen. The recognition came first in the choir and then at concerts, when I was asked to sing the sought-after boy-soprano parts, and was reinforced at Rochdale High School when I joined the Debating Society.

Debating gave me the highly stylised opportunity to exercise my voice before a captive audience and eventually became the most important part of my school life. I only fully realised what an effective weapon debate can be when it won me my first – and only – compliment from our Headmaster, the redoubtable Dr H. F. W. Payne.

'Docker' Payne, as he was known by the boys, was a truly formidable man. Not particularly tall, although quite strongly built, he ran his school with a rule of iron. The boys were terrified of him and so, too, were the staff, as I discovered later. Although I was bigger, on the few occasions I stood before him I felt like the mouse in the eyes of the cat. I have seen him reduce eighteen-year-old sixth-formers to tears with a few well-chosen words. Despite this, or because of it, his school reached a level of academic success that was widely envied in the North-West – not least so in many of the local public schools.

One day he attended a debating society forum when we were addressing a sanctimonious motion in support of the lines from a hymn: *Step by step since time began We see the steady gain of man.*

I had chosen to lead the opposition to the motion, partly because I didn't believe it, but mainly because it gave me the opportunity to be controversial. I had planned a bitter speech on the decline of man's freedom, and then 'Docker' came into the hall and sat down. It was a time to decide – discretion or valour?

Docker had caned me only once before, when I was caught aiming ink from my fountain pen at the back of a woman teacher's gown. My aim was bad, and it was her neck that took the stain, and off I went to the head's study. It was an experience I did not wish to repeat and, although I would never be punished for what I said in a public debate, I had no desire to build up a back-log of 'black marks' for the future.

In fact, I held my breath for a few seconds and launched into the speech I had prepared. It expounded my beliefs –

which I still hold – that many have in fact not gained, but slipped back, in the search for personal fulfilment. Afterwards Docker came striding towards me. He cleared his throat, as though having difficulty in speaking, and muttered gruffly: 'Well, Smith, at least that is an original outlook.' He turned on his heels and stalked away. It was the nearest he could get to an out-and-out compliment.

While the Unitarians were teaching me to think for myself, and the Debating Society to speak for myself, the school's masters were teaching me some of the lessons of history. I became totally immersed in modern history, and in particular those six or seven years before the 1914–18 War when the mighty Liberal governments of first Campbell-Bannerman and then Asquith pushed through some of the great reforms of British history. Gladstone had already introduced primary education for all children, thus destroying the monopoly of learning held by the rich. Campbell-Bannerman and Asquith went on to introduce the first sickness benefits for the poor, old-age pensions and, in 1911, imposed controls on the House of Lords' powers after the Tory landowners in that chamber had twice refused to accept the Liberal Budget.

The history of the seventeenth and eighteenth centuries, with unlimited power in the hands of the monarch and the aristocracy, had seemed colourful but remote. They were part of a glorious cavalcade, but their doings had absolutely no connection with my life that I could see. The great Liberals on the other hand laid down the enlightened ground rules of civilised life in an industrial society, and to me they were very real. Gladstone, the son of a Liverpool merchant, Asquith, a Yorkshireman, John Bright, Rochdale's own contributor to reform, were men with whom I could identify. They were rich men, surely, but one knew that their lifestyles had taken them into contact with the ordinary man, and given them some understanding of his problems.

They were interested in the politics of people, making genuine efforts to improve the lot of the masses who, until their times, may well not have existed at all in the eyes of Britain's rulers. What struck me most deeply, in my lessons on the years before the Great War, was the way in which every reform aimed at helping the ordinary man was fought tooth and nail by the

Tories. What did it matter to them, I asked? They were rich, famous, secure. Why should they grudge a few basic improvements in the bitter, grinding lives of the poor? My upbringing had, of course, done nothing to ally me with Tory thinking. But what was this fear of the working man? A distrust of Tory party motives, born from hours of reading those school books, has never really left me.

Grammar school passed quickly – too quickly – in a blur of debates, swotting and pranks. Although we held many of the masters in great affection, we also felt it beholden on us to make their life as difficult as possible. They tolerated the jokes and the escapades with a kindly patience, knowing, I suppose, that we were young men cutting our teeth, testing authority for the first time. They allowed us to push them to the very limits, but vengeance came swiftly when those limits were exceeded. It was a school that channelled boyish spirits in the right direction, but never broke them.

In my School Certificate I managed respectable credits in Maths, French, English language and History, with passes in English literature, art and geography. I failed chemistry, of course, but that was a foregone conclusion. It was a subject which had baffled me completely. In one class exam, I had scored the school's lowest mark, with three out of three hundred. They gave me the three, they said, for writing my name correctly on the top of the paper.

With that behind me, the time came to make the first major decision of my life. Should I stay on at school and try for university, or go out into the world and earn a living? It was a decision I had to take on my own, because my mother took me aside one evening and said, 'Cyril, I know these are hard times, but if you want to go to college you must stay at school and forget about taking a job. We have managed so far, and we'll go on managing until it's time to stop. It's up to you.'

I was well aware of the value of money, and just how difficult it was to earn. Since my early days at school, I had been contributing to the family pot. I had two daily newspaper rounds, which brought in five shillings a week, and a Sunday newspaper round which brought in another two shillings, and they were only the basis of my schoolboy economy.

For the jam on my bread and butter, I delivered telegrams

for the Post Office for ten hours every Saturday – a half a crown plus tips – and the star of my fund-raising activities was my job working five evenings a week in the projection room at the Empire Cinema for ten whole shillings! So already I had a regular income of nineteen shillings and sixpence a week, which the telegram tips regularly took over the one pound mark. Most of that went into the family budget.

When it came to raising spending money for myself, there were ways and means for a lad who was prepared to keep an eye open for opportunity. I would whitewash a lavatory for one shilling, and paint a hen-house for five, and I provided the lime in that price too, so the owner received a fair bargain. But holiday times, Christmas and Wakes Week, were the occasions for the real killings.

My paper rounds took me round the stalls of Rochdale Market once a day, and I fell in naturally with the raucous, back-chatting market traders. These were the war years, with strict rationing, and life's luxuries were scarce. Many a fowl went onto a family's Christmas Day table thanks to my friends on the market, and many a half-crown went into my back-pocket as part of the deal.

However, it was in Wakes Week, the traditional Rochdale cotton industry holiday in June, when the budding businessman in me reached his peak. Wartime travel on the railways was limited and extremely crowded, and for this reason the railways issued only sufficient tickets to fill a holiday train. Tickets, in Wakes Week, were obviously at a premium.

They were issued, with all the grudging grace of charity, at the Thomas Cook office in Drake Street. It was a time when Britain was a queue-weary nation, men and women patiently standing in lines for hours for bread or for bacon, for butter or – a day of the wildest exhilaration – for bananas. Even the banana queues were the merest caterpillars compared with the snakes of the Wakes Week rail queues. I decided, very early in the war, that this was a situation worthy of exploitation.

So one night before the ticket sale, I took a few orders from family and neighbours, threw a blanket over my shoulders and at midnight walked down to Thomas Cook's. I slept on the doorstep, and had my pick of available tickets at ten seconds after nine am the following day. It became a yearly event, as eagerly anticipated as a camping expedition, and I eventually built up an order list of some eighty, perhaps even a hundred tickets ... at one shilling a time. Remembering lurid stories of the Spanish conquest of South America, I used to call it my 'Drake Street Eldorado'.

With four-score shillings jangling in my pockets, I went off on the five-day family holiday at Cleveleys, a little seaside town near Blackpool, with all the swagger of a Cortes back from the Halls of Montezuma.

Holidays were a time of giggles and tears, jokes and clipped-ears, as the five members of the Smith family staggered off to the railway station heavily laden. We took few clothes – the bare minimum, in fact – but we puffed and heaved under burdens of suitcases filled with such unlikely booty as loaves of bread, pots of fish-paste, tins of beans and perhaps – we were on holiday after all – a couple of tins of salmon.

We could not afford one of those posh boarding houses that provided bed and board. Our Cleveleys holiday outpost provided only the beds, and a kitchen in which the guests did their own cooking. Our journeys therefore took on the character of an army patrol carrying its supplies on its back. We knew the cheaper shops in Rochdale – food is often more expensive in holiday resorts, of course – but more significantly, our ration books seemed to provide a wider selection of the 'scarcity' goods in the shops where we were known. That very word 'scarcity' brings back all the atmosphere of those war years. It's a word hardly ever used now, but in those days many a shopkeeper would drop his eyes in embarrassment and shuffle his feet behind the counter before he said, 'Sorry, young man, but there's a terrible scarcity, you know.'

I remember going off to Cleveleys in my school blazer for the last time. I had plenty of money in my pocket, for Drake Street had been a particular bonanza that year, and I was determined to enjoy it. It meant a week of fish with my chips, and bouncing bus journeys into Blackpool to see the lavish shows on the Golden Mile. I had decided to leave school and get a job.

There have been a few times in my life when I have regretted giving up the chance of a university education. When I was asked if I would consider challenging for the leadership of the

Liberal party, I said, 'No – I don't think I am academically qualified for the job.' I think the disciplined learning of university is something that might have tempered some of my more impulsive decisions, taken by a part of my character which demands instant action overwhelming the other which meekly suggests a period of considered judgement. On the whole, however, the schooling I received at Rochdale has fitted me admirably for the life I have chosen to live.

My motives for leaving school at sixteen – although my family would have fully supported a decision to stay on – seem in retrospect quite complex, although at the time I had few qualms. In a nutshell, I felt that my grandmother and mother had done enough. It was time for me to do my share.

If I have gone to some length to itemise the ways in which I tried to earn money, it is because money *was* important to me then. Money did not mean a new colour television set, or a holiday in Spain, and it most certainly did not mean having a bigger car or a more luxurious kitchen than the Joneses. It meant a new pair of shoes for my sister Eunice, and perhaps a shorter wait until it was my turn on the rota to have some new boots... It meant PAID stamped on the bottom of the electricity card, or the freedom to order another bag of coal. It meant being able to hold up your head when you walked into the corner shop, where others, less fortunate, could no longer show their faces because their 'tick' had run out.

So, eventually, it was my turn to bring home a pay packet. With my School Certificate and a High School background, I found a choice job, as a clerk in the Rochdale Inland Revenue offices, watching over other people's money. The pay was not particularly good, but they do not put civil servants on short-time and, as many a middle-aged adult said to me, 'There'll be your pension to look forward to.' Imagine! A boy of sixteen was supposed to look forward to his pension, forty-nine long years away. I never did take the pension into consideration, fortunately. Politics were about to take a firm grip on my life.

Since that evening in 1941, in the blackout, my determination to involve myself in politics had been growing. It had been reinforced by the satisfaction of the school debates, and whenever I met anyone with strong political opinions I had developed a knack of getting them involved in argument. I was attracted to many Left wing causes, but was growing obsessed with the problems of individual freedom. On Sunday evenings in those days, when the cinemas were closed and, thankfully, television had not become a mass anaesthetic, the Town Hall Square in Rochdale was a centre of entertainment – political entertainment.

Speakers of all political spectrums, plus a handful of religious hot-gospellers, climbed onto their soap-boxes in different corners of the square to berate the evening strollers with their views. I would go down and move from pitch to pitch, sampling the arguments, sometimes congratulating, sometimes heckling. One regular speaker was an old-style Communist who, week in week out, would roundly condemn the evils of Capitalism and urge the workers to unite and rise in revolution. He and I soon became involved in a personal battle of wits. I would start my weekly question time in the same way. 'I have some respect for your views but can you tell me if I could go to Moscow and make a similar speech from a soap-box in Red Square?' I asked that question dozens of times, and the speaker developed a carefully rehearsed, evasive reply. I never did get a *real* answer to that question!

Town Hall Square on Sunday evenings had, for me, all the noise and bustle of an Indian bazaar, but there were other occasions when I became involved in deeper, more personal debates. For some years on my rounds, I had been delivering papers to Harold Chorlton, a local Labour Councillor and textile union leader. My rounds began to get longer and longer as I prodded Harold into giving his views on reform, social change and personal freedom. At the tax office I had similar debates with a well-known local Liberal, Frank Lord. Both men asked me to join their parties and both became eager to persuade this curious, cocky young man that *he* was right and the other fellow wrong.

Finally, as the 1945 General Election campaign got under way, Frank took me to Liberal party headquarters in Drake Street. I was in, taking an active part in my first election campaign at the age of sixteen. I have remembered and taken note of my reasons for joining the Liberals. Two men whom I liked and respected had been trying to recruit me to their flag. One of them took the step of leading me physically to his party offices, and introducing me to the workers there. I was even introduced to Charles Harvey, the Liberal candidate, and I remember the honour of it all: me, Cyril Smith, actually talking to someone who wanted to go to the Houses of Parliament! Suddenly, I had changed from being a youthful, intellectual dabbler into a personally involved activist. Party recruiters would do well to ponder that lesson.

I threw myself into the election with a wild excitement. All the rambling, half-formed political ideas of my youth were given the commitment of a concrete objective. All my efforts could be channelled into a purposeful direction. It is such a shame that the 1945 election proved to be a disaster for the Liberals, politically, and for me, personally.

One of the highlights of our campaign was to be a speech in Packer Spout Gardens – what a name, where did it come from? – by Sir Archibald Sinclair, the party Leader. To my astonishment, I was asked to make one of the supporting speeches, presumably to show that the Liberals had youth on their side. It was a small speech, a minor supporting role, but it was the first speech of my life that *mattered* and I delivered it with gusto.

Unknown to me, one member of my audience was watching and listening with an undue concern. Packer Spout Gardens is overlooked by a red-brick building at the corner of Fleece Street (another curiously apt name) which was the Rochdale office of the Inland Revenue. Standing at a window listening as I spoke, was my boss, Alf North, a man of principle and understanding, but a man who believed in playing life 'by the book'.

I was unaware, until I was called to his office the following day, that one of the stricter rules of the civil service was that its members should not take part in political activities which might be seen to affect their impartiality. Mr North looked at me solemnly over the top of his desk and said. 'Smith, you have to choose – the civil service or politics. I will give you a day to think about it. Bring your mother to the office tomorrow and we will talk about it – I'm sure that she would like the opportunity to have her say.'

I was stunned. I had been in the Revenue for just six months, and although I was happy with the work, I already knew that it could not provide an outlet for the major ambitions of my life. I dragged my feet on the way home that night, and my sad stumbling explanation to my mother is probably the most difficult conversation I have ever had.

'Well, Cyril,' she said, 'it's a good job – but it was your decision to leave school and this one has got to be your decision as well.'

My mother and I were both downcast as we stood before Mr North the following morning.

'Well, Smith, what's it going to be?' he asked.

'Politics, Sir,' I said.

'Is there anything you would like to say, Mrs Smith?'

'No, Mr North – he has made his mind up, and I for one will not make him change it.'

He shook his head, and said with a sad little smile, 'It's exactly what I expected you to do, son.'

As he held open the door of the office, he shook my hand and said more brightly, 'You might like to know, Cyril, that I think you've done the right thing. You would have done well here, if you could put your mind to it, but I think you will do better in politics.'

We were out on the street, a sixteen-year-old unemployed boy and a mother, trudging home in silence, both trying to fight back the tears.

Eventually, she spoke. 'I just hope that you know what you're doing, son.'

'I do Mam, I do,' I replied with brusque confidence, but the fact is I was very unsure.

That political ban on many civil servants still exists. I can imagine that it is very necessary in the higher reaches of Whitehall, where the senior civil servants hold as much, if not more, power and patronage than most ministers. But how Liberal party membership was supposed to threaten the State in the hands of the most junior clerk in the Inland Revenue, I will never know. I have never regretted my decision to quit, except in that it caused my mother a great deal of unspoken anxiety. If I had stayed on then, I would still be there, and this book would never have been written. It was the first of many times that 'they' – officialdom in its widest sense – tried to gag me. In refusing to be silenced, I was set irredeemably on the course I have followed to this day.

CHAPTER FOUR

Breakfasts

The bleak, austere world of 1945 was facing, hopefully, a bright new future. The honeymoon between the West and Stalin's Russia was still at the starry-eyed stage, and at last, Britain was to be a land fit for heroes. This was the glowing promise for me, even though my personal future seemed to involve white-washing lavatories once more at five bob a time. At least being unemployed meant that I could become a fulltime, unpaid Liberal party worker for the duration of the General Election campaign. I was blissfully unaware of the turmoils, both personal and political, that lay ahead.

My first shock came when I found that electioneering is not a glamorous round of stirring speeches, enthusiastic crowds and ceremonial banquets. No, the really successful campaign is based on sheer drudgery, knocking on doors in the rain, listening to unending complaints, addressing by hand hundreds upon thousands of envelopes containing pamphlets and propaganda. In 1945, we even had to collect the envelopes, cadging them by the meagre half-dozen here, half-dozen there, for there was a 'scarcity'. We addressed economy labels, hour in, hour out, until our wrists ached so much we couldn't lift the occasional cup of tea brought round by gaily chatting lady helpers.

The candidates get the glamour, of course. They are photographed in the local press, they shake the hands of the dignitaries, sometimes their sayings are reported in the national press or on the radio. The fulltime agents, too, are in their element, handling a team of assistants brought flooding in by the excitement of the event, discussing tactics and policies, forever on the telephone to head office in London for more publicity material, more background facts, pressing for more visits from nationally famous speakers. Yet it is the unseen, unpaid, *loyal* party workers who are the vital nuts and bolts which keep the machine in motion.

The shock of working so relentlessly hard was compounded for me, a bright-eyed, ideal-flushed teenager, by the minute amount of interest shown by most members of the general public. I realised, for the first time, that the average voter has little interest in this game which gave me so much excitement. The people were jaded with politics, quite naturally as they had just endured yet another crippling war for which, they believed, the politicians were to blame. To be a successful campaigner, a candidate had to raise their flagging interest. A good canvasser had to meet disinterest with enthusiasm in such quantity that it fired the voter with enough energy to turn out on the day and put the cross in the right box. It was a tough election, but I learned many lessons from it.

If, incidentally, you *are* one of those people who dread the knock of a canvasser on your door at election time, there is only one successful way to discourage him: say you definitely will NOT vote for his party. You will go down in the records as an 'anti' voter. No car will call at your door on polling day, no 'Future Reference' note will be made for your name, so that you can be canvassed for some distant pool. If, like many embarrassed people, you prefer to be nice and say, 'Yes, I am voting for you' all these things will happen, at least if a good agent is running the constituency. If you say No to every party, you might never get canvassed again. You might also cease being a drain on the delicate enthusiasm of the party workers.

That enthusiasm is vital to any would-be MP. In 1945, I was totally committed to our candidate, Charles Harvey. There was no way in which he could lose, I believed, although we had not had a Liberal member for Rochdale since 1924. We party workers had complete faith, absolute optimism.

I can barely describe our feelings when the results finally came in, delayed as they were by two or three weeks waiting for the Forces votes from all corners of the earth.

Mr Harvey, director of a local mill, had gone down to Labour by 11,836 votes – and was six thousand behind the Tory. Winston Churchill was out, and Clement Attlee was in on a landslide. Our only consolation in Rochdale was that we had kept our deposit. Throughout the country, seventy-six Liberals had forfeited their deposits and our Parliamentary group was reduced from twenty-one to twelve. Life's irony had decreed that the first election I helped fight under the Liberal banner was to be the same election which started their irrevocable slide to that lamented 'minority party' status.

I had lost a job and I had helped lose an election, or so I thought; and I was just seventeen years old. Even the difficulties of my childhood had not prepared me for a blow like this. All my life, people had been telling me, 'It's a cruel world.' In the optimism of youth, I had always disregarded them. Suddenly, in July 1945, I realised that there might be a grain of truth in the saying... not a whole truth, but perhaps a grain. I think I had believed that if you wanted something badly enough, and you were prepared to work hard enough, it would eventually come your way. I now knew that wanting and working were not enough. You also needed something else: stamina. The dreams of life were still there to be fulfilled, but they were obviously going to take a great deal longer to achieve.

It was time to look for a job, and a hard time for such a task. Industry was running down from its full war footing, and not yet changed back to civilian production. Men were coming back from the Forces demanding, quite correctly, their old jobs. I tramped the streets of Manchester hoping to become a copy boy in one of the newspaper offices, with the ambition of becoming a reporter. Nothing doing. I tried the ads in the local papers and, feeling in some way that I had let the family down, often went for work I knew I would hate. It was no good. Turner Brothers, the large Rochdale asbestos company, rejected my application to be a correspondence clerk. At least I was to have the last laugh on that one.

Shortly after I became MP for Rochdale, Turners – the town's biggest employers – entertained me in their board room. With some delight, I explained that once upon a time the firm had not considered me worthy of a lowly job. I have to confess that I took some pleasure at the discomfort this story caused among the directors. Eventually, someone looked up the records and it was explained that I had been too highly qualified for the job on offer which, thought the personnel department of the time, would lead to my becoming unhappy with the work. It was a nice reply. I hope it contained more truth than flattery, but I doubt it.

After several weeks trudging the streets – I really did consider going back to whitewashing lavatories fulltime – I was taken on as an office boy at Fothergill and Harvey, a big textile mill at Littleborough, on the outskirts of Rochdale. Charles Harvey, our Liberal candidate, was a director of the company but I must hurry to point out there was no 'Old Boys' influence at play: I answered an advertisement and was taken on without mentioning Mr Harvey and – as far as I know – without his knowledge.

Forthergills was to be a good training ground for me. It introduced me to the ways of a large, private enterprise company, and also to girls – girls by the score. I was by this time very obviously overweight, edging near the twenty-stones mark, and my relationship with females was, to say the least, wary. Fat men do not make the most presentable companions, socially, and my first, hesitant advances had met with rebuff. I had that fierce, adolescent pride which would not accept rejection and – although it was never a conscious decision – I imagine I had simply stopped making the initial advances. I discovered with dismay that I was to be the only male in an office of eleven girls!

At first, I was embarrassed almost to the point of speechlessness, an unusual state for me even at that age. After a few days, however, my tensions eased and I became, if anything, the office mascot. The girls certainly relaxed, for they talked openly and loudly amongst themselves about the most intimate details of their lives, as though I were not there. I no longer have any illusions about the gentility of 'ladies talk'.

There was one girl there, strikingly beautiful, better dressed than most, who took little part in the general banter. I would sit and stare at her when I knew she wasn't looking, only to turn hurriedly away if she glanced in my direction. She became part of my fantasy life, and I would dream of walking arm-in-arm with her down the prom at Blackpool. In real life, though, I never did approach her. She was too good looking, too smart, to be interested in a fat youth like me. I will not mention her name, for she is married now and I know her to be very happy, but I sometimes wonder what might have happened if I had summoned the courage to ask her to 'walk-out'.

The girls in the office presumably decided that I had more use than I thought, for they quickly elected me as the office-staff representative on the works council. This was one of the more enlightened institutions of the Fothergill management, which met regularly to discuss future plans by the company and to air some of the grievances of the shop-floor. It was not a militant body in today's accepted sense, but it did represent a useful line of communication between management and staff. Ever searching for ways of expressing my ambition to be 'somebody', I became secretary of the canteen committee and the entertainments committee and, by the time I was eighteen, secretary of the works council itself – an eighteen year old representing the views of some four hundred workers. It was a job of little power and considerable extra work, but it put me at the centre of things.

With the workers, I suppose I was fairly popular. I helped reorganise the works cricket teams, spoke up, and they rewarded me in one of my stranger youthful adventures. Looking for attention in any form, I had entered the Carrol Levis Discoveries Show as a singer. To my amazement, the old Theatre Royal in Rochdale was packed the night I appeared. I learned the following day that more than two hundred Fothergills' people had paid to see me. I won nothing in the show, but they gave me a great cheer.

How popular I was with the Fothergill management is not so certain, and for the first time in my life I began to encounter the petty jealousies which, for some reason, always seem to surround any person who decides to take a vigorous part in any human activity. This is one of the mysteries of life to me.

In any group of people, there will be found those with grievances, petty or serious, real or imagined. From time to time, these people will choose a leader who, they hope, will put those grievances right. The man who accepts that leadership, in my experience, almost always finds himself on a hiding to nothing. If he fails to right the problem, he has let the group down, yet if he succeeds, he can face even worse. Allegations of 'bossiness' or 'big-headedness' seem to be the automatic rewards of winning a point.

As a teenage secretary of the works council, I was painfully open to criticisms from older employees, and some of them took the opportunity to go behind my back for revenge. One of our few real grievances at the mill was that the buses, which ferried the workers the five miles or so back to Rochdale, were always ten to fifteen minutes late. Although this seems incredibly trivial in today's climate of open industrial warfare, that wait for the buses, particularly in the harsh Pennine winters, became a major 'grouse' among my fellow workers. One day, over a cup of tea in the canteen, I suggested that the works council should raise the matter with the management. The remark was overheard and someone reported my proposal to the boss, in terms that I can only believe were exceptionally colourful. I was summoned to see Mr Alec Harvey, the managing director, and accused of 'inciting the works to rebellion'. I was angry and not a little anxious, because I thought I was going to be sacked – an experience which, after the Inland Revenue débâcle, would have been a serious blow to my self-esteem. However, Mr Harvey was a straight-talking man, quick to see injustice, and allowed me to argue my case.

From then on, the buses arrived on time and, I believe, a small victory had been won in the cause of good industrial relations. Too often managements allow trivial but irritating issues to cloud the whole spectrum of worker morale. Many times, however, it is *not* the managers' fault, because an issue can be grumbled over in the canteen, groused about in the toilets, but no one has the sense – or is it the courage? – to report it to the boss.

The bus queue affair was my first lesson in industrial relations. It had all the classic ingredients of a mutiny – grumbling below decks, treachery in the ranks, misunderstanding and incomprehension on the bridge. It is minutiae like this which dog British industrial relations, with each side constantly pin-pricking the other until the multitude of tiny wounds eventually opens a running sore.

That is an observation about industry in general, and not aimed particularly at Fothergills, a family firm run in general on the very best lines. Nevertheless, the experience gave me my first warning of the dangers of taking a leading role in any walk of life. It put on another self-protecting layer. Some of my detractors have, from time to time, suggested that I am so rotund because my skin is so thick. Perhaps they are right. Could I be like some human onion, with layer upon layer of thick skins?

The latter half of the 1940s became a time for packing in experience, putting flesh on the bones of my education at school, church and home. In 1945, the family were forced to move from Falinge Road, the dark, cramped house which had been the only home I knew. It was a forced move of the most graphic kind: the cottage next door simply fell down, wornout by age and neglect. With the rickety support of next-door gone, our own place was endangered. We lived briefly at a couple of addresses, before moving to the slightly larger terraced house in Emma Street, Rochdale, which is my home to this day.

In 1947, I had my first encounter with grief when my grandmother, one of the twin pillars of my childhood, died in the front room at Emma Street. She had been so much to me – to be fair, she took the place of a father – but I could not cry at her bedside. She was seventy-nine, and I drew on all my youthful courage to rationalise that she had had a good life, if a hard one. My resolve could not last, however. At the funeral, I wept inconsolably. I wish she could have lived long enough to see some of the earlier successes of my life, she deserved that: she, as much as anyone, made me what I am.

There were other blows, too. Some of them, I suspect, were dealt out by other hands than those of an unkind fate. For some time, I had been taking steps to achieve the growing ambition of becoming a teacher. The preliminaries were successfully resolved, and I found myself a place for the following year at a Chester teachers' training college, on the condition that I spend the intervening months as a student teacher in a Rochdale school. To become a student teacher, I had to take a medical examination.

The medical, of course, was a worry to me and I consulted my family doctor: did I have a chance of passing? Dr Scarr reassured me. I wouldn't make a jet-pilot or even a coal-miner, he said, but I was perfectly fit to teach in school. Despite my obesity, my heart and lungs and limbs were in first-class shape. Warmed by this confidence, I went off to see the doctor appointed by the Education Authority. The blow was that much more sickening when I was told I had failed. Heavy with disappointment, I went back to tell Dr Scarr the news and was surprised at how angrily he received it. He strode from his desk and, from a room next door, telephoned the Authority's doctor.

I could hear his half of the conversation, because he was almost shouting in his anger, and the phrase which stuck in my mind – it was repeated two or three times – was, 'What the hell has that got to do with it?' He slammed down the phone and returned to the surgery, his face flushed. Nervously, I asked him what was wrong. He gave me a long stare, as though hesitating, but finally said, 'I'm sorry, Cyril, but my professional ethics prevent me from telling you.'

It was only many years later, as a Councillor, that I was to get an intimation of the real cause for my rejection. Applicants for teaching posts were, in those days, judged on harsh moral yardsticks. Teachers must set a good example to the children. Added to this was the fact that one of the most powerful men responsible for the selection of teachers was a staunch Methodist who, in the past, had made several bitter attacks on the Unitarian Church. Yet here was an application from a youth who was not only illegitimate, but also a Unitarian. What obstacles these were! When I later became chairman of the Education Committee my earlier rejection was, naturally enough, a considerable embarrassment to officers who could remember the incident. Even in my position as chairman, I was never able to extract a completely satisfactory answer. The nearest I ever came to an explanation was a hurried, crestfallen confession from one officer who said: 'I don't think the reason was connected with the medical, Mr Chairman, but that is all I know.' I didn't need to push further.

That short sentence, taken along with the assurances of Dr Scarr, may not be complete proof, but I remain convinced that a teaching career was taken from me out of prejudice. Recent corruption cases have shown beyond all doubt that local government is not always the haven of considered justice it was once thought to be.

I do, however, have this major consolation, once again the last laugh. I have no doubt that had I been allowed to become a teacher I would have thrown all my energies into the profession. I may have become a headmaster and perhaps something of a personage in the world of education. It would have given me a highly satisfactory career. It would also have sapped much of the energy I have thrown into my political work, and deprived me without doubt of the intriguing, if not extraordinary, life I have actually led.

If there is anyone still alive who allowed blind prejudice to stop a wildly enthusiastic youth taking up his chosen career, read this – *and accept my thanks*. I do wonder, however, if there were other young men and women whose lives were irredeemably blighted by a similar disregard of basic Christianity.

While I was suffering setbacks in my work and sadness at home, my political career was beginning to turn in a purposeful direction. Despite the bitterness – or perhaps because of it – I had recovered from the shock of the 1945 defeat and immersed myself totally in Liberal party affairs.

I was chairman of the Rochdale League of Liberals, and won a North-West area debating competition. I helped form a Rochdale youth 'Parliament', where between three and four hundred teenagers divided in loyalties between Conservative, Liberal, Labour and Communist met regularly in the Pioneers' Hall to take part in debates run exactly on House of Commons lines. Can anyone imagine that many youngsters turning out for a political 'game' today? I did have the satisfaction, when the Liberals wrested control of the Parliament, of being elected Prime Minister – the nearest, no doubt, I will ever get to the role.

By 1947, I was an executive member of the North-West Federation of Young Liberals, a member of the National Executive of the Young Liberals and a Young Liberals representative on the party's National Council. I was beginning to stretch out my arms from Rochdale, to get my fingers near the pulse of *national* politics. It was a time not just for talking, but also for watching, and listening, and learning.

I may have been edging towards the party's vital nerve centres, but I was still to see my twentieth birthday. And what is more, despite defiant speeches, I was still a product of my background. A born radical, I was coming into contact for the first time with the elite sections of the party, the rich, the famous, the well-educated and – I was beginning to see it even

On right, front row, is my grandmother; with her, on the left, is my aunt; my brother is between them, and standing behind are my mother and me.

A real family group. This is us on holiday at Cleveleys, with our landlady, my sister, my grandmother, and behind, my mother, brother and me. I was fourteen years old.

The four of us – my sister, my mother, myself and my brother, on holiday at Cleveleys.

Centre: The mayoral lamps outside my home, 14 Emma Street, Rochdale. The lamps stay for one year only.

Bottom left: Me and my mum having a paddle.

Bottom right: My brother-in-law, Ken, and me relaxing on holiday. I was seventeen years of age.

The photo I used for my first council election in 1952.

Enjoying a drink (notice it's lemonade!) with the late Ralph Williams, a former Rochdale Mayor.

Left: One of my earliest holidays in London, with me and my mother feeding the birds in Trafalgar Square.

Below: My mother and me, as Mayor and Mayoress of Rochdale, in our chains and robes.

The declaration of the result of the 1951 General Election in Ashton-under-Lyne, where I was Labour Party agent.

On my way from church, on Mayoral Sunday 1966.

Lord Rhodes (then Hervey Rhodes) outside Ashton-under-Lyne town hall after the 1951 election, which he won. I was his agent.

Clement Attlee addressing a meeting, which I had organised, in Ashton-under-Lyne. Attlee was Prime Minister.

I visit David Steel's constituency. This is my mother, brother and me with David and his wife, Judy.

The count in Rochdale town hall at the February 1974 General Election. I indicate my majority in thousands and my secretary, Judith, keeps an eye on my votes.

I enjoy a drink with Harry Secombe when he came to Rochdale.

I welcome a party of Rochdale children to the House of Commons. These children came from my own primary school, Spotland, which I attended as a child. Miss J. Lees, the headmistress, is in the back row, next but one on my right.

Top: My present factory – opened in 1966, and purpose-built.

Bottom right: My first factory, opened in 1963. Outside my colleague, Mr Harrison, and me.

Bottom left: An internal view of part of my factory. As opened in 1966.

then – the political dilettantes. Socially, I was still a wide-eyed boy.

My jobs on the National Council and the Young Liberals Executive began to take me regularly to London, expeditions into wonderland for a boy who, only two years previously, had thought the world ended at Cleveleys. There were the sights, of course, Parliament, the Tower, the Palace, the walk down Horse Guards Parade as I made a slight detour on the way to the National Liberal Club. There was that fine building itself, a baroque Victorian confection built to the memory of Gladstone, with a library containing more leather-bound books than I had ever seen in one place. There were also the breakfasts.

I may have been a young man on his way to make a name for himself in politics, but I was also a young man with a hearty appetite and – for the first time – a few shillings in his pocket to indulge it in a modest sort of way. To be in London for a morning conference meant catching the midnight train from Manchester. It was a dusty trip, in hot crowded compartments on trains run near to destruction during the war, and it deposited me on the platform at Euston at some unearthly hour in the morning.

No matter, I set off at a purposeful stride through the just stirring streets, my mind set on my ultimate haven – Lyons' Corner House in the Strand. I was to be one of the privileged few. I would be at the head of the queue for the first serving of breakfast. And the first serving meant *bacon* with your egg. Food rationing still had an iron grip on the land, and bacon was as prized as lobster and fillet steak are today.

There were other breakfasts, too, which I remember well. At National Council meetings, it was the custom to farm out delegates from the provinces to the homes of the party faithful in London. On the first occasion it happened to me, I looked down with horror at the name and address on the scrap of paper which had been handed me and bleated: 'There must be some mistake – you can't send *me* here.' Oh yes they could, they said, and off I went on the tube to a magnificent house, overlooking Lord's Cricket Ground, the home of Sir Andrew McFadyean, who was then party treasurer.

It just couldn't be true, I thought, as I looked up at the great door of the house. Me, not yet twenty, staying at the home of a real-life *Sir*. The house had a servant who called *me* 'Sir', and I couldn't help thinking what my mother would say. They, too, had hundreds of books, and velvet curtains, and huge reading lamps that stood on the floor by your chair. It was the first time I had known of the existence of such a thing as a standard lamp, much less seen one.

Yet Sir Andrew seemed completely unaware of the deep impression his home was having on me. If he had treated me with the condescension a man of his style and wealth often reserves for awkward youths from unfashionable towns, I don't think I would have been offended. I rather expected him to treat me in that way. In fact, he spoke to me with great charm, as if addressing an equal in age and wisdom, and listened attentively to my views. I rose early the following morning, for I wanted to walk round the streets of London, and breakfast had been laid on for me specially. Sir Andrew came down in his dressing gown and we continued our conversation about the state of the party.

That breakfast had a profound effect on me. I realised that despite my ungainly size, despite my awkwardness, I could finally talk to anyone, anywhere, and express my views without fear of being laughed at. If I ever had any inverted snobbery, it left me that morning.

The views that I had been discussing were the foundation of my very first attempt to sway Liberal party policy as a whole. A hobby horse was beginning to grow underneath me, and it is one that I still ride today – a deep-down, emotional belief that workers have the right to a much bigger say in the running of their own industries.

In the late forties, the majority of British management had still refused to learn the lessons of the General Strike and the misery of the thirties. The war had allowed them to push many unpalatable truths into the background, hopefully – from their point of view – to be forgotten. Instead of seizing the immediate post-war years as a golden opportunity for a fresh start, to make industry a genuine partnership of interests for both management and labour, they appeared to have gone back to the very worst attitudes of the Bad Old Days. Workers were once again to be mindless serfs, really little more than machines built of muscle and bone rather than of steel. A start button would be pressed, and these human machines would begin to produce the goods until someone pressed the button marked stop.

These men-machines, so it was thought had neither minds nor mouths. Just to be at Peace again was their bonus, a paypacket the sole reason for their existence. The Attlee landslide should have warned the industrial establishment that they were misinformed. The new Labour government's sweeping nationalisation programme seemed to produce in boardrooms a terror of the workers, a feeling that they should be prevented from expressing any opinion on the future conduct of their industry. The factory floor was to become the new battlefield, but this was to be a civil war.

My deep interest in the problems of working men stemmed from the many youthful conversations with men from my neighbourhood about the profound indignity of being treated as an inconsequential robot. The Them and Us syndrome had been an integral part of my youth, a cause of burning resentment. Were we not all free men, living in a free society? Were we not equal partners in producing wealth?

Although these feelings were Left wing, I could see the value of shareholders. It was a time when investment to replace warworn machinery and plant was desperately needed. But were shareholders' interests really the be-all and end-all of industrial life? A factory which lost money might cost a wealthy stockholder an extra week in Cannes, perhaps mean bets at Royal Ascot. A factory which lost money would cost a worker his job, the money to put shoes on his children's feet to forestall the landlord's eviction order. Surely, in a free society, these, too, were considerations worthy of the most serious attention?

These were some of the questions which tormented me in the last years of my teens. One other query was: *should I join the Labour party?* Although a passionate Labour government was enacting some of the greatest reforms in the history of Parliament, many of which I welcomed with youthful fervour, its obsession with nationalisation worried me. I could not easily forget my school lessons on the great Victorian Liberals, concerned as they were with personal freedom. Nationalisation, to me, represented the inexorable growth in power of the State, ever-spreading tentacles snaking their way deeper and deeper into the workings of everyday society. It was anathema to my radical creed.

Nationalisation also offered, it seemed to me, an opportunity for the Liberal party to claw back some of the power it had lost. The electoral humiliation of Mr Churchill had proved that the country was tired of Tory ways, yet here was a Labour government terrifying huge sections of the public with the ogre of State control. Surely, if the Liberals could come forward with a radical, but just industrial policy, one which gave shareholder, manager and worker a right to fair rewards and a fair hearing, we had an electoral trump card? I set out, innocent of political machinations, to help sway the Liberals towards a policy of worker-participation.

In my eyes, that meant a workers' council in every factory, where the employers and the employed discussed company policy, future production problems and methods of improving productivity. The man on the shop-floor would no longer face a *fait accompli* that his working life had been radically altered in some direction – without his consent and participation. It meant that if he had an idea of how to improve his working life and that of his factory, he could freely express it. It also meant profit-sharing, for nothing motivates a man or a woman better than the thought that there is a bonus on the way. I earnestly believe that few workers would strike over a trivial issue – a mild rebuke from a foreman, the taste of the canteen tea – if a stoppage were to threaten a generous bonus just before Christmas or the summer holiday.

Perhaps my arrival at my first Liberal party Annual Conference at Hastings in 1949 should have warned me of the pitfalls ahead.

A Rochdale Liberal friend, Frank Gill, drove me to Hastings in his ageing Austin Seven. As we rolled down a hill into the town, there was a strange bump and, with no little amusement, we watched a lonely wheel overtake us and go skidding off down the road. It was some seconds before we realised that the wheel was ours. Obviously tired at the little car's laborious progress, it had decided to go off on a pioneering mission of its very own. Our amusement changed to consternation as the ancient brakes brought our three-wheeler to an unbelievably tardy halt. Frank chased off after the wheel, and in a sweat of relief we bolted it back in place.

It so happens that Frank was a diminutive man and, of course, I was no featherweight. As we finally trundled into Hastings, he could not resist turning and saying impishly: 'I suppose we should give a little prayer of thanks that the wheel came off the driver's side, and not from under the ballast.'

Three wheels or not, the car had not turned over. It would appear I held the balance!

Already, my brand of politics was raising a few lofty eyebrows within the Liberal party. I had, for instance, led a Young Liberal delegation to a crowded May Day Rally on Manchester's Platt Fields where we, too, had expressed our solidarity with the workers, surrounded as we were by perhaps five thousand Socialists, Communists and supporters of other far Left causes. Despite murmurs of disapproval, I was determined to keep the offensive alive.

I made my first-ever conference speech at Hastings that year, on my beloved subject of worker-participation. I returned to the attack at Blackpool the following year. To my intense joy, conference accepted the proposals. At last, I had made a national impact, helping to commit a major political party to what was then a truly radical policy. BBC radio even broadcast one of my conference speeches. Cyril Smith, it was apparent, had arrived on the national political stage.

I felt I had been rewarded with due recognition when, in 1948, I was appointed fulltime Liberal agent for Stockport, Cheshire, a town with the truest of blue Tory traditions and two Parliamentary seats. I was prepared for an uphill battle politically, but I had not realised that a Liberal agent is expected to be at least as good at raising money as he is at raising votes.

All political parties, except possibly the Tories, continually profess to be short of funds. The Liberal party, for as long as I have known it, is genuinely hard-pressed financially. I found that my job as agent in Stockport was not merely steering the political fortunes of two constituencies. It was also organising garden fetes, bazaars, social evenings here, extracting a few shillings there, to feed fighting funds suffering from acute malnutrition.

I was not only expected to cover my own salary – which, as youngest fulltime agent in the country, was far from lavish. There were also bills to pay, for the printing of posters and pamphlets, for postage, phone bills and hall bookings. On top of this, we were also expected to contribute to the party's national funds. As a bit of an expert in finding unexpected sources of income – my Thomas Cook bonanza years were still fresh in my mind – I think I succeeded reasonably well. I also learned a few much-needed lessons on grass-roots diplomacy.

Liberal party workers, because it is such a small party, tend to be totally dedicated. In a town like Stockport, where the electoral battles against the Tories were so thin in victories, the workers were dedicated almost to the point of obsession. The ladies who held the bazaars and the coffee mornings to raise our desperately needed funds, knew their worth and were eager that it should be recognised. Tact is a good agent's most vital weapon. It is a trait which I possess in minute quantity. A large part of whatever store I have built up I owe to the ladies of Stockport.

Tact aside, I was also painfully beginning to absorb some of the real facts of political life, like the simple axiom that there are times to speak out and times to stay silent. I stayed silent about my most important political venture in Stockport, a municipal elections pact with the Labour party.

I had been filled for some time with a growing concern that the post-war Liberals were becoming, not a party in their own right, but merely an anti-Labour group. This was reflected in the attitudes of scores of people I met, from Rochdale and Stockport to the leaders in London. To me, it was – and still is – a nonsensical policy. If people wish to vote anti-Labour, then they should surely vote Conservative if they live in a constituency where the Tory has a realistic chance of victory. There are very few towns – Rochdale is one – where the Liberal is the most effective anti-Socialist. Apart from that simple tactical truism, I dislike the principle that parties should gather votes for what they oppose. That is the politics of the negative, and can often lead to sterility in party thinking. 'Let someone else put forward policies, and we will oppose them.' That gives the opposition carte-blanche to push the best ideas. Surely it is more effective, if more arduous, to put forward the best policies in the first place.

In Stockport, it was naturally assumed that our job was to oppose Labour. I could see no reason why we shouldn't oppose the Conservatives. So in municipal elections, we quietly dropped out of wards which Labour had a chance of winning. Labour allowed us a straight contest where we might have a chance. It was a plan which met with a modest success but, sadly, it was a plan I could not talk about – I was beginning to realise that it is much easier to upset your own supporters than the opposition ranks.

These doubts about the true effectiveness of post-war Liberalism were beginning to loom large when the 1950 General Election was declared, but were quickly pushed aside in the excitement of the contest. After all, wasn't one of our Parliamentary planks to be the worker-participation scheme for which I had striven so hard?

When the first bundle of the national party manifesto arrived at my office, I was trembling with excitement as I cut the string. Hurriedly, I skipped from page to page. I remember the puzzlement when I didn't find the worker-participation clause first time: I thought they would place this prize policy nearer the top of the list. More slowly, this time, I read through the document again. It took me a long time to find – a tiny, oblique reference so watered down as to be irrelevant.

There must have been some mistake. Could it be rectified in time for the policy to be included in the later, vastly bigger, issue of the manifesto destined for the eyes of the general public rather than committed party workers? I telephoned Liberal head office in London, to be passed from one official to another. Eventually, one of them coughed uncomfortably, and admitted: 'Sorry, old boy, we thought it would lose us votes in the South. If you think it would be any good to you up there, by all means go ahead and use it.'

I protested vehemently. This was official party policy, I pointed out, passed by the national conference and reported widely in the press and on radio. There was a silence, and then the official added almost sardonically: 'That's politics, old boy – the art of the possible.'

I slammed down the phone, and spent the next few days

ruminating on the remark, 'if it's any good to you up there, go ahead and use it.' I was reluctant to accept the full meaning, but eventually it became unavoidable: the promises you made to voters were to be judged, not on their merits as policies, but on their merits as vote-catchers. Potential Liberal voters in the South of England were judged to be different from Liberal voters in the North, so make them a different set of promises. It was as though people in different parts of the country were taking part in different elections. If the party had gained real power – unlikely, even to us, then, but a possibility – would there have been legislation to introduce worker-participation in the North and not in the South? That, of course, was an impossibility.

It was my first, jolting introduction to the realities of party politics. You don't actually tell lies, if it can be avoided, but you can tell as little of the truth as is thought prudent. You arrive at the art of the selective truth, feeding a piece here, a piece there where you judge it to be of the biggest electoral advantage. Worker-participation had been judged too Leftist for the Southern suburbanites, so keep it quiet. If it would appeal to the hard-headed Northern industrial worker, shout your head off. Perhaps no one really thought we had a chance of winning the election, anyway, so that we would never have to face the legislative problem of which voter to satisfy: the Lancashire mill-hand or the Wembley clerk?

I am not saying that the art of the selective truth is the sole prerogative of the Liberal party. In truth, the Liberals are less guilty of using it than either Labour or Conservative. How many times have we all heard the parrot-like protests of broken electoral promises? I accept that in 1950, I carried a great bias in favour of worker-participation, having spent so long working in its cause. To me, it was one of the few 'nitty-gritty' policies which could give the great mass of working people a reason to vote Liberal. But it was the way it was rejected, cynically and without consultation, in the interests of electoral expediency, that soured me. The young idealist in me took a near fatal knock. Politics, I realised, was truly a dirty business.

In the event, the 1950 General Election was an unmitigated disaster for the Liberals. Our candidates were massacred in a poll which, probably more than any other, polarised British politics along class lines. Of the four hundred and seventy-five candidates we fielded in a massive show of strength, not less than three hundred and nineteen forfeited their deposits. We were left with a mere nine MPs. It was the end of the moderate centre. From then on, party doctrine, rather than individual conscience, was to rule at Westminster.

My candidate in Stockport South, Reg Hewitt, was a man of great standing in the town. A former Socialist who had been director of the International Labour Organisation, he had fallen out with Labour dogma, embraced Liberalism and in the meantime became a director of a prosperous manufacturing business. He managed to hold his deposit, but only after I demanded a recount from an astounded returning officer. The recount gave Reg the handful of votes needed to carry him over the required figure of twelve and a half per cent of the poll. That was to be my last act for the Liberal party for seventeen years – saving the hard-pressed Stockport Liberal Association a much-needed one hundred and fifty pounds.

After the announcement of the poll, Reg and I sat down for a mournful lunch at Stockport Reform Club. Reg, a man of great worldly experience, was the man who had lost, but it was I who needed the most consoling.

'Reg,' I asked dolefully, 'what does the future hold?'

He gave me a long, sympathetic look.

'You are twenty-one years old, you have a lifetime ahead and you already know more than most about politics, good and bad,' he said. 'If I were you, I would join the Labour party.'

Within weeks, before my resignation from the Liberals had been formally accepted, I was involved in municipal elections in Rochdale – speaking in support of Labour candidates.

CHAPTER FIVE

Gas-lamps and Grammar Schools

Turncoat is the word they used, of course, the inevitable shorthand slur aimed at everyone who changes his mind. It is a word that has been aimed at me twice in my life – the second time more vociferously than the first, when I eventually went back to the Liberal fold, but by then I was fairly immune to insults. In the spring of 1950, when I was at the vulnerable age of twenty-one, it was thrown out in stage-whispers from behind china coffee cups whenever I attended a social function in Rochdale – and it hurt deeply.

It hurt because although I had changed parties, I had not changed principles. There were changes to be made in the world, changes to help the sick and the old, the badly housed and the poorly educated, and at that time the Liberal party did not seem willing, let alone able, to help. The Labour party had flung itself into a frenzy of social reform, and I was faced with an inevitable choice: should I try to achieve at least some of my objectives within a party pledged to positive action, or give up this intriguing game of politics completely? Yes, the choice was inevitable.

The fiasco over my cherished worker-participation policy had brought about the glum realisation that I couldn't change the world alone. If you wish to tilt at windmills, a bulldozer is a better weapon than a lance. I was beginning to understand the basic tenets of power. To effect change, you either have to have the power yourself, or be in the position to influence the people who do have it. Power, that is what politics is about. It is fashionable today to ignore this truism, to sweep it under the carpet as the Victorians did with sex. Without power, or the ability to sway those in power, a politician is useless, however high-minded his policies or brilliant his speeches.

On 15 April 1950, the *Rochdale Observer* reported: 'Labour supporters in the Falinge Ward got a surprise at the adoption meeting on Wednesday night of their municipal election candidate, Mr Alfred Kaufman, when Mr Cyril Smith, a former active worker of the Liberal cause in Rochdale and now Liberal agent for Stockport, came to the meeting and asked if he could speak on behalf of Mr Kaufman.

'Mr Smith was invited to the platform and said he had come to the meeting "completely unexpected" to speak in support of the Labour candidate. He assumed that the election would be a straight fight between Labour and Conservatives and that being so, he felt compelled, as a Liberal, to support the Labour candidate and to urge all Liberals in the Falinge ward to do likewise...

'...Mr Smith went on to say that if he understood his basic principles of political creeds correctly, Conservatism meant a static state, Liberalism was a progressive radical force, and Socialism was at least a progressive force whether he would agree with its method of progress or not. Therefore, on these grounds, he would urge all radical Liberals to vote Labour if there was not a Liberal candidate in their ward. "I cannot conceive any Liberal in accordance with his Liberal principles voting Conservative," concluded Mr Smith.'

The report led to a spate of letters to the paper, indignantly attacking my appearance at the meeting. The letters came, significantly enough, from both Liberals and Conservatives prominent on the local political scene, and vitriol seemed to be the basic ingredient. Among other allegations was one that I was 'angling' for a top job in the Labour party. It was the first time I had been at the centre of the hornets' nest of local party politics, and I was stung into a lively self-defence. One letter I wrote gives me great satisfaction today, for it relieves me of any charge of hypocrisy... On 13 May, I wrote: 'I would join the Labour party tomorrow only for its nationalisation programme.'

I was, in fact, seeking membership of the Labour party, but my grave reservations about nationalisation were troubling my conscience. Unwilling to be dishonest, I had explained my doubts to the local party leaders, despite the fear that they would disbar me from becoming a member. I explained at length the point of view that I hold to this day: membership of any party does not necessarily commit a man to total support of each and every declared policy.

I see no reason why a man should not have the right to a wide spectrum of beliefs under the same 'umbrella' movement. For instance, I strongly support comprehensive schools and just as strongly support the use of corporal punishment in those schools for serious breaches of discipline. Children who steal, who interfere with another child's right to learn or who make a habit of constant bullying, should be caned. Here are two basic beliefs, one Left wing, one Right wing, which I hold with equal firmness and in which I see no dichotomy. Many politicians profess to worship every idol on their party's shrine, and perhaps they are telling the truth. If they are, they are either truly perfect, or they have the minds of sheep. Personally, I think they are more likely to be lying.

My view is that, if you are broadly committed to the majority of a political movement's long-term aims, you should join it, and help work towards those aims. At the same time, you should declare your opposition to policies in which you do not believe, and work towards having those policies changed. It is not the easiest way to progress in a party, but it is the only positive way. Asking the Labour party firstly to overcome their suspicions of a Liberal 'turncoat', and secondly for absolution from the sin of not worshipping the Golden Calf of nationalisation, was asking a great deal. It is to their credit that they accepted me.

On 21 June 1950, the *Rochdale Observer* carried the headline: 'To Join the Labour party: Mr Cyril Smith's Decision'. My membership was confirmed soon afterwards. It was the beginning of twenty-six years of intensive local politics which, to be honest, were probably the most productive years of my life.

The mere mention of local government is likely to bring a barely suppressed yawn to the lips of the vast majority of the British people. A country which shows little day-by-day interest in its national politics can hardly be expected to be wildly exhilarated by the goings-on down at the town hall. In many ways, this is a very great shame, for local government is often the most intimate point of contact between the citizen and his elected representatives. Few people seem to grasp the fact that their lifestyles are fundamentally affected by the decisions made by their local council. The way in which their children are educated; the roads they drive on and the lighting which illuminates them; the books they are allowed to read from the local library; the flowers they can gaze on in the local park; the houses they live in – if they are council tenants, or the houses they are allowed to build if they are owner-occupiers; the distance between bus-stops, and the fares those buses charge; the siting of those damnable parking meters or the policeman who one day books someone for speeding and the next returns his lost dog; the fireman who saves their houses or rescues their cats from trees; the water that fills their baths or flushes their toilets; the men who come or don't come to empty the dustbins; the men who ensure that their beer measures exactly a pint and their butter weighs exactly a pound; the very shape and size of the city or town centres they work or shop in; the rivers they fish in or the National Parks they walk in or the baths they swim in; all these things and many more are controlled by local government in one way or another.

Most people are deeply interested in some or all of these things; *few* show any interest in the men they elect – or allow to be elected by failing to vote – and who control the shape, size, quality and efficiency of all these services. The ratepayer complains about the rates, the tenant about the rent, but few give any support or, more importantly, offer any constructive criticism to their Councillor. In some ways, it is the fault of the people. In others, it is the fault of the Councillor.

There is a small number of very good local Councillors, anxious to work, hopeful of improving the lives of their communities. There are many who are adequate, dutifully attending meetings, diligently following through complaints but, sadly, carefully following the party-line. There are also a number of very bad Councillors, some self-seeking, some unthinking, some downright dishonest, who have clambered onto the public bandwagon from entirely unacceptable motives: for personal gain through business contacts, for vanity, for a desire for a small amount of power lacking in their everyday lives. The Councillor who spends a committee meeting handing out dictatorial orders to paid officials is often the man who goes home to be ordered to do the washing-up by a dictatorial wife!

Anyway, it was to be almost two years before I was asked to stand for the council by the Rochdale Trades and Labour Council – a body which in those days represented Socialist political and trade union interests in the town – and even then I was given an 'impossible' seat: Falinge Ward, the ward in which I had been born and lived, but which had elected anti-Labour Councillors almost since living memory. The ward had its slums, the district in which I had been brought up, but it also included large areas of solid Victorian and Edwardian houses owned by mill families and their senior employees. My Conservative opponent, Fred Greenwood, had held the seat for some eighteen years, during which he had been Mayor and, for many years, Chairman of the powerful Finance Committee. He was the very epitome of the old-time Councillor, a man of substance and stature, a pillar of the community. He was, I believed, unbeatable, and I am sure the Labour leaders thought so too.

I did, of course, have three important weapons at my disposal: a knowledge of political organisation, a thirst for hard work, and the youthful energy to carry that hard work through. I set out to make myself personally known to every voter in the ward.

In the six months before the municipal elections, I canvassed every single house in the ward, spending every free evening, every weekend hour, knocking on doors, talking, lecturing, wheedling. Young as I was, I already appreciated the fickleness of electors in conversation with a canvasser. Yes, I'm going to vote for you, but I'm in the middle of my tea. Yes, I'm going to vote for you, but I'm just going out to visit a sick relative. Yes, I'm going to vote for you, but I'm just going out to/just coming in from my night shift. The ones who seemed in a genuine hurry were noted down, to be visited again. The ones who seemed reluctantly able to spare a few minutes were cajoled to invite me into the house.

Entry into a home, the escape from the doorstep and the easily closed door, is a major breakthrough for any electoral candidate, at whatever level. The barrier of the front door has been removed. The candidate becomes, if not one of the family, at least a guest, and therefore must be listened to – or even argued with – on a serious rather than a casual level. The candidate becomes, not a face in the street, but a face in the sitting room, and therefore a part, however small, of the family's life. He has changed from being a faceless nonentity into a human being. He must then be considered and judged: serious or flippant, pleasant or unpleasant, interesting or shallow. Inside their own homes, voters make these decisions. It is the job of the canvasser to ensure that the decisions are the right ones.

It may seem cynical, like the attitude of a door-to-door salesman, but that in effect is what a candidate is. The sales-pitch is necessary to get the vote; but unlike a salesman's transaction, the sale is the beginning, not the end. The vote gives the politician the opportunity to show off his goods. If he lives up to his promised performance, he might make another sale at the next election. I have often wondered, in these days when the nation is so bereft of leaders, how many great statesmen have never reached Parliament simply because they did not have the technique, nor the advice, nor the straightforward effrontery, to canvass properly.

In that 1952 municipal election, I was experimenting with these techniques. I realised that once I was in the home, and once I had satisfied the voters' questions, there was one more obstacle to overcome: how to maintain any hard-won loyalty at such a pitch as to ensure the 'sale', the turn-out and the cross on the ballot paper on polling day. I took to carrying with me a sheaf of nomination papers, and when I received a favourable response, I would say: 'In view of your promised support, perhaps you would be kind enough to sign a nomination paper for me – it would give me great pleasure if you would?'

This, I admit, was a cunning mixture of cheek and good sense. People presented with a paper to sign could hardly refuse. If they were genuinely committed to my cause, it gave them a sense of importance to scrawl their signature on an official document. If, in fact, they were wavering, and only talking to me out of the inherent British sense of courtesy, it placed them under a feeling of obligation. Even then, with the signature on the dotted line, my campaign was far from finished.

Every evening, after many hours of tiring and often trying canvassing, I would return home, and, by hand, address an empty envelope to every family whose signatures were on the nomination papers. I stored the envelopes away, and gloated like a miser over his gold as the piles of beige paper grew. In the week before polling day, I drew up a duplicated letter, which read something like: 'I am very grateful for your support in signing my nomination papers. I know that, having given your word in this way, you will turn out and vote for me on polling day. In return, I will guarantee that, should I be elected, I will represent this ward and your interests to the very best of my ability.'

I 'topped' every letter with a hand-written, 'Dear So and So' and I 'tailed' every letter with 'Kindest Regards, Cyril Smith'. In the days before the poll I delivered one thousand, eight hundred and fifty letters in a ward of five thousand voters, by hand.

I suppose when you spend your entire life living in one small town, it is inevitable that certain people, certain places, will keep figuring in your life. The municipal election count for Falinge Ward in the Borough of Rochdale was held in 1952 in the sombre premises of Spotland School, the building which had seen many of my pranks, and from which I passed my eleven-plus examination. That night, I walked across the school yard where I had fallen and grazed my leg, thus causing the illness which transformed me physically, and peered into the classrooms and remembered the books which had transformed me intellectually. I noted how small the desks and chairs were, even for a man of normal stature.

Spotland School was yet again to be the scene of a major event. When they eventually announced the count that night, for that impossible seat, C. Smith (Labour) was the winner by a majority of five hundred and twenty votes. C. Smith (Labour) an overweight youngster with a reputation for having a big body, a bigger head and an even bigger mouth, had defeated the un-defeatable pillar of the council. This was to cause a major stir in the town, and probably a sense of ill-ease even among my own Labour colleagues. It left the *Rochdale Observer* in a flurry, for they had already prepared their page of pictures of the successful Councillors... and C. Smith (Labour) was not among them. They didn't have my picture – it wasn't thought necessary. Their photographer spent a hectic morning the following day, pursuing me around the town, looking for a 'head-and-shoulders' of Rochdale's newest, and then youngest-ever Councillor.

As the result was announced, I remember pushing my hands into my trouser pockets and rocking back on my heels in a daze of surprise and pleasure. It was the first *real* election I had ever won, the first time I had squeezed votes out of *real* people, instead of members of some identified society or political party. As I rocked, my fingers closed round a ha'penny coin, my total wealth that night. We left the school in a mood of jubilation, and went down to one of the local pubs, the 'Highland Laddie', which had been adopted as our election headquarters. I couldn't even buy a round of drinks for my supporters and, protecting my pride, would only accept a gill of mild from a member of the ward committee. I was a Councillor, I had been given a voice in the future of my home town, but I still did not have two ha'pennies to rub together.

Comparing elation over long periods of time is a difficult exercise, but I believe winning that council seat in 1952 gave me the greatest sense of victory of my life. The sheer impossibility of the task, the discouragement I had received from older local politicians, the suspicion and the 'turncoat' jibes, had all been overcome. All my work had been rewarded, and my methods had been vindicated.

It will be easy for many who read about my election campaign to sneer about 'pushyness' and even 'electoral blackmail'. Perhaps I did 'force' myself onto undecided voters but I felt no qualms then and feel none now; in fact, I still fight elections with the same single-mindedness. A politician's job is not *winning* elections, but putting those victories to useful purpose once achieved. Too many candidates exhaust their energies before the poll, and even if they win coast through half-asleep until the next election. But the rules say – quite rightly – that elections must be won before a politician can even begin his real work, and I feel that any methods used in winning are acceptable if they are reasonable and legal. I set out to become a good Councillor for Falinge Ward, and even though I was to represent it as a Socialist, as an Independent and as a Liberal, I was never beaten there. The folk of Falinge voted not for Cyril Smith, politician and speech maker, but Cyril Smith, worker.

I began as I intended to go on. At my first meeting, the council's

'Mayor Making', I proposed that in future the full council and the majority of committees should meet in the evenings. These were the days when Councillors could not even draw compensation for loss of earnings caused by their public work, never mind the handsome – and much abused – allowances offered to them today. Local government is very demanding on time, an average of three meetings a week, many of them lasting three or four hours, and the effect could then be seen on the composition of the council. The Conservative and Liberal side was packed with professional men, the owners of small businesses, or managers allowed time off because being on the Corporation was 'good for business'. Our benches were largely filled by full-time trade union officials, and a housewife or two, with the occasional night-shift worker who would drag himself to a meeting after perhaps two hours' sleep. The day-meetings system gave local government 'club' atmosphere, open as it was only to the few. It excluded many potentially brilliant Councillors who couldn't afford to win an election. Nevertheless, at that first meeting, my resolution was rejected – and was in fact rejected at every subsequent meeting for fourteen years! The Rochdale Corporation Club was to remain in business.

It was the first of many of my resolutions to be rejected. A new Councillor is expected to sit down quietly, listen to his superiors and learn the ropes. He can make speeches in support of motions proposed by the wise-old-men, dutifully toeing the party-line. That was taken for granted ... by almost everyone but me. I still had only a lance, but there were many more windmills to tilt at. I won a reputation for having gas-lamps erected to give some feeble illumination to the hideous back yards between the rows of industrial cottages, which many old people were genuinely frightened to cross on the way to their distant lavatories. I fought for – and eventually had established – a municipal baby-sitting service, which would issue the names of capable baby-sitters to young parents, who desperately needed a few hours of relaxation away from the kids. I had 'Paradise Flats' demolished, a particularly sweet triumph, for the name was a mockery: the families who lived in this appalling slum shared the food with rats, had to climb many stairs for running water, and wished that there were mushrooms, instead of hideous yellow fungi, growing from the walls.

These little victories salved some of my failures, but did not deter me from starting battles which I had no hope of winning. I remember, for instance, attacking the rates of pay of council officials, the beginning of a long and intriguing battle of wits with officers which I will describe later. It was a subject which had long exercised my mind; even before being elected, I had started a 'letter campaign' in the local press complaining about Corporation salaries. In these days when the ten thousand a year senior official is more of a commonplace than a rarity, some of those 1951 letters raised an ironic smile.

Registering a formal protest – 'formal because that is all one seems able to do' – I wrote to the *Rochdale Observer* on 14 August: 'It does seem ridiculous to me that an official who is already receiving a wage of £20 a week should receive ... a further £2 a week. There will inevitably be wage restraint in the country, but I fail to see how we can logically ask a man receiving £5 or £6 a week not to ask for more pay in these circumstances. The levelling of wages should commence at the top, not at the bottom.'

Haven't we all heard that somewhere before? Wage restraint? Levelling down of wages? The one thing that seems to have changed is the value of the money under discussion. That letter indicates the council officers' *raises* were to be equal to roughly a *third* of a working man's pay. That is the second change. In these inflated times, particularly since the reorganisation of local government, senior local government officers do not receive increases of that size, say twenty pounds a week given an average wage in the region of sixty pounds a week. They do not receive one thousand pounds a year increases because that, it seems, is not enough! I know of one man who was earning about four thousand pounds a year before local government reorganisation – he's now earning more than eleven thousand for doing a similar job!

This is a problem in which I have always taken a close interest, and perhaps the most controversial resolution I put before Rochdale Corporation as '*l'enfant terrible*' Councillor was my proposed reduction on senior officials' salaries of five per cent. The resolution was not accepted, of course, and it did not make me particularly popular with officials, but it did demonstrate that I had a healthy concern in the runaway growth of public expenditure which was only just beginning to snowball in the early fifties.

It was perhaps an omen for the future, because my first job of real power in public life came in 1954 when I was elected Chairman of the Rochdale Establishment Committee. I say 'real power' because it often happens that it is the Chairman of committees who makes the real decisions of local government. The quality of local government, the value ratepayers get for their hard-earned cash, depends almost entirely on the quality of the committee Chairmen. It is a job which calls for an alert and, to some extent, a suspicious mind, a deft political touch, a high resistance to flattery and a positive approach to dealings with officials.

The Establishment Committee was, in effect, the personnel department of the council. It decided the size of council staff, approved promotions, and interviewed applicants for new posts. In many ways, Establishment Committee decisions controlled the quality of the borough's administration and, as such, it was the committee with the most intimate contact with senior officials. Would-be 'empire-builders' had to put their expansion plans before the committee. As Chairman, I made a very strong point of being extremely reluctant to recruit extra staff. If my modest example had been followed throughout the country, Britain's harassed ratepayers might today be slightly less so.

Make no mistake, the plight of Britain's ratepayers is now a national scandal. It is causing hardship in thousands, perhaps millions, of homes throughout the land, in a manner which is entirely new. People have never liked paying rates – it has been the source of public displeasure ever since I can remember. In those days of the early fifties, however, when vast school building and housing projects were under way, I think the complaints were unjustified. Local councils were doing much of the work which revolutionised the standards of housing and education in the country; as a general rule, I feel ratepayers received more than adequate service for their money. Sadly, I do not think that is so today.

It is no surprise that building societies, when considering applications for mortgages, are now rejecting would-be buyers who have the income necessary to justify the purchase, but do not have the necessary surplus to meet the rates on the property involved. Many families are being forced into selling established and well-loved homes to move into smaller properties where the rates are less usurious. The property-owning democracy has long been one of the golden aims of our civilisation; it is being undermined by the insatiable demands of local government which has lost the ability, or the will, to control its spending. The roots of this ungovernable growth go back to the period of the 1950s when I became personally involved. I think I have as good a claim as anyone in Britain to understand what went wrong, and why.

Not all council officials, or committee chairmen for that matter, are empire-builders. It is natural, I suppose, for any ambitious man or woman to enjoy having control of an important department and it follows that the bigger the department, the greater the sense of power and achievement. I do not, however, believe that the explosion of local government recruitment came as part of a considered policy but more as a gradual, unrecognised mistake. Senior council officials, the town clerks, the engineers, the architects, the treasurers, are busy people, and in the 1950s they were being worked at full stretch. Long dreamed-of plans, delayed by the war and the austerity years immediately afterwards, suddenly became a reality. Concentrating, as they were, on the massive building and development programmes which mushroomed throughout the country, many officers were too occupied in looking outwards – at the blossoming housing estates, the schools and the swimming baths, and spending too little time looking inwards at the workings of their own departments.

If someone further down the line asked for an extra clerk, another gardener, a few more bricklayers or painters, the request was only cursorily examined, and passed on to the council for approval. That was the point at which the Chairman of the Establishment Committee should have become involved. Too often, he or she failed. Maybe the Chairman was too busy also, or perhaps suffered from an empire-building complex.

I think, in fact, the failure of proper supervision lies in one of the root evils of local government, the relationship between officials and committee Chairmen. Senior officials tend to be highly qualified and tenacious men – that's how they won their jobs. Usually, they outshine their Chairmen both in intelligence and in the ability to put a point of view. One has to add to this unfortunate and uneasy relationship, the proprietorial attitude which many Chairmen take towards their work. They talk of 'my chief officer' and 'my department'. All too often, the committee Chairman unknowingly works to a position in which he defends his department against the criticisms of the general public, forgetting that his appointed role is to protect the public – the ratepayers – against the wilder ambitions of the department. It was in this incestuous atmosphere, I believe, that the monster of a bloated local government system was conceived. It was nurtured, and brought to manhood, by another set of circumstances.

First, there came the growth of 'professionalism' in local government work, the organisation of engineers, public health inspectors, librarians and others into professional bodies. These bodies began to set down high standards of professional qualifications for entry into local government. These standards sent rates of pay up and at the same time created a scarcity of suitably qualified youngsters. It has now reached a stage when too many officials are too highly educated and too highly paid for the work they do. *All* social workers, for example, do *not* need qualifications in psychology and sociology. Much of the routine visiting could be done by people of average intelligence and education. In fact, one of the basic needs of social visiting – the easing of the pain of loneliness in old people – could be done happily by volunteers. This suggestion of course, would be condemned out of hand by many of the so-called 'professionals', who tend to look upon voluntary workers as meddling amateurs.

In addition to the growth of 'professionalism' came the gravity of the trade unions among the rank-and-file of council workers. It is the arrival of the politically orientated trade union militant onto the local government scene which causes me the greatest dismay now as I survey the world in which I spent twenty-two years of my life.

I think that, by now, most Councillors and senior officials have finally realised that the limits of public spending have not only been reached, but have been substantially exceeded. The realisation, I fear, may have come too late. The monster is too big, too firmly established. I doubt now if councils have the power to cut public spending radically in the face of opposition from their own trade union employees. It would call for a major confrontation between councils and the TUC with threats to public health, transport and welfare services, and I have little doubt that the TUC would win. It is my profound but unhappy belief that local democracy has been fatally wounded, if indeed it is not already dead. The Councillor for whom you vote no longer has the power to control the destiny of your community: that is in the hands of the local secretary of NALGO or NUPE or some other union.

The Establishment Committee gave me the experience in dealing with officials and staff which, I hope, I put to good use in later, more important offices. I hope I found the right balance in my attitude to both encourage and motivate the staff, and at the same time protect the voters' interests. I found that good officials can accept criticism if it is fair criticism, but woe-betide you if your criticisms are ill-based – you are 'put-down' before your fellow Councillors in committee in no uncertain terms, and in those circumstances, a wise man apologises. By the time I was asked to chair some of the 'big spending' committees, my dealings with officials were being carried out in an atmosphere of cordial, if wary, respect.

In 1963, I was voted Chairman of the Estates Committee, a key job I held for three years. Estates was the committee which, among many other roles, was responsible for Rochdale's council house building programme. The programme had not been progressing well. In the five years previously, we had built a total of only four hundred and thirty-two houses. I staggered the corporation officials by publicly promising to build two thousand in the coming two years, in an attempt to reduce the town's pathetically long waiting-list. We did it – at least we built one thousand, nine hundred and eighty homes but only because the committee cut every piece of red-tape possible, changed some of the older building regulations, let contracts quickly, and ensured that contractors delivered on time. Local government can be a slow, ponderous process, and much of the blame must lie with the council: the hours of repetitive debate, the constant referring back of important decisions, the politicking on issues which are strictly un-political, can be the despair of architects, planners and builders. I think the Estates Committee showed that Councillors can act speedily, given a big-enough bully at the head of the table. I was big, and I made myself a bully, to get those houses built.

Britain's council house building programme has, I think, been one of the quietest revolutions since the war. The estates themselves, particularly the concrete jungles, changed the face of the country, sometimes not for the better, but one should remember all those red-bricks at least replaced even uglier slums. Apart from the physical change, I think the council house has revolutionised society itself. It made millions of people aware, for the first time, of the advantages, the pleasures, of living in a well-built, well-equipped home. In my youth, a young couple planning marriage looked round for a house to rent in the same street as their parents, the same streets where their grandparents and great-grandparents had lived. The thought of trying to get away from the home neighbourhood, the same two-up, two-down with the lavatory across the yard, the same landlord with the same reluctance to repair the same leaking roof that grandma has complained about forty years previously, that thought had just never occurred. The council house changed that: I am happy to know scores of couples in Rochdale who were brought up in council houses and who are now buying their own homes, many of them, I am glad to say, in the more expensive parts of the town. The council house lifted people's sights, and that was a major advance for our society. When they were first built it was said 'People will use the bath to put coal in' – but you know they don't, they use it to bath in.

In all honesty, however, I cannot say that the council building programme was an unqualified success. I think the evils of the high-rise blocks of flats are now well recognised, but too late. In Rochdale, while I was Chairman of the Estates Committee, we built seven tower blocks which, when you look down on the town from the Pennines around, are now our most obvious landmarks. These flats – let at economic rents to more prosperous families – have not been beset with as many problems as one sees in other towns and cities. That, I think, is because they are directly adjacent to the town centre, so that people can reach their places of work, their shops, their favourite pub, within minutes, hence preserving some of the old intimacy of the former terraced streets.

To move people many miles from their work and their friends, and to cage them in tower blocks in the back-of-nowhere, is now proved to be lunacy, but many towns and cities went on doing so long after the problems were known. In the College Bank flats in Rochdale, there is no talk of life reaching crisis point, but there is vandalism, people do complain of loneliness, mothers do worry about their children playing out of sight scores of feet below.

The biggest failure of the housing programme, on a national scale, has not, however, been the high-rise flat but the almost unbelievable failure of planning departments to do just that — to plan ahead. The vast programme of the fifties and early sixties provided the country with a fairly adequate stock of two- and three-bedroomed houses. What the planners failed to plan for was the simple, human fact that people grow old, that children grow up, and when they grow up they get married and leave home! Then they need homes of their own too, but they can't get one because, for miles around, there are hundreds of couples in late middle age living alone in three-bedroomed houses. So what must the council do: build more houses for the youngsters, borrow more capital at cripplingly high rates, destroy more agricultural land?

The answer is *no, no, no*! What they should do is build more small maisonettes, more old people's bungalows, so that the older people can move into cheaper, more manageable homes, and the young ones with their small children can have the three-bedrooms left vacant. It is so incredibly simple, so incredibly obvious, but it has been overlooked by housing authorities throughout the country! It is one of the cheap, simple answers to the country's housing problems, but we have probably lost this opportunity too. This plan will only be successful if the smaller units are built on the same estates, or at least in the same neighbourhood as the bigger houses. A middle-aged couple whose children have left home are often happy to find a smaller place, cheaper to rent, cheaper to heat, easier to clean, but they will not leave the area where they have lived for many years, where they have raised their children, made their friends, become, in fact, part of the community. It would be a grave breach of the democratic ideal to evict couples simply because their children have left home. They will only leave voluntarily if they can remain among their friends and neighbours. While I was Chairman of Rochdale Estates Committee, I spent hours touring the town, looking for tiny bits of land here, tiny bits there, just big enough to allow us to squeeze in a couple of bungalows, a small block of maisonettes. We had some success, but not nearly enough: the original estates had not been planned that way.

Housing was the second great love of my career in local government. The greatest was education, the field into which I had been denied entry as a teacher, but over which, in Rochdale at least, I was to exercise supreme control. That is a boast, but I do not make it idly. Education mattered to me in a way which almost caused pain, it was virtually my *raison d'être* as a Councillor, and I set out from the very beginning to dominate educational planning in the town. Education was to me the ultimate reform, the ultimate social change. By all means you should house people well, look after their health and welfare, tear to bits their environment and rebuild it full of air and light, but it was all a waste of time unless you educated their minds to appreciate the change.

I was elected to the Education Committee when I joined the council in 1952, and was Chairman for six years from 1966. It was a period during which the British educational system went through some of its most traumatic changes and it was a period I spent – surprisingly, many people think, in view of my own schooling – working towards the introduction of comprehensive education.

Why should a man who had benefited more than most from the grammar school system spend a large part of his life trying to destroy it? Why should a man who escaped from the slums by passing the eleven-plus feel that selection by examination at that early age is wrong? Most people who ask me those questions assume that it is a matter of political ideology, that I was going along with Labour party dogma in order to smash privilege. That is not true. I was opposed to the eleven-plus simply because I felt too many able children failed through simple 'exam-nerves', suffering from a few days of over-anxiety which could – and often did – irrevocably shape their lives. To decide that a child is fit to be either a doctor or a docker at the age of eleven seems to me to be patently inhumane.

I was also opposed to the grammar school system, even though I accepted that they gave the top four per cent of children an excellent education. What concerned me was the effect that 'creaming-off' the more brilliant pupils had on the less able or, indeed, on the very able, who nevertheless lacked the ability to pass examinations. I believed very strongly that the brighter, go-ahead pupils in a school act as leaders, pace-setters, in a way in which even the best teachers cannot emulate. To deprive entire generations of their natural leaders seemed to me to be little short of criminal. At the same time, it also deprived those natural leaders of the chance to lead, a skill learned only by painful experience, a skill which, learned younger, is learned better.

The argument for comprehensive education is as much a social one as an educational one. I wanted to destroy class barriers, but in no way did I support the theory of 'levelling-down' educational standards, by robbing the intellectual 'rich' of opportunities in order to give to the poor. As an Education Committee Councillor, I always pushed for the best possible teachers and equipment for every single pupil, cream or otherwise. As Chairman, I demanded them. In this way, I hoped that the range of subjects and interests offered to the top four per cent would, firstly, rouse a feeling of envy in the less able children which, secondly, would give way to a determination to compete for those same educational 'goodies'. That, in simple essence, is my theory on comprehensive education: give the very able the very best in a way which motivates the less able – or the nervous, or perhaps even the lazy – to drive themselves harder for a place among the elite. It is a theory which does not readily fit in with the trendy views of many modern educationalists who condemn competitive education. I believe a school should use every urge present in a pupil in order to achieve the optimum educational results. Competitiveness is very strong in children: it should be turned to good effect.

In 1963 Rochdale took its first step towards a more egalitarian educational system when we abolished the eleven-plus. The grammar schools continued more or less unchanged, except that their pupils were chosen on the basis of preceding years' work in the classroom rather than a few cold-sweat hours poring over examination papers. In 1968, as Chairman of the Education Committee, I began a massive programme of consultation with teachers and parents, councillors and council officials, sitting down together at regular meetings to discuss methods of implementing a fully comprehensive education system. Each school staff-room elected a member to the committee considering the problem. Public meetings were held at every school in the borough, to which every single parent was invited. Some of these meetings passed in an atmosphere of calm accord, others became angry enough to verge on the riotous. I discovered then that the most civilised, the most clear thinking of people can change into raving Mr Hydes when the future of their children's education is under discussion. In some areas of the town, usually the more prosperous areas, I began to accept personal insults of the most wounding kind as a routine part of any meeting.

However, the policy of giving the town, its teachers, its parents and its pupils, two years to reach eventual agreement succeeded. In 1970, Rochdale went fully comprehensive without a single contrary vote: Labour, Liberals, Conservatives and Independents voted unanimously for the change. I think that was probably the biggest single achievement of my local government career.

In too many towns, education had been, and is still being, used as a political football, to the dismay of teachers and the confusion of children. The Thameside débâcle would never have happened if political parties had not insisted in thrusting their own pet policies down the throats of their enemies. Education is too big an issue for politicking. It is an issue for constant and genuine consultation, an issue in which the parent should have a bigger say than the administrator. Rochdale based its system on primary schools, middle schools for the ten to thirteen age groups, and custom-built comprehensives with sixth-form facilities equal to anything in the country. A report by the Institute of Borough Treasurers was to show later that, comparing educational qualifications gained with the amount of capital invested, the Rochdale schools system was the third most efficient in England and Wales. That report, of course, was a major triumph for me. But the greatest elation came from the fact that the town consulted, talked, compromised and eventually, as a single unit, said *Yes*. We achieved a minor revolution without spilling a drop of blood. It should be remembered, I think, that any blood spilled in an educational war tends to be the blood of children!

Because of my efforts, my old school had ceased to exist. In 1954, it had moved from its Victorian premises in Fleece Street to a new building, and changed its name to Balderstone Grammar School. At the opening ceremony of that new building, I had been seated next to my old headmaster, 'Docker' Payne. We exchanged a few words, for I had already made known my hopes for comprehensives. After the ceremony, I asked the organising official why I had been placed next to Docker. 'He was the only man we knew who could keep you quiet for a few hours,' he laughed.

When the first comprehensive pupils moved into Balderstone years later, I fell to wondering how my actions had effected the life of 'Docker' Payne, one of the men of total integrity who had been a major force in my own development. I happened to mention to a veteran Councillor, 'I hope "Docker" Payne will forgive me.'

The Councillor's eyes opened in surprise, and he said: 'Don't tell me you don't know.'

'Know what?'

'That Dr Payne agrees with you. He led a deputation to the Education Committee in 1945 asking for the implementation of comprehensives. He must have been too much of a visionary – we laughed him out of the town hall.'

When this piece of information had sunk in – and it took a few seconds – I exploded with astonishment. 'The tricky old bugger. He never said a word to me. The only doubt I've had all these years was that I might be hurting "Docker" Payne.'

The old Councillor's eyes twinkled as he said: 'Perhaps the good doctor thought it was a good idea for you to have just one doubt!'

CHAPTER SIX

The Mayor Walks Out

Gracie Fields, that other Rochdalian, once looked back on her childhood and wrote: 'I was taught to respect God, the King and the Mayor of Rochdale in that order.' When I met this legendary entertainer for the first time, I gently chided her on the remark, saying it was obviously meant as a joke but had been presented in a manner of great seriousness. 'Joke?' she retorted. 'Joke? That was no joke. When I was a lass, that was the order of things – in fact, the King was lucky to scrape into second place!'

Her reply set me thinking. All my conscious life, I had been working towards my ambition to become Mayor. I had taken it as a foregone conclusion, the natural zenith of my progress. At no time, however, had I looked upon the office with a sense of awe, as though donning the red robes and the gold chain somehow changed the wearer into a different sort of person. The Mayor to me was simply Chairman of the Council and, as such, had been given the role as the just and proper reward for years of work on the town's behalf. Gracie's attitude made me aware for the first time of the real feeling towards the Mayoralty held by many of the older townspeople.

Rochdale is very much a community. Its members will fall out among themselves, but will present tight-closed ranks to any criticism from an outsider. It is a town which, when its cotton heart stopped beating, was forced to build itself a new identity. Make no mistake, Rochdale could easily have died a spiritual death. Its great families, their fortunes made through cotton, moved down to London or bought great estates away from the debris left by their drive for wealth. Capital accrued from the mill-workers' toil was invested elsewhere, so there was none left for new mills and new looms. The cotton families themselves, for a century effective leaders of the town's society, were no longer present locally to set the pace in social life, welfare schemes or charitable organisations.

The people who were left could have sat back and let the town wither, but with their good-humoured toughness they refused to do so. They began to build themselves a new social order, based on voluntary work, religious activities, sporting and leisure groups and the local pub. They needed a new focus of civic pride and they chose, almost in a medieval sense, the Mayor. At least he is one of us, they seemed to say. For one year, give him the pomp and circumstance, let him live like a lord. Then take it all away from him, just to show that he is still one of us.

Many times I have been asked to lecture to local societies on the duties of a Mayor. Many times, I have started with this story which, I think, demonstrates a town's attitude to its Chief Citizen. It goes:

'The morning of the big day arrives and a chauffeur-driven car sweeps up to your house to take you to the Town Hall. Waiting round the corner in a large blue van, which pulls up as soon as the limousine sweeps away, are a group of workmen who step out and erect two symbolic gilt lamp-standards, which are to burn outside your door for the length of your office. You are taken to the Town Hall, where you are given a Master key which opens every office in the building, you are taken to the Mayor's Parlour where your maid shows you your drinks cabinet and says, "Whenever you want anything, Mr Mayor, just ring." Finally, more practically, they give you a free pass for all the town's buses.

'Twelve short months later, the chauffeur again sweeps the limousine up to your door and whisks you off to the Town Hall. (Just round the corner waits a blue van.) After the new Mayor is installed, you walk automatically to the Mayor's Parlour, only to find it is packed with the guests of the new man. You sit alone in some corner, drink a cup of tea, and decide to go home. But there is no chauffeur waiting, and on the bus you find that your free pass is no longer valid. So you feel in your pocket and hand the conductress your five pence. When you finally get home, the blue van has gone – and so too have the fine gilt lamps that stood by your doorway.

'It is only two hours since you left home. These two hours are at one time the shortest and the longest of your life.'

I became Mayor of Rochdale in 1966, in just less than the twenty years which, as a boy, I had decided would be my time-limit for the task. My year of office began on a note of high farce caused, inevitably, by my rather extraordinary Mayoral girth.

The Town Clerk of Rochdale, Mr Kenneth Moore, was a resourceful man of considerable foresight. Months before the problem had occurred to me – indeed, months before it was confirmed that I would become Mayor – Mr Moore had anticipated trouble with the Mayoral robes. This red flowing garb, along with the lace jabot collar, is not bought every year, as most ratepayers assume, but is skilfully altered year in, year out, to accommodate the figure of the new Chief Citizen. But Mr Moore, with his magnificent foresight, decided, quite rightly, that Rochdale's robes would not fit Rochdale's Mayor-to-be. What to do?

In an exercise in local government cheese-paring which could well be adopted as a classic of its kind, Mr Moore wrote to every borough in Lancashire, asking if they had ever had eh, hmm a rather large Mayor and if so, would they be prepared to eh, hmm loan or sell the robes concerned to the Municipal Borough of Rochdale. In this case, however, Scrooge was thwarted. The only town which could be of any help was Stockport and – I must admit to much amusement – when I was asked to attend a top-secret fitting, the garments proved to be a good four inches too small across the chest.

Even the thrifty burghers of Rochdale were not prepared to see their next Mayor going about his Worshipful duties with a piece of string tied round his waist, so another line of attack was deemed necessary. The ever resourceful Mr Moore contacted a firm of legal tailors in London – they manufacture robes for judges – and was told, Yes, we could make an outsize Mayoral robe but, sorry, No it could not be ready in less than four months.

This time-gap in itself represented a minor constitutional crisis for Rochdale Corporation. It had been the custom for years for the Mayoral Selection Committee to meet in March to name the Mayor elect, a mere two months before the Mayor

Making Ceremony. The needs of the hour meant a change of plan, and Mr Moore used all his extensive powers of persuasion to get the committee to meet in January. The meeting itself was a bit of a sham, for its deliberations were virtually *fait accompli*: the next Mayor was always appointed from the political party whose turn it was to take the honour, and the successful applicant was always the most senior serving Alderman or Councillor of that party who hadn't yet had his turn.

Traditions, however, are supposed to be traditions and, officially, I wasn't supposed to know that the committee was even meeting. The fact that I had been telephoned by the Town Clerk and told to be in the committee ante-room at such-and-such a time was all part of the game. It was no great surprise, therefore, when the door opened, and out came Mr Moore saying: 'Ah, Alderman Smith, how fortunate that you are here. The Mayoral Selection Committee has a request to make to you. Perhaps you would be kind enough to come in?'

This was the point at which, had I decided to follow tradition, I should have told the committee that accepting the onerous task of becoming Mayor was a matter for considerable deliberation. Could I have a few days to think it over? That was one bit of bogus modesty I could not accept. The Chairman asked: 'Alderman Smith, this committee has decided it would give us great pleasure for you to become the next Mayor of Rochdale – do you accept the office?' 'Certainly,' I said. 'Thank you very much.' It was my first break with civic hocus-pocus. It caused a bit of a stir among the members but, knowing me as they did, I think they would have been a little disappointed had I done anything else.

The next break was to come on the day of the Mayor Making 23 May 1966, a milestone date in my life. It was a day which began normally in the Smith household in Emma Street, with my mother leaving home before six am to carry out her duties as a cleaner at the Town Hall – tidying the Mayor's Parlour which, that very evening, her son was to occupy as the rightful tenant.

I think the earlier chapters of this book spelled out fairly clearly that my mother is a rather determined lady. If there is any remaining doubt about this, it should be dispelled by her attitude towards her son as Mayor.

Towards the end of the war, she had left private service and taken a war-work job in a local factory. The war over, she took a cleaning job at the Rochdale Infirmary and eventually became Matron's maid – they had such things in those days. Deciding on another change, she then became a charwoman at the Town Hall, daily scrubbing scores of stone steps which I was later to dirty as I went about my business as a Councillor. Promoted again – and I rush to say it was some years before I became Mayor – she was put in charge of cleaning the Mayor's Parlour, the opulent hidey-hole where VIP visitors to the Town Hall were entertained.

It was a post which caused an obvious embarrassment for, being a bachelor, it was assumed that I would make my mother the Mayoress. Was it right, some people were asking, for the town's First Lady to do her own cleaning up? I had hesitantly broached the subject to her, to get the tart reply: 'Let's get two things straight, Cyril. I have worked all my life to get a pension, and I'm going to carry on working until the State is willing to pay me my due. That's the first point. The second is that I'm not going to be Mayoress. I'm not going round this town speechifying and making myself a laughing stock in front of all my friends and neighbours.'

What could I do? I could hardly have my own mother sacked, so she continued to get up at six am every morning to clean the Mayor's Parlour through my term of office. She did, however, relent and agree to become Mayoress halfway through the year. By that time, local organisations had drawn up their future engagement lists, so no requests came in for her to speak. She enjoyed dressing up wearing the Mayoress's chain of office, and attending the dinners and the dances, the bring-and-buys and the boys' clubs. Few people ever called her 'Your Worship' however. They stuck to the pet name by which she was known in the Town Hall – Hetty. Hetty, Mayoress of Rochdale, enjoyed the office. She enjoyed being the Mayor's char-lady too.

On that day of 23 May 1966, Hetty came back early from her work so that she could attend another function: the opening of the new factory of Smith's Springs (Rochdale) Ltd, the result of four years' work in building up my spring company. I intend to discuss my business career at length later, so suffice it to say here that it gave me the greatest satisfaction to achieve two major objectives on the same day: the new factory, which cost the then stunning figure of seven thousand pounds, was the final demonstration of a successful working life; the Mayor's chain was the final symbol of a successful political life – as I thought then. It was a day on which I actually thought I had achieved my life's work.

The Mayor Making took place in the evening, for the first time in the history of Rochdale Corporation. It was my second break with civic tradition, and it was made, not from a desire to break rules for the sake of it, but out of my strongly held conviction that daytime meetings of local authorities disbar many ordinary people from participating. Anyway, as I joked in my speech, I had invited the entire seventeen-strong staff of Smith's Springs to attend, and I didn't see why I should have to give them a day's pay to attend a public junket.

The Mayor Making itself was a delectable mixture of pride, emotion and hidden humour. I recited a passage from the Boy Scout's prayer, asking for help from God to make me equal to my task, and was barely able to stop myself bursting into tears. There was the overwhelming self-gratification as the gold chain was slipped over my head. There were also the barely disguised smirks from the uniformed members of the Rochdale Band which, from time to time, took me to the point of a schoolboyish giggle.

There had been raised eyebrows when I announced that the Rochdale Band would play at the Mayor Making, rather than the magnificent organ in the Town Hall presented by Sir Samuel Turner, founder of the Turner Brothers asbestos firm. A brass band, Cyril? The Town Clerk had asked. Is that really the proper thing at such a solemn occasion? I was Chairman of the band, I said, and I was determined they would be there. The Town Clerk relented, but I doubt he would have done so if he had realised the second, secret, reason for my insistence. I had originally drawn up a guest list of one thousand two hundred people to attend the ceremony, all close friends, but had been forced to slash the figure to a mere three hundred because of pressure of space in the Town Hall. I don't suppose anyone was counted that evening, but there were forty men in the uniform of Rochdale Band. A strange figure, when the normal complement of any brass band is twenty-six. Fourteen of these men dutifully lifted their instruments to their lips, and made a great show of bulging their cheeks, but they played not a note. It was my way of slipping an extra number of guests into the chamber, and the humour of a shared secret added a rare piquancy to the evening.

It is difficult for me to say how good a Mayor I was, so I will leave that to other people. Firstly, the official side of the matter – the expectations of my fellow Aldermen and Councillors as they were expressed in speeches at the Mayor Making. You will note that all the flattery did not come without a sting in the tail.

The *Rochdale Observer* reported the event under the headline: BOYHOOD PROPHECY HAS BECOME A REALITY FOR TOWN'S NEW MAYOR. Their story began: 'A boy of nine years stood on the Town Hall Square and said, "One day I'll be Mayor of Rochdale." That boy is now Alderman Cyril Smith and on Monday he saw the prophecy come true ...'

The paper goes on to report that speeches made in my support, with speakers listing some of the activities of my life: paper boy, cricket umpire, brass-band enthusiast, fund-raiser for Rochdale Football Club, table-tennis player, welfare and youth organiser, businessman – the praise was fulsome and not a little embarrassing.

I thought it fitting that the official motion that I should be installed as Mayor came from Alderman Harold Chorlton, the same trade union leader who, when I delivered his newspapers as a boy, had tried so hard to enrol me into the Labour party. We did not know then that, tragically, it was to be one of his last speeches.

The motion was seconded by Councillor Clifford Parker, who went so far as to describe me as a latter-day Dick Whittington, before going on: 'All qualities that are the ingredients for greatness are possessed by Alderman Smith. Administrative ability, boundless energy, strict attention to detail and a contagious enthusiasm *that can only be improved by a touch of the bearing rein from time to time.* These outstanding qualities lift him far above the rank and file. Add his great and all-embracing love of Rochdale and its people and his genuine desire for progress and you have a man admirably fitted for the office about to be bestowed upon him.'

I had crossed swords on occasions with Clifford Parker, a Liberal Councillor, and his remark calling for 'a touch of the bearing rein' brought one of the laughs of the evening. I laughed too, because – well – he was right.

So these were the right and proper sentiments, albeit a little too sugary for me, of the official face of the Mayoralty. To get the unvarnished, ordinary man's attitude, I asked Fred Rothwell for any memories he had of my term of office. Fred, Mayor's Attendant and chauffeur to eighteen of Rochdale's Chief Citizens, is a plain speaker not given to obsequiousness. I think I had better just quote what he said:

'When we knew it was going to be Cyril as Mayor, my wife and I half-died with apprehension. We knew what a busybody he was – working day in, day out – so we thought we would never get a minute's rest. It was, in fact, the busiest year we ever had. Cyril attended something like eighteen hundred to two thousand functions, often doing as many as ten a day at the weekends, but strangely enough, it was one of the years we enjoyed the most.

'We certainly had a lot of fun, and some of the laughter was at Cyril's expense. I don't think he knows to this day that we had to adjust the headlamps of the civic Austin Princess. With himself and Hetty in the back, the springs were so far down that the headlamps lit up the roof of the Odeon Cinema across the road from the Town Hall.

'One of the first official functions was to attend a match of the Rochdale Hornets, the town's rugby league team. Now the seats in the Hornets' director's box had been taken from a cinema which had closed down, and they were separated by those hard wooden arms. Cyril just couldn't get into them – he had to watch the match from a wooden bench on the touchline. The next time we went to the ground, they had sawn one of the arms off, so that Cyril could have two seats side by side. I remember the fans, no respecters of persons, these, turning and shouting, "Watch the gap in the middle, Cyril, you could do yourself an injury." He took it, as he takes everything, in good heart, Mayor or no Mayor.

'When Hetty became Mayoress, we had two characters on

the team, because Mrs Smith had a crisp tongue when she cared to use it. I remember at one charity function, a small display of flowers which had been on the top table was auctioned off – it's a regular custom in Rochdale to raise a few extra shillings. Cyril, as Mayor, thought it was his duty to buy the flowers, even though I know he didn't have much money at the time – he had just opened his new factory and had sunk almost every penny he had into the business.

'I suppose the flower arrangement must have been worth five bob at the most, but when Cyril made his bid a woman's voice piped up from the other end of the hall with a bigger one. Cyril wasn't to be beaten, of course, and the bidding went on heatedly until Cyril finally took the flowers for thirty-five shillings. You can imagine his reaction when, in the car on the way home, he found that the woman he had been bidding against was his mother! You should have heard the language. To cap it all, she dropped the flowers into the gutter as she got out of the car. There was no one about at the time, which was a good thing, because I wouldn't have liked the town's good citizens to have heard their Mayor and Mayoress going on like that.

'Cyril was always a fanatic for raising money for charity. He single-handedly collected something like twenty thousand pounds for a post-graduate medical centre at Birch Hill Hospital. It was called the Bateman Centre, and I think it was Cyril's pet project when he was Mayor. I wouldn't say he actually blackmailed people out of money, but it wasn't far off. He came up to me at another dance – which people had already paid heavily to attend – and said, "Fred – go round to so and so's shop tomorrow and pick up a colour television set. He's giving us one to raffle." A colour TV. They cost a fortune in 1966, and I told Cyril that I didn't know how he did it. "That's nothing yet," he said, and disappeared back into the dance like a tiger going after its prey. He came back half an hour later, beaming like a Cheshire cat.

'"Have we got a tow-bar on the Mayoral car?" he asked.

'"No, Cyril, we haven't," I replied.

'"Ah," he said. "Well, we'll have to make some other arrangements."

'"Why? What for?"

' "Someone's just given me a caravan for the raffle; we'll have to think of some way of moving it."

'That Bateman Centre was one of his big successes, although it did cause certain problems. At one stage, a man turned up from New Zealand saying he was a doctor and, as a trustee of a large charity "Down-under", was looking for worthy causes he could put money into. When Cyril heard, he was onto him like a leech. He was entertained in the Mayor's Parlour, signed the distinguished visitors' book, and went round with Cyril on a series of speaking engagements. He finally coughed up a cheque on a New Zealand bank but, as the weeks passed, there seemed to be trouble in getting it cashed. Then one night at another function, in came the Chief Constable and nervously told Cyril that our friend had in fact escaped from an asylum and the police had just taken him back. I expected Cyril to go mad, but he just roared with laughter. There aren't many people who can con Cyril Smith, but this one did. That night, Cyril and I went into the Town Hall and found the distinguished visitors' book. Ceremoniously, we inked a black border round this fellow's name.

'It's still in the book, black border and all.

'My duties were to dress Cyril in his ceremonial robes, and sometimes that was no easy task. The tricorn hat, for instance, was too small for him, and the slightest wind would whip it off. In the end, we stuck it to his head with Sellotape. In the robes, with the lace jabot hat, and the big gold chain, he looked like the reincarnation of some medieval king.

'One of the highlights of the year was a visit to Tourcoing, Rochdale's "twin-town" in Northern France. No Mayor had ever taken the full civic regalia there, but Cyril decided we should put on a bit of a show, particularly as one of the duties was to lay a wreath on the town's War Memorial. We dressed him that morning with special care, in the hotel bedroom which was at the top of a narrow flight of stairs. All prepared, Cyril swept down those steps like a red avalanche. A maid was coming up carrying a tray of breakfast pots. She took one look at Cyril, let out an hysterical scream, dropped the tray and fled.

'Tourcoing was a marvellous trip, and Cyril was very keen on this idea of foreign exchanges to build up international relations, even in such a small way. The Mayoress liked the place too, sometimes a bit too much for Cyril's liking. We had to take her back to the hotel in the evening, and make a great show of getting ready to go to bed. When Hetty was safely asleep, Cyril and I would sneak out and go to one of the pavement cafés for a drink and a chat with the locals.

'Oh, yes, Hetty really enjoyed being Mayoress when she got over the first nervousness. She was still working in the Town Hall as a cleaner, but she revelled in the official functions. I remember her telling me about a Royal Party they attended at Buckingham Palace, when Cyril was to receive his MBE. Actually inside the palace, walking up a flight of stairs, a women tried to push her way in front of Hetty.

'"I suppose it was Lady this or Lady that," she said with satisfaction. "It made no difference though, I gave her a right clout across the shins with my walking-stick. That put a stop to her little games."

'But I must not give the impression that Cyril's year as Mayor was all fun and games. We did a lot of hard work: there were always hundreds of electors and children and teachers and pensioners swarming in and out in the Mayor's Parlour, and he spoke to them all. I think he didn't like all the pomp, and was trying to show as many people as possible that the Mayor was only a human being like themselves.

'He was certainly very kind, in a way that the public never got to hear of. He suffered a major personal loss when his old friend, Alderman Chorlton, was hit by an open train door on Rochdale Station and was killed. I think Cyril had known him since he was a kid. He couldn't do enough for Mrs Chorlton. He took me off all civic duties for three days, and put me and the Mayor's car at her disposal while she made all the arrangements for the funeral.

'He was also very kind to me. He gave me a day off every week, which was very unusual, and drove himself round his engagements. I won't mention any names, but some Mayors treated me like some sort of personal slave. Many's the time I have sat in the car for three or four hours while the Mayor was inside wining and dining, and I've never had so much as a cup of tea. Cyril wouldn't let that happen, he made it clear that if he accepted an invitation to any function, I was to be well looked after too. The only complaint I have was that he didn't buy me a present at the end of the year. Instead, he gave my wife an expensive coffee service. I think he thought I was being paid to do my job – my wife wasn't.

'And while we're at it, there's one little secret I must tell. I don't know if people realise that the town had to buy a special robe for Cyril, because he was too big for the old one. For some reason, there's a law against buying new robes from the rates. I probably shouldn't say this, but they put down the cost of the robe – it was about one hundred pounds – to the soft furnishings account. I think that's pretty apt, don't you?'

Well, so much for Fred Rothwell's summing up of my year of office – and, incidentally, thanks, Fred, for the tip about the soft furnishings account. I have always thought I would buy that robe back from the Corporation as a souvenir, for it has never been used since. Perhaps I had better do so before the District Auditor starts getting edgy!

As Fred makes clear, it was a very happy year in many ways. It was also a hard year, because I was determined to make the Mayoralty work for the benefit of the town, both internally and externally. On the external front, I met and entertained as many businessmen as I could, in an effort to attract sorely needed industry to the borough. Internally, I set out to show that the Mayor belonged to the town and its people, and not vice versa.

Gracie Fields' remark about respecting God, the King and the Mayor of Rochdale, had made a deeper mark than I at first appreciated. The idea of a Mayor as a feudal lord did not appeal to me at all. In particular, I became very impatient with the bowing and scraping approach from many people who, I knew only too well, wished that I personally were at the bottom of the ocean in a large sack weighed down by a substantial weight of concrete.

If I had any overriding aim, it was to bring the Mayor – the office, not myself – down into the everyday lives of the ordinary people. I invited every voter from Falinge Ward to meet me in the Town Hall, dividing something like four thousand names into four large parties. I visited every school in the borough, and went into every classroom of every school, so that the children could meet the Mayor, speak to him, and understand that he, too, was just an ordinary man like their fathers.

It was a year, too, that cost me a sum of money which, with my business commitments, I could barely afford. I was given a Mayor's allowance of one thousand pounds mainly to cover the cost of entertaining guests in the Mayor's Parlour. The uninitiated who resent civic leaders splashing out money on entertainment should know just how great a source of worry this is to the civic leaders concerned.

Because I was spending public money, I opened the drinks cabinet as rarely as I could, bearing in mind that it was not in the interest of the town to be downright mean with guests such as important industrialists. I may have had a Mayor's Parlour, and a Mayor's Maid to hand out the drinks, but every time I offered Joe Bloggs a cup of tea I received a bill for tuppence. One previous Mayor had warned me that his year had cost him ten thousand pounds of his personal cash. With my arrogant assumption that the office would eventually be mine, I had been making financial preparations for ten years: I had been paying half-a-crown a week into an endowment insurance policy which matured when I took office, giving me an extra two hundred and fifty pounds leeway. I spent that, too, but there were never any allegations that I was an extravagant Mayor. I gave heavily in time and effort and that, I thought, was sufficient.

It would be pleasant to record, also, that the year passed in serenity on the political front, but I am afraid that was not to be. Huge rifts were beginning to split the Labour party following the death of Hugh Gaitskell, a politician for whom I had held the greatest respect. I had once been asked by Frank Cousins, Transport and General Workers' Union, to join its Parliamentary Panel, the 'short list' of potential Parliamentary candidates the union sponsors; but the union opposed Gaitskell's policies – a case of Gaitskell versus Cousins. The Labour movement was beginning a steady, irreversible swing to the extreme Left. The Labour party was becoming a monolith, an Establishment in its own right, and I was growing increasingly unhappy.

In the sixteen years I had been a member of the movement, it had changed from a brash, battling youngster, facing the realities of power as a regular phenomenon for the first time, to an introspective, smouldering, schizophrenic adult. The movement had played the class-warfare game with great skill, but instead of smashing the class-system apart, its avowed intention, it had only succeeded in polarising public opinion to such an extent that class differences were fossilised in the same way that prehistoric plants can be found in perfect condition, but made of stone, not living tissue. The ideal that the working man could be lifted from drudgery by the use of his own gifts and talents seemed to have been forgotten. The men and women who had progressed were to be ignored, because they were probably voting Conservative or Liberal.

The new, ideal Labour voter was to be either a mindless worker who never questioned his shop-steward, however idiotic the shop-steward's demands were to be, or the unemployed worker, able-bodied but lazy, who was prepared to live in his subsidised council house on social security payments issued on the assumption his vote went to the Left. At the other end of the Labour spectrum were to be the elite, the ministers, the loyal MPs, the senior trade union officials, who no longer needed to consult the masses before imposing their views on the State. George Orwell prophesied it in *Animal Farm* – and I make this point in earnest concern, not out of rancour – when he wrote: 'All animals are equal, but some are more equal than others.'

The biggest disaster the British public ever imposed on itself was the creation, often by apathy, of so called 'safe seats', whether at Parliamentary or local government level. The safe seat means that 'safe people' can be slotted into the House of Commons or the Town Hall, safe in the sense that they need neither the wit nor the will to resist the manipulations of their party elders. The Labour party has become particularly vulnerable to this sort of manipulation, and that inevitably led to the re-emergence of an eighteenth-century cancer, corruption.

It is no accident that the recent corruption trials which shocked the nation almost always involved Labour Councillors in areas where they had been in total control for many years. Automatic re-election often takes away the need for honest endeavour. Once the need to satisfy the electorate is removed, the politician is free to pursue his own, rather than his community's ends.

Rochdale did not suffer from this problem, because the

leadership of the council has changed hands regularly every few years, sometimes to Labour, sometimes to a loose Conservative–Liberal coalition. In the quarter of a century I spent on the council, I can only recall one Councillor about whom I had suspicions, and those could well have been ill-founded. But it is not true to say that approaches were not made from disreputable sources.

I myself once received a letter from T. Dan Smith, then the well-publicised and highly respected planning Overlord in the North-East. He asked for a meeting but, I was puzzled to note, not at the Town Hall, but at the offices of the Rochdale Trades and Labour Council. Nevertheless, I was impressed that this important man should wish to meet me and I asked the Town Clerk to reply. We organised a small reception at the Town Hall, and I asked the local press to attend. He did not arrive, leaving me with the humiliating task of making excuses to the council staff and journalists present. When Dan Smith went to jail some years later on corruption charges, taking with him the reputations and sometimes the liberty of several prominent North-East Labour politicians, I think I received my answer for his non-appearance. The Town Clerk had answered on my behalf, therefore making the meeting official business. I often wonder what would have happened had I replied privately, and agreed to meet him at party headquarters, rather than the Town Hall. I do not know, of course, what the meeting would have led to: I am just highly relieved that I never became involved.

There was one other approach, too, which leaves me with suspicions as I look back with hindsight. The only foreign trip I ever made abroad as a Councillor, except for official visits to Rochdale's twin-towns, was at the invitation of a building firm which was interested in importing a European prefabricated building system. I went on this trip, but carefully noted my reasons for doing so in the council minutes. In the event I voted against the introduction of the system on a large scale into Rochdale's housing programme because of a technical doubt. Years later that firm – I cannot name it for legal reasons – is still at the centre of a lengthy and widespread investigation.

I cannot pretend that I led some sort of crusade against corruption, for at the time I did not know it existed. It certainly did not exist in Rochdale, possibly because no one – Labour, Liberal or Conservative – could guarantee to stay in power long enough to force an illegal contract through to fruition.

But as I was saying, by 1966, and indeed for some time before, the growing monolithic power of the Labour party had become steadily more offensive to my principles of individual freedom. In a minor way, I had become one of the targets for that attack.

The Rochdale Trades and Labour Council was an unusual organisation in that it represented both trade union and local political aspirations, a small-town hybrid of the Labour party and the TUC combined. The trade unions had, on a count of votes, the greater power and I suddenly found myself under attack from this direction. There were grumbles that, because I had become an employer with my own small factory, I could no longer be considered representative of the working man. This seemed arrant nonsense to me on two counts. Firstly, I was working at least as hard as any of my employees and, secondly, wasn't it the sacred policy of the party for working men to improve their lot in life, as I had managed to do? My arguments did not prevail, and I was voted out of the Chairmanship of the council after the most powerful union delegate – the man who controlled the biggest number of card votes – told me privately: 'I have no doubts about your competence, Cyril, but I think you are getting too bloody powerful.'

It seemed a ridiculous argument, because surely any organisation wants its Chairman to have as much power as humanly possible? However, I accepted the dismissal philosophically, marking it down as another offspring of the many petty jealousies in local politics. What I wasn't prepared for – and this came in the middle of my Mayoral year – was an internal attack from the political wing of the local party.

As Mayor, as I have already said, I was also Chairman of the Corporation, and it was my duty to ensure that the Corporation acted within the limits of the law. One of the statutory duties of the time was to ensure that the Borough's housing budget balanced at the end of the financial year, and in 1966 we were sorrowfully facing a hundred and twenty thousand pound deficit on the housing account. We had two alternatives: to impose the whole amount on the rates, which would have meant the then outrageous increase of one shilling in the pound for every ratepayer in the town, or to increase council house rents. I proposed a compromise: put half on the rates, half on the rents, because I believed – and I still do – that although council housing is a vital social service, the owners of private houses, struggling to pay off mortgages, have a right to equal consideration *whether they vote Labour or not*.

It was a fashionable belief that all council house tenants voted Labour, and all owner-occupiers voted Conservative or Liberal, a belief which from my years of face-to-face canvassing I knew to be an utter fallacy. At this stage of the argument, national government – in the figure of Mr Richard Crossman, then at the Ministry of Housing – stepped in. It was a time, as ever, of a prices 'freeze' and the Labour government had appealed to councils not to raise rents. Not accepting the 'freeze', I set off to London with a deputation to demand the right to put our own house in order.

The meeting was a shambles. Dick Crossman had suddenly changed office, and we were met instead by Bob Mellish, then a junior housing minister, who I was later to meet as Labour Chief Whip while I was Liberal Whip in the Commons. Bob, on most occasions a sensible enough man, was a bit out of touch with the events that day, because he chose to give me a patronising lecture on the duties of local government.

'I'm not being talked to like a schoolboy by anyone,' I declared, incensed, and turned to walk out of the room. Only the intervention of the Town Clerk persuaded me to stay, but even that achieved little. The case had attracted national attention, and the following day I was quoted in the *Daily Express*: 'It was a waste of time. I was confused and frustrated. The government got us into this mess and they have got to get us out of it.'

Despite the angry confrontation in Whitehall, I still persuaded my Labour colleagues to go ahead with the rent increases... that is until halfway through the council meeting of 20 August 1966, when a piece of paper was handed up to the Mayor's dais. It informed me that the Labour group had met informally before the council, and had decided to vote against the rent increases. Blazing, I stood up and told an amazed chamber: 'From this minute, I no longer consider myself a member of the Labour party.'

THE MAYOR WALKS OUT

For a Mayor to resign from his party halfway through his term of office caused, not unnaturally, something of a sensation. The *Guardian* – how I wish I could still call that paper the *Manchester Guardian* – quoted me the following day: 'I have resigned because they went behind my back. This is probably the end of my municipal career.'

In that, I was wrong. My resignation had seriously wounded the Labour party, because at the time they held control of the council only by my casting vote as Chairman. If that were not enough, four other members resigned from Labour and joined me in setting up an Independent group which was to sit as an important 'balancing' vote for the next four years. As an Independent, with a small but robust following, I was able to maintain many of my Corporation offices including my high-prized Chairmanship of the Education Committee.

All that ended in 1972, when Labour regained full control of Rochdale Corporation. Almost their first move was to dismiss me from the Education chair, which I accepted, because all controlling groups wish to chair the more important committees. But there was more, much more, to follow. I was sacked from the Youth Committee, of which I had been Chairman for twenty-one years, and from the Youth Employment Committee, which I had chaired for twenty years. I was sacked from the Committee of Rochdale Youth Orchestra, which I had formed to give the children of Rochdale an opportunity to play music, an opportunity which had been denied me by the lack of cash for music lessons. I was sacked from the Committee of the Youth Theatre Workshop, which I had helped to found, to encourage drama and the visual arts in the town. I was sacked from the Boards of Governors of no less than twenty-nine Rochdale schools, which I had visited so assiduously as Mayor. I would no doubt have been sacked from the Human Race if Rochdale Labour Party had had its say.

I had known the pomp of local government. It was a time to learn the spitefulness, though I had, and treasure, hundreds of letters from Rochdale teachers thanking me for my efforts.

What no one knew at the time was that there was to be a Parliamentary by-election for the Borough of Rochdale later that year...

CHAPTER SEVEN

'The Cart-horse will Win this Race'

It was a time for taking stock.

I am a great believer in ambition. Striving towards a definite goal has the effect of immeasurably enriching life, even if the goal is never reached. A man might decide to become Prime Minister, the Archbishop of Canterbury, even General Secretary of the Transport and General Workers' Union, and good luck to him. Ambitions such as these are beyond the limits of reality for the average man, however, but if he likes his garden, his gardening will be greatly improved if he tries to produce the prize marrow at the local show; if he likes a game of darts, he will practise more assiduously and his game will improve if he is selected to play for his local pub team.

In June 1967, the *Rochdale Observer* carried a lengthy two-part interview with me, and they published it under the headline: AN EMOTIONAL HARD NUT WITH A DESIRE FOR POWER – *Cyril Smith's self analysis*. It was a fair headline, and it still applies. But what it did not reveal, however, was although that desire for power was still strong within me, I no longer had a way to express it. As this great believer in ambition, I had discovered that a major fault of the trait is ambition achieved. I had, after all, been Mayor at the age of thirty-seven, and had been awarded the MBE for my services to local government. Where to now? The answer at the time seemed to lie in industry.

My childhood poverty had left me with an urgent need for the security of a sound financial base. My early departure from school and the subsequent squandering of energy in local politics, had for many years deprived me of any real idea of how to achieve that end. I had no professional training, and for years no opportunity of steady promotional advancement because I was never a member of any structured organisation long enough to advance. In short, my progress through working life had shown slightly less sense of direction than the average grasshopper's travels through a hayfield.

The civil service was out because of my political work. Teaching, the only profession which interested me, had been barred. It seemed for a time that the professional side of politics, a job as a party agent, was the sole possibility.

After leaving the Liberal party in 1950, I became agent to Hervey Rhodes, the Labour MP for Ashton-under-Lyne, Lancs, for long enough to become embroiled in my first national political row. Hervey, a mill-owner and junior minister at the Department of Trade, had a deep knowledge of Egyptian politics through his contacts in the Egyptian cotton industry. The early fifties was a time of growing tension in North Africa, with Egypt laying strong claims for territory in the Sudan. Prime Minister Attlee, his control on Parliament growing weaker by the day, had called a General Election and wisely decided to avoid any entanglement in complex foreign quarrels. Hervey, however, was deeply interested, although his government post had no connections with foreign policy. One day, in an unguarded moment, he told a reporter: 'Egypt will have the Sudan over my dead body.'

It was time for another 'Government Split' field-day in the press. All hell was let loose. Phones were continually ringing, and reporters and photographers camped on our doorsteps. Clem Attlee became anxious to paper-over any signs of a new rift. Hervey was, of course, considerably chastened, but there was a major problem looming on the horizon. Weeks before, the Prime Minister had arranged to appear at a political meeting in Ashton in support of Hervey. When news of the proposed meeting leaked out, the press were unready to accept that the meeting was a prior engagement. Here, they thought, was a Prime Minister preparing to travel to a little-known constituency to admonish a rebel minister. It was to be a big story.

Hervey and I sat down to discuss the problem. Advice was sought from Transport House. The event would have to be arranged, it was decided, so that the Prime Minister and Hervey could not meet in private, and it was my job to set the timetable. In what must have been one of the most curious public meetings ever, Hervey eventually gave his own speech before Mr Attlee arrived. As Clem walked into the hall, Hervey thanked his audience and sat down. Clem climbed into the vacated space on the podium, made his speech and left – while Hervey remained fixed in his chair.

In the tension of the evening, worried about split-seconds on my timetable, I met the Prime Minister's car and attempted to bundle him into the hall. He would have none of it. 'Don't forget the crowd, Cyril,' he said. 'They're the voters, you know.' I was in a sweat of anxiety, but he calmly waved to the crowd and the press photographers, and chatted to bystanders, before going in. That show of political 'nous' demonstrates, I think, what a master Clem Attlee was – a politician history has greatly underrated. From my point of view, the meeting – or should I say, the non-meeting – was a considerable success. The two men did not even shake hands, a strange state of affairs I must agree, but the press were never able to write: 'PM Carpets Rebel Minister.'

It was exciting working for Hervey Rhodes, later Lord Lieutenant of Lancashire, but I was to leave him in 1953, on the offer of the first capital I ever acquired – two hundred and fifty pounds. My benefactor was Alan Tillotson, one of those rare but truly delightful people, a very rich man with a deep concern for the welfare of ordinary people. Alan, whose family own newspapers and many other interests, desperately wanted to become Labour MP for Heywood and Royton, the constituency bordering Rochdale, and he offered me the bonus if I would join him as agent. That amount of money was probably twenty-four times greater than any amount I had ever had in my pocket at any one time. I went.

Alan who, like me, had started his political career as a Liberal, never did win that seat, but he made a speech which has always stuck in my memory. It was at an election rally, and he was being niggled by a wise but acerbic old lady.

'I see, Sir,' she said, 'that you are an ex-public schoolboy?'

'I am,' Alan replied.

'I also see,' she said, 'that you are a director of more than twenty companies?'

'I am, Madam.'

'That means, I suppose, that you are rich?'

'I cannot pretend that I am poor.'

'In that case,' said the woman, trying to set the barb, 'how can you be a Socialist?'

'That is simple, Madam,' Alan replied, with great charm. 'Socialism comes from the heart, and not from the pocket.'

I could have echoed those feelings myself, except that my pocket was lamentably thin at the time, despite my carefully guarded two hundred and fifty pounds. I was in my mid-twenties, and longing for independence. The opportunity which finally came up appealed not only to my desire to be my own boss, but it also had a certain piratical charm – I bought the newsagent's shop where I worked as a boy. In truth, it was not a particularly good buy, but I could not resist the imagery of the boy turning boss.

The shop, in St Mary's Gate, Rochdale, had been a thriving concern, but in 1955 was due to be demolished to make way for new housing and road developments. I bought it for two hundred pounds down – the bulk of my precious capital – and paid off another two hundred pounds by instalments. It was a declining business, because every day one of my customers would leave to make way for the bulldozers. I could only afford to hire one paper boy, so I did the bulk of the round myself – back pounding the same pavements I had trodden fifteen years earlier. But I was my own man, and the experience proved to be doubly useful. I was by this time an active Councillor, and the shop and the round gave me countless opportunities to meet people and listen to their problems. Councillor Smith made bigger gains than Businessman Smith at the time, but the businessman was storing away lessons of great value for the future. I learned, mainly, that a shopkeeper can only make a good living if he can afford a very big shop. I decided there and then that any real financial success would have to come from the manufacturing industry.

When the bulldozers finally smashed through my little shop in 1959, I was just fractionally better off. My compensation from the Corporation was four hundred pounds, the very price I had paid, but I was able to split the newspaper rounds and sell those for two hundred pounds. This capital gain for four years' work didn't put me quite in the league of the property speculators who were then piling up their millions, but it was a definite, if slight, improvement. In the meantime, I was out of work again.

For some years, one of my interests – some would say it was masochism – had been Rochdale Association Football Club, beavering away in the Fourth Division totally overshadowed by the giants twelve miles away in Manchester, United and City. The car, however, was yet to become the universal means of transport, and local loyalties were stronger than they are today, so the club could still draw gates round the six thousand mark. Respectable as that figure was, it was still two thousand short of the club's break-even point, and I had taken an active interest in raising funds to cover the gap. It was an interest which was to lead to one of my more colourful careers as an entertainments entrepreneur and sometimes bingo caller.

There is an archetypal figure in modern football, without whom many a club would have joined Accrington Stanley in leaving the ranks of the Football League for the less heady, but less expensive pastures of semi-professional or even amateur soccer. These men tend to be self-made, possess a fierce local loyalty and exhibit a thinly disguised streak of toughness – if they bother to disguise it at all. One such man is Fred Ratcliffe, owner of a large spring-making works in Rochdale, and Chairman of Rochdale AFC. My fund-raising activities had brought me into contact with Fred and when he learned that I was looking for a job, he offered me the work fulltime. I said yes.

At the beginning, it was little more than an extension of my work as a political organiser... raising raffles, recruiting agents to sell our weekly pool coupons. It seemed simple enough, but it was soon to bring the wrath of the law down on my head. The laws governing lotteries and sweepstakes present a minefield of problems ranging from simple ambiguity to crass idiocy. I trod on one of those mines when I reached the simple conclusion that the best way to get bigger returns from a raffle was to offer bigger prizes. The club bought a small car from a local garage at cost price, and I set out to raffle it off.

Someone – I never did find out who – had the initiative to sell a ticket to the wife of the Chief Constable of Rochdale, Frank Gale, a personal friend of mine who was, nevertheless, a stickler for doing things strictly by the book. I didn't know the law demanded that tickets for raffles with prizes over a certain cash value should be sold only to members of a legitimate club or organisation. I don't suppose Mrs Gale knew, but Frank or someone on his staff did, and I was dragged before the magistrates in the very Town Hall where I spent most of my time, to answer charges of breaking the public lottery laws. The club hired a barrister and defended the case, but we were 'bang to rights' as I believe the criminal classes say. I was bound over to keep the peace for twelve months, twelve months in which I was subjected to constant leg-pulling. 'Are you behaving yourself, Cyril?' they shouted in the streets. I wasn't particularly annoyed about the ridicule – but I was annoyed at the waste of public money. Hours and hours of magistrates' time, lawyers' time, police time seem to be wasted every year prosecuting people who have made simple, human mistakes. Surely a warning from the police would be sufficient?

My other wheeling and dealing activities in the nether-regions of soccer were more profitable. I introduced wrestling bouts on summer evenings at the ground, and developed a love of the entertainment – I don't call it a sport – which I have maintained ever since. I still pay to see wrestling matches, and watch them avidly on television, although I know only too well that the 'fights' are 'fixed'. That doesn't spoil my enjoyment – it is the skill of the performers, both in an athletic and a theatrical sense, that gives me the pleasure.

The star of my fund-raising activities, however, was the introduction of bingo to the town some years before the big entertainment chains moved in. I heard one day that Oldham Athletic were making a lot of money from a new style of Housey, Housey, that Christmas-time party game. Incredulous, I went to Oldham and saw that, indeed, they were packing a small club-house with serious people head-down in concentration over pieces of cardboard. If Oldham could do it, so could Rochdale, I decided, both bigger and better. So I hired a disused cinema from the Corporation – it was due for demolition – and we were soon packing the house. The law, since changed, would allow only a maximum of £2 prizes per game, and our only charge was two shillings for admission, but the public came flocking in. The cinema rent was only thirty pounds a week, and all the 'staff' were volunteers from the supporters' club. I took my turn, being cashier one night, checker another and bingo caller on yet another.

At one stage, we were raising a thousand pounds a week for the club, much of it from bingo. I sometimes regret I did not become a bingo entrepreneur in my own right. I may never have entered Parliament, but I would have made an awful lot of money! Such is the state of pay equality in Britain. There was I, raising the wages of men being paid more to kick a football about for, at the most, three hours a week, than men producing machinery in a factory, or food from the land for forty hours. Yes, there was I, raising more money as a bingo operator than I do as a reasonably successful industrialist and an MP to boot! Is it any wonder when one hears complaints that men of real ability no longer choose careers in politics?

My abilities as an organiser must have impressed my boss, Fred Ratcliffe, for he soon offered me a job in his spring factory, continuing the football fund-raising activities as a sideline. Being paid for the two jobs gave me, for the first time, enough money to begin adding to my capital of six hundred pounds. It also gave me a knowledge of spring making and, just as importantly, an insight into the general activities of British industry.

I was eventually promoted to one of the key posts in the factory – production controller. I say key post, because in this very department lies one of the serious ills of our industrial system. The work entails ensuring that ordered goods are delivered on time, and I was to learn that the goods involved – any product on the open market – may be of the right quality and at the right price, but they will not continue to sell if they are not delivered on the right date. This is certainly not a direct criticism of F. S. Ratcliffe (Rochdale) Ltd, but a general complaint I was to hear time and time again from my opposite numbers in other firms. To do my job successfully, the deliveries into our factory – the machinery, the raw materials – had to be on time so that we could meet our deadlines. All factories face the same problems, yet too often there are delays which can have a chain reaction throughout an entire industry, as hold-ups at one factory disrupt production schedules at the next, building up from days into weeks and even months as machinery and men are switched from job to job dependent on the materials or spare-parts available.

It is very easy to say these delays are caused by strikes, and undoubtedly many of them are, often for outrageously petty reasons. To blame all disruptions on trade union agitation, however, would be a major falsehood, a disservice to industry itself. Since leaving Ratcliffe's, I have realised that throughout Britain, week after week, managements are making totally impossible promises on delivery dates in their desperation to win orders. Too often, British industry sells promises, not goods.

By the time I had learned these lessons, my dream of entering the manufacturing industry in my own right was coming to reality. I knew there would be occasions when my deliveries would be unavoidably delayed, but I resolved I would turn down an order rather than make an impossible promise of delivery.

My entry into the spring industry was not accompanied by any fanfares. There were no stirring speeches outside a shining new factory, no free junket in the works canteen. It all began with a meeting of six men in the cramped front room of my house in Emma Street in 1963 – myself, Geoff Harrison, an expert spring maker, and four Rochdale businessmen. I had one thousand pounds and some organisational ability. Geoff had great technical skills, but no money. It was our job to persuade the other four to put up another two thousand pounds – we needed this sum for equipment and a further thousand pounds to cover our anticipated losses for the first three months of trading. I, of course, had very little business experience ... but I could talk. Talk, I did, that night and my sixth paid career – as opposed to unpaid political career – began.

Smith's Springs (Rochdale) Ltd started its life in an old joiner's shop as the ideal industrial partnership; capital and admin. ability as raised by me, and skill as supplied by Geoff. I *was* the management, and he *was* the shop-floor, for we were to be the only two active workers. We bought our small amount of machinery secondhand – a lathe, a furnace, an oil bath and a grinding wheel. Our rent was five pounds a week, and our address was 3 Flannel Street, yet another of those old Rochdale street names with more than a touch of irony! Geoff was to produce the springs, I was to sell them. This time I was to pound the streets, not just of Rochdale, but of all England, and parts of Scotland and Wales looking for orders.

Going 'on the road' as a commercial traveller presented its own problems. For a start, I couldn't drive – I didn't take my test until 1966 – but fortunately, my brother Norman had a small taxi business and his slack period was in mid-week. He agreed to chauffeur me around for three days in the middle of the week for five pounds a day, including petrol. There was little money to spare for hotel bills – and the hotels we did use were the very cheapest – so it was of the essence to cram as many calls as possible into those three days. It was a time for energy and perseverance, two qualities which, I am sure, will eventually bring success in industry. If they are combined with a modicum of luck, however, the success comes that little bit more quickly.

My first breakthrough was, in fact, pure luck. Springs, of all shapes and sizes, are used in vast quantities in almost every industry – in pumps, in machines, in cars and aeroplanes, in almost anything that carries or lifts or compresses. The manufacture of springs had been going on since the dawn of the Industrial Revolution, and the major producers are well entrenched in the market. A new firm, an unknown firm, had really only one way of breaking into that market ... offering equal quality at lower prices. My first major order came at a ridiculously low price because of a basic mathematical error. Someone divided my tender for five hundred springs and came up with the answer that they were one shilling and threepence each. The firm Marshalsea Bros, of Taunton, Somerset, accepted the tender with delight ... until someone ran a check on the long division. I remember the phone call that followed.

'Hello, Mr Smith, this is Marshalsea Bros from Taunton. I'm sorry to say there has been some mistake.'

My heart sank. 'Oh, yes,' was all I could say.

'Yes, I'm afraid there has been a miscalculation. We worked out your price at one and threepence per spring, and we have discovered that in fact it is really two shillings and threepence per spring. At that price, I'm afraid, we will have to cancel the order.'

If my present-day arithmetic is correct, we were talking

about fifty-six pounds and twenty-five new pence but it was one of the most important sums of my life. I was desolate.

'How much do you normally pay?' I croaked.

'I don't think we can go much higher than one and fivepence.'

My hesitation was only momentary. 'All right, you can have them for that – if other firms can make them for one and fivepence, so can we.'

I put down the phone and forced the courage to tell Geoff. We would no doubt make a loss on the deal, but it would keep him working for about twelve hours and at that stage in the business, we needed as much production as possible.

Geoff was philosophical, if a little wry. 'I thought we were in this business to make money as well as springs,' he said. 'But I suppose if we can't make both we might as well make one of 'em.'

The order was delivered, on time, and I thought I should capitalise on the contact. I set out one winter evening with my brother to drive through a night of heavy snowstorms to Taunton. We were outside the office at eight am the following morning, waiting for the buyer to arrive. Eventually, one of the staff came out to apologise. Sorry, but the buyer had been taken to hospital.

I was explaining the journey we had made when a wellspoken voice said from behind: 'Any man who has been prepared to drive from Rochdale in this weather at least deserves a hearing. Come into my office – we'll talk it over.'

The voice came from Squadron Leader Sidney Fields, the Managing Director. In his office, we established a trading liaison which continues to this day. It was our first major contract, and it probably would never have happened if he hadn't been passing by that day. As I said, energy and perseverance will achieve ultimate success, but it is much easier if there's a little bit of luck as well.

Smith's Springs now employs seventy people – a size which, in my mind, is ideal. I know every one of the employees, and they know me. Because of my political work, I handle only the financial side of the business, and Geoff Harrison is Works Director. I pay him three times more than I pay myself, because he does three times more work. It is, I think, a happy company, and building it has given me an inside knowledge which has helped me immeasurably as an MP. It gave me – this is a boast, but I do not apologise – a chance to put into practice what I preach, and I think this would be a better governed country if there were more politicians, particularly ministers, who could make the same claim.

I made a speech at a recent Party Conference saying that Liberals were in favour of trade unions taking a responsible place in industry. The speech brought a letter from the Transport and General Workers' Union, pointing out that I owned a non-union company. Would I mind if their local organiser approached my workers to ask them if they wished to join? It was, of course, an open challenge, and I passed the letter to the Works Council. How do you feel about it? I asked. If you want to join, by all means join.

The council, which is elected by the employees and meets in secret without management interference, considered the proposal. It gave me some considerable pleasure when the council voted unanimously to reject the union's advances. It was pleasure drawn not from any inherent dislike of trade unions, but because they have become such a rallying point – and a recruiting ground – for so many industrial misfits. I have found, and many people share the experience, that the unions are often at their strongest, their most militant, in an unhappy factory. Whether one follows the other is a 'chicken-and-the-egg' conundrum. Does bad management create unhappy workers who then become union militants? If that is so, the managements are to blame and the unions are doing their right and proper job. But are there cases where it is the unions, not the managements, that are causing the discontent, for sinister political ends? Although it grieves me to say so, I feel the answer to this last question is an overwhelming *yes*.

My policy for keeping shop-floor morale high is quite simple. I pay above the minimum pay rates laid down in national negotiations between bodies like the Confederation of British Industry and the unions. At the same time I discourage overtime unless absolutely necessary, for I feel time off is at least as important as time spent working. We were given the five-day week in this country to spend the weekends with our families or at our leisure, not in order to be paid time-and-a-half by working on Saturdays.

In addition to higher pay rates, I have also followed-through on one of my near-sacred Liberal philosophies, profit-sharing. Each year, fifteen per cent of our gross profits – which works out at nearly twenty-five per cent of after-tax profits – is shared out among all workers who have been with the company for more than twelve months. Even in the difficult trading conditions of the past few years, our employees have received bonuses of as much as a hundred and fifty pounds or more in August, the height of the holiday period. Seventy bonuses represents a fair sum of money, but we feel the workers are just as entitled to the bonus as the directors.

We offer other so-called 'fringe-benefits', such as pension and life insurance schemes.

At Christmas time, all employees are given a turkey and a bottle of whisky – not so much as a perk, but as a gift given in a spirit of friendship which, I hope, pervades the company.

All these things are the nuts-and-bolts of good industrial relations. The oil that keeps the machine turning smoothly, I think, is provided by the direct personal relationship Geoff Harrison and I have with the staff. I may not go to the factory as often as I would wish – I can't when I spend four days a week in London – but when I do go in, I am available to anyone who wishes to see me, to discuss a grievance, help in a family matter or (I am their MP as well, of course) take up a political point. Like everyone else, my employees call me Cyril if they wish to do so. That seems a pretty fair start to a sound industrial relationship.

While my business had been growing steadily in the late sixties, my political career had changed to the grasshopper style of my early working life. My abrupt departure from the Labour party was something of a seven-day wonder, and our little band of five Independents on the Corporation, although highly vocal and reasonably influential in the council chamber, was unable to expand its membership. We fought several council elections and by-elections and, although we managed to force ourselves into second place in most counts, we took no new seats. One of the hypocrisies of the British public is the regularly repeated condemnation of 'too much politics in local government'. It's the public's fault – they continue to vote along political lines in their municipal elections!

In the meantime, things were beginning to stir in the Liberal party. Younger men were coming along with new, radical ideas, and were beginning to wrest control of party thinking from the upper-class dilettantes who had reigned supreme at the end of the war. The new impetus worked its way down towards the grass-roots, and eventually the almost moribund Rochdale party – which had not even fielded a candidate in two recent General Elections, began shaking itself back to life. It was inevitable that I should go back into the fold. In January 1968, along with the four Independents who had supported me on the council, I re-joined the party of my youth. Our little party received a guarded, but sincere, welcome – they shook our hands rather than kissed our cheeks. This time the turncoat jibe was supplemented with cries of, 'How many more parties are you going to try, Cyril?' By this time, as I have said elsewhere, my skin had thickened. But how many other parties? I had merely re-joined an old love, not embarked on some passionate romance with a new floozy. This time the jibes were met, if not with laughter, at least with smiles. There were certainly no tears.

To repeat the slick answer, a man who changes his mind is wiser today than he was yesterday. I was in fact wiser, not by a day, but by nearly two decades. The growing cynicism of the Labour party was giving me graver anxieties day by day. The new thinking of the Liberal party, committed as it was at last to worker-participation in industry, to the wider horizons of Europe, to personal liberty within a free enterprise system, offered me new hope. I may have changed my personal outlook a little, but I had moved, politically, neither to the Left nor the Right. It was as though the parties themselves had changed the boundaries, like rivers switching beds. One day, I found myself back in the mainstream of Liberalism, because the social-democratic waters of the Labour party had washed elsewhere – or had been drained away.

I must make it clear, however, that my rejoining the Liberals in 1968 was not part of a long-term plan to capture, as I eventually did, a Parliamentary seat. Nothing was further from my mind. If anything, I believed my political career, at its strictly

'THE CART-HORSE WILL WIN THIS RACE'

small-town level, was already past its zenith. I had been Mayor, my business was growing at a satisfactory if not lightning pace, and I was in a mood to spend the remainder of my life offering what service I could to Rochdale, giving any benefit of a long experience back to the town that I could, without totally exhausting my ability to live a full personal and social life. It was time, in fact, to sit back and enjoy some of the fruits of my labours.

The offer to fight the 1970 General Election came as a surprise, and at a time of acrimony among Rochdale Liberals. Our Parliamentary election record had been abysmal for many years, and after some fairly bloody infighting we decided to adopt a new candidate, but who? The election was just weeks away, and we were denied the luxury of a long series of interviews which normally characterise the search for a new electoral spearhead. I was still looked upon with some suspicion by a selection of the local party, and I was by no means the unanimous choice. It was not a good way to start a General Election campaign. The sheer lack of time forced a 'paper-campaign' onto us – electioneering done by pamphlet, rather than personal contact – and at no time did I think I could win. As I described in the first chapter, I was right in this belief. We lost by some five thousand votes, and I found the taste of my first-ever election defeat bitter indeed. But we did take the Liberal vote into second place in the poll...

This second place must have set cogs in motion in the Liberal party organisation, but any machinations went ahead without my knowledge or even interest. Any faint desire to enter Parliament had died in that defeat. The thought of spending four or five days a week in London, away from my family and friends, did not thrill me. The potential disruption it posed for my business life could in no way be outweighed by the parsimonious salaries being offered to MPs. I was still Chairman of Rochdale Education Committee, which I had long considered the pinnacle of my life's public work. I had all the benefits, I admit, of a very large fish in a rather small pond.

My first intimation that a conveyor belt had started under me came at the Liberal party Conference in 1971, when Jeremy Thorpe sat down at the dinner table in my hotel and announced: 'There could be a by-election in Rochdale in the next year or so – will you stand for us, Cyril?'

It may seem macabre – it is macabre in fact – but one of the constant occupations of a party leader in Parliament is the health of other members. In times of low majority government, the Prime Minister and the Leader of the Opposition must spend many hours preoccupied with rumours about the state of health of the Right Hon. X or the Hon. Y, because a death means a by-election, the possible loss of a seat, and perhaps a change in legislative plans. For the leader of the Liberal party, with its only record of outstanding success being in by-elections, the health – or ill-health – of MPs is a matter of crucial concern. In Scarborough that year, Jeremy, who is above all a brilliant campaigner, had heard that Jack McCann, Rochdale's Labour MP, was ill.

I was not keen to be drawn into the discussion. Jack McCann had been a friend of mine for years, although we had fallen out in the 1970 campaign when I attacked his speaking record in the House. But irrespective of his ill-health – which I recognised, despite myself, raised a valid political question-mark – I did not wish to stand again.

'If anything does happen to Jack, will you get in touch with me?' asked Jeremy.

'If you want me to – all right,' I said, wanting to end the conversation.

'Does that mean you would agree to stand?' asked Jeremy, his face showing a little hope.

'No – it just means that I will get in touch with you,' I answered.

Nothing more was discussed until early 1972, when I received a letter from David Steel, then Chief Whip of the party, saying that he was extremely anxious that I should fight the next election. I wrote back, declining politely. David wrote again, asking me to reconsider. I replied, yet again, saying No.

The early months of 1972 were among the happiest of my life. I faced a comfortable future, I had important work to do both publicly and privately, I had – for the first time in my life – peace of mind. No one, I thought, was going to shake my own little ivory tower. Then came the municipal elections, a Labour-controlled council, and the spite. The loss of the Chairmanship of the Education Committee I could bear, because it was a valid political move. But the stripping of all my other council-controlled offices – the Chairmanship *and* the Committee of the youth orchestra, the Chairmanship *and* the committee of the theatre workshop, the ejection from no less than twenty-nine school boards, were humiliations that I found difficult to accept. To remove me from a Chairmanship was one thing – to remove me from Committees another! My ivory tower was not just shaken, but shattered into splinters. I withdrew into myself, nursing my wounds like a wild animal, determined never to expose myself to public hurt again.

The phone call came two months later on a Sunday morning in July, just before I went to church. Jack McCann was dead.

When I returned from church, the phone in the house was ringing again as I went through the front door. It was Jeremy Thorpe, expressing his regrets, and asking: 'Will you fight the by-election?'

I was still numbed by my treatment from the new Rochdale Corporation, still highly protective of my self-esteem. I had no desire to be hurt again, so once again I said I was not anxious to stand. I put forward, instead, the name of Dr Michael Winstanley, the Cheshire GP who had managed to combine medicine with a career as a TV personality and who had, until 1970, been Liberal MP for Cheadle, a constituency only the other side of Manchester from Rochdale. Michael seemed the ideal choice because, among other things, he had affectionate links with Rochdale, even to the extent of being captain of one of the town's many cricket teams.

That day, I sat down and wrote to Michael, asking if he would be interested in becoming our Liberal candidate. The reply came by return of post. To précis its contents, it said: 'There is only one man who can win Rochdale for the Liberals, Cyril, and that is you!'

The pressure was building up. Jeremy Thorpe telephoned again, promising massive backing from the party – a top agent, money, a multitude of voluntary supporters – and his own personal contribution: he was prepared to live in the constituency for three days during the campaign.

The persuasiveness was enormous, but the way in which it eventually triggered me into saying Yes has never been known before. If there was any one single motive which made me fight that by-election, it was the motive of *revenge*. My treatment at the hands of the Rochdale Labour party that spring had left me with a totally unaccustomed feeling of impotence. My home town, for which I had worked so hard, seemed to have turned its back on me. I went through a long period dogged by other emotions new to me, lack of confidence and self-pity. Then the by-election was called, and once again people were flattering me, cajoling me to get up and fight. The self-pity disappeared – after all, if those people had faith in me, why shouldn't I? The self-confidence which had always been a major driving force came roaring back. And if I did win, what then ...?

Could revenge possibly be sweeter? The Labour party had taken from me jobs which I considered vitally important. How would it be if I took from them the most important political job the town had to offer? By the time I said Yes to the nomination, I was already in a fever of excitement at the prospect.

I entered the by-election with two advantages. Firstly, Labour were to enter a new man, so it was no longer a case of weighing my record against that of Jack McCann, but a case of mine against no opposition record at all. Secondly, and most importantly, I had established my *viability* as a candidate by coming second in the 1970 poll. This is the particular millstone of any Liberal candidate, however talented. We have to prove, not that we *will* win but that we *can* win – for people do not like to 'waste' votes on candidates whom they believe to have no chance. One of the stranger public opinion polls of recent years showed that eighty per cent of the British electorate would like to see a Liberal government at some time or another, but as they thought this to be an impossibility, they wouldn't vote Liberal. In Rochdale, at least, I had overcome this particular hurdle.

From an organisational point of view, Jeremy Thorpe lived up to his word magnificently. The help and money came pouring in, and I was given the fulltime services of one of the Liberal party's top agents, John Spiller. John, formerly John Pardoe's agent, was working in Switzerland, and was sent into Rochdale especially for the fight. He brought with him his girl-friend Angela and, so dedicated was he to the campaign, that he only mentioned by off-chance one morning that they intended to get married in Rochdale Register Office that week. Absolutely no arrangements had been made to celebrate the event: I hurriedly organised a cake and a few bottles of champagne, and we held the reception in Emma Street. I was best man, and we had a good time.

In political circles, men like John Spiller are regarded with the sort of awe which must have been directed at top-guns in the Old West. As well as being a superb organiser, he has an astute political brain. It was he, for instance, who pointed out that there were some nine thousand immigrants in Rochdale, mainly Pakistanis, and asked: 'What are we going to do about their votes?' It was a question of fundamental importance, for the issue was being clouded by the entry into the contest of an anti-immigration candidate, one of the early manifestations of National Front thinking in serious politics.

My views on the matter are straightforward. It must be the duty of every sane person in the country to fight racialism at every turn, but at the same time, it would be ridiculous to pretend that racial problems do not exist. Different cultures, different religions, different lifestyles, cannot be thrown together without some misunderstandings on either side. It will take time before the immigrant populations of this country can be fully integrated, and that integration must be allowed to go on with as much understanding and as little interference as possible. It must be a natural, not a forced, process. It will not be helped by opening the floodgates of unrestricted immigration, placing even more pressure on housing and job availability in our industrial towns and cities. When people say to me, 'That's all right, Cyril, but you don't have to live next door to them', I have the ultimate answer: my neighbours in Emma Street for twelve years have been a Pakistani family, and I could not wish for nicer people next door! But equally to stop immigration totally is immoral and un-Christian.

It was John Spiller who pointed out this area of political action. It was a matter in which Jeremy Thorpe took a great interest. Jeremy and I met all the leaders of the immigrant community in Rochdale early in the campaign, explained our views, and asked for their support. I am sure we got it, for by the time the Labour party decided to tackle the immigrant areas, 'SMITH THE MAN' posters were staring from the windows of house after house. Their star 'attraction' for immigrants was John Stonehouse MP, whose large-scale trading empire with Bangladesh was yet to fall in ruins.

Another arena in which the Parliamentary candidate must do battle lies in the bloodstained sands of press relations. The press in this country has always shown a healthy disrespect for politicians. Newspapermen sometimes reflect the opinions of the voters with a much greater accuracy than the voters' own representatives. My relationship with the press, until the by-election, had mainly been on a local level, and had always been cordial if not self-idolatory. My 'gimmick', if I ever needed one, was always to tell the truth, a thought so alien to many politicians as to be almost revolutionary. But would this simplistic attitude be as effective with the national press, which was by then beginning to take an eager interest in the by-election?

With all the luxuries always made available to a by-election candidate, the party had supplied me with a personal assistant, Aza Pinney, who was an expert in press relations. He sat down with John Spiller and I to discuss our tactics in the newspapers. I was determined to go my old way, telling the truth as I saw it, casting out the spur-of-the moment opinion which, so often, can lead to a major newspaper storm. They urged caution. It was necessary, they said, now that Rochdale had become a centre of national interest, to present myself as a man of national stature. We came to a compromise: each night, we would sit down and discuss the agenda for the following day's press conference. Aza, with his knowledge of the newspaperman's mind, would consider the day's events and attempt to anticipate likely questions. I would then be briefed on the most acceptable answers to those questions and, should I be tempted to 'shout my mouth off', at least the answers would be accurate.

We decided to base our campaign on winning the 'popular' press to our side, for Rochdale is a town where they read the 'pops'. I remember my trepidation when John announced one evening: 'The *Daily Mirror*'s coming tomorrow afternoon. I've cancelled all your engagements, give this chap all the time he needs.' The interview, my first in-depth talk with a national political journalist, lasted three hours. At the end, I thought I had established a reasonable relationship with the fellow, but I had no idea what he thought of me. I bought the paper the following day with all the anxiety of a budding starlet waiting for the reviews of her opening night. It was good, very good in fact. I had not only been taken seriously, but I had even been given a good chance of winning!

From there on in, the campaign never looked back. Pressmen trailed me wherever I went. The *Daily Express* sent one of its best Northern photographers, Brian Duff, to dog my footsteps. He got the best picture that has ever been taken of me, a view of my outstanding feature – my backside – next to my car which carried a banner proclaiming: 'You are right behind Cyril Smith.' I hasten to add that I was wearing my trousers!

Things were going well, and at this stage I must pay due tribute to the enormous help I received from Jeremy Thorpe. Jeremy, although I did not know it then, was one of the men with whom I was later to cross swords. Our disagreements, which I will discuss later, have discoloured our friendship, which is for me a matter of profound regret. But I will never deny the charismatic presence he brought to my by-election campaign in 1972.

He is a man of acute political grasp, of great flair, but his biggest asset is the possessing of an electioneering gift verging on genius. He spoke for me at meetings, he knocked on doors for me as a canvasser, he toured the town in a Land-Rover shouting for me over a loud-hailer. He is the sort of man who can stop an old lady in the street, give her an unembarrassed hug, and leave her as a Jeremy Thorpe fan – and a committed Liberal voter – until the end of her days. With Jeremy on my side to woo over floating Conservative voters the campaign became a foregone conclusion.

At the eve-of-poll rally in the Town Hall, I thumped out my message time and time again: A vote for the Conservatives was a wasted vote. It was a sweet phrase for any Liberal. There were only two possible victors – Liberal or Labour.

'It is,' I roared, 'a two-horse race.'

Then came an inspiration which, to me, brought the memorable phrase of the campaign...

'... *And it is a race that the cart-horse will win.*'

By the time we drove to the Town Hall for the declaration the following night, we knew we had won. Our canvass returns from the polling booths made it inevitable – only the size of the majority was in doubt. Before leaving Emma Street, I telephoned Jeremy to give him the news. He was so overcome with emotion that he could hardly speak. 'I'll ring you back later, Cyril,' was all he could say.

My win at Rochdale was to do for Jeremy what Orpington had done for Jo Grimond, bring back a sense of hope, give the leadership of the Liberal party a concrete importance. It was the start of the latest, and the biggest, Liberal revival.

I arrived at the Town Hall to a storm of cheering from a huge crowd, the pop-pop of photographers' flashes, the glare of the television floodlights. The press, too, were in no doubt as to the winner. They asked me to pose giving the victory salute, although the official declaration was still an hour away, so they could rush their pictures back to Manchester for the night's last editions.

So, in the early hours of 27 October 1972, Cyril Smith, former paper boy, civil servant, party agent, newsagent, bingo organiser and factory owner, was declared Member of Parliament for the Borough of Rochdale, by a majority over Labour of five thousand and ninety-three votes.

Of course I was proud. Of course I was emotional.

But as I looked over at the crestfallen faces of the Labour group in that chamber – faces I knew so well in a setting I knew so well – I was barely able to control the urge to make a gesture quite unfitting to the modesty of victory.

I was sorely tempted to turn my V for Victory sign round!

CHAPTER EIGHT

'The Longest Running Farce in the West End'

The Members' Entrance to the House of Commons lies on the north end of this huge building, and is reached through New Palace Yard. The 'New' in New Palace Yard has always struck me as being symbolic of all that is good with Westminster, and much of which is bad, for it was created by William Rufus between 1097 and 1099, which must make it about the oldest new place in Britain. The New Palace is so called to distinguish it from the Old Palace, which was once the residence of Edward the Confessor, and its surviving parts are better known today as Westminster Hall – scene, among many others, of the momentous trials of King Charles I, Sir Thomas More, and Guy Fawkes.

It is a place of awe for anyone with the slightest knowledge of English history, a place of pilgrimage for people who have a love of democracy from any corner of this troubled world. It is the sort of place which intimidates visitors by its very presence, even men and women who have the greatest right to enter, the right given by the people of Britain at the ballot box. It certainly intimidated a twenty-eight-stone Alderman and small-time businessman from an almost forgotten cotton town in Lancashire, a man, I might say, not easily given to intimidation.

History, however, is not restricted to the towering stone walls. There are those who believe that a modern industrial state should be governed by a more modern machine. By this, I am not attacking the pomp which serves – or should serve – as a constant reminder to the workers in this grandiose factory that their job is to protect the people of Britain. I am attacking, however, the pomp and ceremony which can at times become downright obstructive to good government.

The Members' Entrance off New Palace Yard serves as a good example of this, for it was the place in which I was first confronted, as a new member, with the hocus-pocus of 'tradition'. The Members' Entrance, despite its sombre, proprietorial name, is really little more than a cloakroom. Inside, I was solemnly given the single coat-hook, my name written by it, which is the right of every MP. It was there that I saw my first piece of Parliamentary red-tape, an actual piece of the stuff hanging below the hook. What was that for? The serious attendant explained that I should hang my sword from the tape should I ever decide to attend the House of Commons wearing a sword. My disbelieving guffaw of laughter was met with doleful eyes: it was, Sir, *tradition*.

I do not really mind this senseless frippery, because at least it provides a small but regular source of amusement in a building not known these days for its scintillating wit, but there is another *tradition* about the Members' Entrance which I find decidedly offensive. The name of the glorified cloakroom means exactly what it says: it is the *Entrance* for *Members*, and no one else but members and House of Commons staff are allowed. If I wish to take visitors into the House – family, friends, constituents, business or commercial contacts of importance to Rochdale – they have to enter by a side entrance hidden away in the corner of the New Palace Yard. Some members choose to demonstrate their superiority by pointing guests round the corner, arranging a meeting inside the building, and then using the Members' Entrance themselves, a habit which immediately sets the MP apart from ordinary mortals. I take my guests in through the undistinguished side door, which successfully robs them of any sense of occasion, a pity considering they are entering one of the most hallowed buildings in the world. That is annoying enough, but it is the symbolism of these separate entrances which appals me. Many a citizen's first arrival at *his* or *her* Parliament is marked by a show of MPs' *privileges*. I was always led to believe that MPs are the *servants* of the people. Shouldn't the voters, then, enter through the privileged entrance, with the MPs banished to some humble side-door? After all, we are the hired help, paid to go to Westminster to practise our trade. Let us use the tradesmen's entrance!

The snobbery of the Members' Entrance is, admittedly, a minor failing in the daily operation of the Palace of Westminster, but I think it illustrates the attitude of many of today's 'defenders of democracy'. The Commons was once called the 'Best Members' Club in the World', a title it should well jettison, but which is in fact guarded with a cast-iron jealousy. Surprisingly (or is it, really?) many of the most vociferous defenders of these meaningless privileges are those members who take the greatest pains through their public appearances and statements in the media to prove that they are truly men or women of the People.

With my uncanny genius for upsetting stuffed-shirts, it took me only a matter of days, back in 1972, to raise the gall of my working colleagues, both politicians and Westminster staff. On the Friday of my very first week in Parliament, I was interviewed on BBC television's *Nationwide* and asked my views on working conditions at Westminster. Quite good, I said. There were restaurants and bars, a hair-dressing salon, showers and sun-ray lamps, and on top of that you were paid four and a half thousand pounds a year for going into the place! Not a bad way at all to earn a copper or two, I opined, and most people in Rochdale would have agreed with me. The following week, having eventually been assigned an office which I was to share – more of this later – with two Conservative and two Labour members, I dropped in to meet my new 'room-mates'. The mood was less than cordial. Eventually, John Prescott, the Labour member from East Hull lashed out. 'I hope that TV broadcast was the last, rather than the first, expression of those sort of opinions.'

What did he mean?

'We don't like new boys ridiculing all we stand for,' he replied. 'It isn't the done thing, when you've been here less than two minutes, to go around in public criticising codes of behaviour which have grown up over centuries.'

I assured him, in no uncertain terms, that if I wanted to say something in public, I would say it, no matter how many layers of decorous gentility were stripped off. To be less wordy, I think I told him to 'get knotted'. From there on in, few MPs bothered, like sixth-formers at some expensive public school, to be my tutor in the art of Westminster niceties. To be fair, Prescott and I eventually became friends, but I have to stress the word 'eventually'.

These opening skirmishes, aimed on my part at showing the denizens of this strange new world that I was my own man, were by no means confined to my meetings with fellow members. I ran foul of a dozen and one *traditions*. I was critical of the toilet situation in the House, which reserves umpteen tiled palaces for MPs, but causes visitors from outside to tramp the corridors in a tormented daze looking for a *public* lavatory. As someone who once whitewashed such abodes for five shillings a time, I do not believe that ordinary people have habits unacceptable to the refined attitudes of their elected representatives. I was critical of the cafeteria rules, which permit an MP a maximum of three guests when buying a cup of tea and a bun! If a Rochdale couple visit me, and bring their two children, I am supposed to ask another MP to accompany me to the cafeteria if I wish to share a 'cuppa' with the entire family. What rubbish!

I was critical of the 'lobby correspondent' *tradition*, which allows only certain journalists to enter the Commons Lobby to talk about matters of public interest, but at the same time lays down that these privileged reporters can sit on only three of the chairs in the lobby. To me, that was a grave insult to the importance of their role in disseminating news to the general public, yet it came as a personal shock that these lobby correspondents were, themselves, contributing to the privilege system. When I invited John Sheard, my collaborator in this book, into the Lobby Bar for a gill of beer, we were asked to leave before we had finished the first drink. The complaint came, not from an MP, but from a journalist. Yet John has been working for Fleet Street based newspapers for more than fifteen years – four of them, I might add, on the troubled streets of Belfast and Londonderry rather than in the becalmed cloisters of Westminster.

Pinpricks like these are an everyday part of life for an MP who goes to Parliament to work rather than to relax in the insulated womb of the Best Members' Club in the World. Most of the time, because of the inexorable weight of traditions, a member cannot change them, although he may occasionally

'THE LONGEST RUNNING FARCE IN THE WEST END'

be given the opportunity to fight back. Mine came when one of the figureheads of tradition, the Sergeant at Arms, refused to allow me four tickets for the Visitors' Gallery on a particularly dull day in the House of Commons.

As soon as I became an MP, I vowed that the people of Rochdale – the people who put me there – would be given every opportunity to savour the experience of my office. When constituents visited London, I did everything humanly possible to show them round Westminster, to explain the workings of the place, to help them observe 'democracy in action'. It made me a regular seeker of tickets for the Visitors' Gallery, which are guarded only slightly less carefully than the Crown Jewels, and I soon learned the *modus operandi*.

Tickets are issued by the Sergeant at Arms, the ceremonial Keeper of the Peace, whose other main public task seems to be carrying the Mace into the Chamber at the beginning of each daily sitting and watching over it for the relentless hours that follow. Is it perhaps the boredom which the poor fellow must undergo that justifies his five-figure salary? The issuing of tickets begins immediately after the prayers which open each sitting, and I soon became one of the few regular attenders at these daily devotions. I stood next to the Sergeant at Arms so that, prayers over, I was first in the ticket queue. There came the day when I wanted four tickets for a Rochdale family visiting London, a day when I was the head of a queue of just two MPs. The Sergeant at Arms, Rear Admiral Sir Alexander Lennox, KCVO, CB, DSO, refused my request.

I was furious, but the Rear Admiral would not relent. Eventually, my visitors went to the House of Lords Gallery – to watch a funeral, rather than a wedding, as the saying goes – although the Commons Gallery was almost empty. I wrote a letter of protest to the Speaker, Mr Selwyn Lloyd. Selwyn must have passed the letter onto 'Sandy' Lennox, for I received a letter from the Rear Admiral which began: 'Dear Smith, It is my practice never to issue more than two tickets per Member before 4 pm ...'

The reason for this practice was not, as far as I can recall, explained, but the opening address of 'Dear Smith' did nothing to assuage my feelings. I think I made my point when I replied with a letter which began, 'Dear Sergeant ...'

It brought an official complaint, of course. David Steel, then Liberal Chief Whip, suggested that I should apologise for a breach of Westminster etiquette. I refused, and never did apologise, which meant that Sandy Lennox and I were not on speaking terms for many months although, I must admit, we did become very friendly before he retired.

In the meantime, I was trying to make my minor contribution to the effective government of this country ...

To this end, the antiquity of Parliamentary etiquette was a mere hindrance compared with obstacles created by the antiquity of the building itself. Facilities for members and staff at Westminster are a national disgrace, and more so when one considers that it is in this building that the laws governing safety and working conditions in factories and offices are made.

As I have already said, I shared my first office with four other MPs, two Tory, two Labour, and this in itself made the practice of party politics an extremely sensitive procedure. The room was small, private telephone calls were virtually impossible, and the dictating of letters to my secretary – particularly when the others were also trying to dictate – produced an atmosphere of bedlam. Eventually, I suppose, we abandoned the pretence of secrecy and adopted an unspoken code of Honour, so that anything overheard in our particular rabbit-hutch was not used as political capital outside those constraining walls.

It was not, however, the claustrophobic atmosphere of this office which caused the greatest difficulties, but its geographical location on the third floor of a building on the Victoria Embankment. Every time the division bell sounded on the closed-circuit TV system linked to the House, I had a frantic eight minutes to walk the half mile or so to register my vote. The system would have been almost intolerable if this had been a direct journey, but, as the quickest route threaded through the subway system of Westminster underground station, it became impossible. I would puff and pant my way through the evening crowds, often being forced to refuse autographs or ignore friendly offers of handshakes, as I scurried to the Division Lobbies. I will never know how many of those people I was forced to brush-off said to their friends: 'That Cyril Smith is as bad as the rest of them. He makes out he's just an ordinary fellow, but I saw him in the tube station the other night and he just pushed me out of the way.'

On occasion, this performance could be repeated as many as seven or eight times a night, with divisions coming every forty minutes, and I began to believe that an MP's greatest asset is not a good brain but a good pair of feet. What other country in the world imposes this sort of ridiculous strain on its legislators? The threat to my health was beginning to worry my Liberal colleagues, particularly David Steel who, as Chief Whip, spent every free minute prodding and prying into the myriad tiny rooms, corridors and closets which skulk forgotten in the darker corners of Westminster. Eventually, he made a discovery which, to my mind, rivalled the opening of Tutankhamen's tomb by Lord Carnarvon and Howard Carter: a tiny room at the top of a stone spiral staircase leading off the Commons Lobby. The discovery of the room, used for storing brushes, mops and buckets, had to be a closely kept secret, because there were other, much more influential groups of MPs, constantly on the lookout for office space within the precincts of the Palace. It was only by producing a medical certificate showing that the dash from Victoria Embankment was a potential danger to my health that the Liberal party were able to occupy our glorified brush cupboard, which was to become home to Clement Freud, Richard Wainwright, Alan Beith and myself. I was able to negotiate the spiral stairs with a leeway measured in fractions of inches. I was, as some wag pointed out, the only MP in Britain with a made-to-measure staircase.

But as I was saying, in the meantime, I was still trying to make my contribution to effective government of this country ...

If the pettinesses of Parliamentary tradition were galling, and the inadequacy of working space exhausting, my growing awareness of the hypocrisy of Parliamentary procedure was positively alarming. The first two complaints, though serious, could be endured with a little stoicism and a larger measure of humour. The gravity of the third charge – the cynical hypocrisy of the House of Commons itself – cannot be brushed aside, for it represents a cancer which is eating away the very heart of our democracy. I do not hesitate to declare that Parliamentary democracy in this country, if not dead already, is in the latter stages of a terminal sickness.

I wonder how many of the British public know what *actually* happens during the so-called 'great debates' they read about in their newspapers? I can only imagine that the number is very, very small, otherwise I would have to accept that the British public is very, very stupid, a premise which I totally dismiss. The answer, I fear, is that the British public is being deceived – 'conned', to use a word which, though unpleasant, is in this context absolutely accurate. The Great Parliamentary Debate is a *sham*, an empty public relations exercise to persuade the public that its interests are being protected. Its value is measured in the number of column inches won in the press, the number of seconds engendered in the radio or television news programmes. Its value as an influence on the process of government is nil. Debates are a showy waste of time, because their conclusion has been decided weeks, or months, or even years before – on the day of the previous General Election. Once a party has been given control of the government by the voting public, every item of important legislation from thereon in has been finalised. The two-party system, and the Party Whips, have decided that an MP's presence on the floor of the House of Commons is, at best, of nuisance value: at worst, a charade in the ever-continuing game of party politics.

I am quite sure that the average voter believes the man or woman being paid – at the time of writing – a hundred and twenty pounds a week plus up to sixty-five pounds a week expenses to represent his or her area in the Commons spends most of the time doing just that. This, I am afraid to report, is not true. The amount of time spent by many MPs actually in the Commons is incredibly short: one has only to watch the scores of cars pouring into Palace Yard just before the ten pm division bell – and pouring out again at ten fifteen – to realise this. Fifteen minutes a day actually spent in the House can, for the majority of a session, justify an MP's existence in the eyes of his most important judges: the Party Whips. So long as he walks through the proper lobby at the proper time, a member of the two majority parties can justify his pay-cheque. On the nights when Bills are being voted – and this only happens perhaps twenty times a year – an MP might be forced to put in all of *four hours* in the House, poor fellow (or lass!). He or she doesn't have to speak, only vote. There is one chestnut about a Tory

'THE LONGEST RUNNING FARCE IN THE WEST END'

MP who spent many years in Parliament and the only words he ever spoke were: 'Could we have the windows closed, please.' This story may be apocryphal: it may not have happened but it *could* have happened. No one would have objected!

These fifteen-minute attendances, with the occasional night of several divisions, suggest that there is at least a bare minimum of time that a member must spend in the House to keep his party bosses happy. Even this, however, is not the case, for one of the great luxuries of life for a Labour or Conservative member is the pairing system. The two majority parties 'pair', so that one Labour and one Conservative MP can take the night off without affecting the balance of power in the House. It is a privilege not extended to the minority parties: in days of low government majorities, every absent Liberal or Nationalist is a bonus for the administration of the day. Whichever party is in power, Labour or Conservative, jealously protects the cosiness of the pairing system. On some nights in the Commons, there can be more than one hundred and fifty 'pairs' – more than three hundred highly paid and privileged people who have given themselves the night off! Is the business of running Parliament a serious business, or is it not? Or is it merely a ritualised mockery?

While not actually recommending a clocking-in system for the House – and even that would not be a terribly bad idea – I do think that we MPs could do a great deal more to earn our pay, certainly to earn it more effectively. I know that Parliamentary work is not the be-all and end-all of the role, because there are always letters to write, constituency matters to be examined, committees to attend. But I sometimes wonder how much time some members devote to these other activities. It takes me between two and three hours each morning to read and answer my mail, yet I have heard of one MP who says that a dozen letters a week would be considered a heavy post. I receive many letters from people outside Rochdale which contain the line: 'I have asked my MP to help but he doesn't seem to get anything done ...' I am strictly forbidden, of course, to take action in these cases – interference with another member's constituency is one of the cardinal sins. But if anyone from Rochdale wrote to another MP asking for help I would be mortally offended.

Even the much despised local government system publishes a yearly report of attendances by Councillors, so the electors can obtain a fair assessment of the effort being put in. In local government, too, a Councillor can lose his seat for failure to attend meetings over a period of six months without an adequate excuse like a serious illness. Parliament only publishes a *voting* record of its members, but as I have shown, this can mean as little as fifteen minutes' 'work' – dare we call voting work? – per day. Is an MP really filling his role just by satisfying his party masters? Aren't we forgetting someone else ... Mr and Mrs British Public?

I wonder what Mr and Mrs Public will say when they realise that the so-called 'Great Debates' rarely take place with an audience of more than fifty MPs? That for hours upon end, the green leather benches of the Mother of Parliaments are occupied by a dozen members or even less? That Adjournment Debates, often well publicised and, in fact, a useful opportunity for airing grievances, are almost invariably attended by just *two* people, the lucky back-bencher who has won a ballot to speak for fifteen minutes, and the junior minister who has been appointed to answer him? I am not saying that the majority of MPs shirk their duties by constant non-attendance, or that the majority ignore their constituency problems, but there are still far too many who take advantage of the laxity of the rules. Let's face it, six thousand pounds a year, with up to sixty-five pounds a week in allowances, isn't bad pay for a part-time job!

The most outrageous factor of this whole issue is that it is *not* an issue: the majority of MPs take the cosiness of their working lives as a matter of course. In the middle of 1976, during a particularly bitter Parliamentary fight over the Labour government's plans to nationalise the shipbuilding and aircraft industries, a major row did break out over the pairing system. A Conservative member was away on holiday in Crete, and his Labour 'pair' was accused – unfairly, I think – of voting. Margaret Thatcher went into a sulk, and withdrew from the pairing system, which produced the ludicrous situation of Ministers on missions abroad being recalled so that their votes could prop up the government's slender majority. If ever there is a need for a 'pair', it is surely when a man is representing

British interests abroad or when another member is dangerously ill; ambulances bringing sick MPs into Palace Yard are, to me, one of the ultimate symbols of the degradation of the system. On this occasion, a Labour man was pilloried for voting, whether he did so properly or not. Yet isn't this what he is paid to do? Has he or has he not been elected to the House of Commons to attend its important business? And why was that Tory away on holiday at a time of high controversy? Isn't the three months a year holiday MPs have voted themselves enough? The row reached incredible heights of bitterness, with allegations of 'dishonourable behaviour' being bandied back and forth. Dishonourable to whom? To the two-party system of course.

The galling truth about that particular nationalisation vote was that a rare chance was missed to demonstrate that the House of Commons could still be an effective democratic force. There was a real opportunity to stop Jim Callaghan's Left wing imposing on Britain legislation which was undoubtedly contrary to the wishes of the vast majority of the British public. For once, the splintered Opposition was prepared to *oppose* and Mr Callaghan only scraped home by the skin of his teeth. What a triumph it would have been if the House of Commons had, for once, acted in the interests of the people, rather than in the interests of party politics.

Sadly, the elected members of Westminster handed over the Bill into the delaying hands of the unelected members of the House of Lords, which set out to do the questionable – not illegal – work of sinking the Bill in a sea of procedural red-tape. Once again, the elected representatives had proved that Britain is governed, not by Parliament, but by Cabinet, and a cabinet more likely to be influenced by the views of Left wing trade union leaders than by the views of its own supporters in the Commons. It confirmed to me once again – although by this time I needed little confirmation – that the carefully orchestrated 'battles' on the floor of the Commons have about as much effect in changing the lifestyle of the British people as a drunken argument in a Rochdale tap-room. For this sad state of affairs, those men and women on the floor of the Commons must take the blame. The majority of MPs have allowed themselves to become nothing more than numbers on a voting role, making a contribution to national policy similar to 'Clickety-click, sixty-six' in a game of bingo.

The House of Commons as a political force has been rendered impotent. Its speeches are made, not to sway policy, but to persuade a gullible public that its interests are still being guarded. It is no longer the muscle of the will of the people. It has become, it grieves me to say, little more than a flabby public relations man, peddling the shabby wares of its omnipotent masters in the Cabinet Room at 10 Downing Street, the CBI or the TUC.

These are very serious allegations, and will no doubt cause considerable rancour, but they must be apparent to anyone who examines the procedural workings of the Lower House.

Once again take the example of the 'Great Debate'. To me, an ardent debater since my early years at grammar school, the singular purpose of taking part in any debate is to persuade another person to change his or her view. Without that purpose in mind, a debate merely becomes a worthless opportunity for shouting-off. In Parliament, of course, the two-party system forbids the changing of minds: MPs vote as their party machine tells them to vote, irrespective of individual consciences, and recent events – particularly in the Labour party – have shown that the expression of conscientiously held individual views is the quickest route to the political graveyard.

In four years, I have never witnessed one case in the House of Commons when a passionate speech brought about a change of viewpoint. If this is so, what is the point of holding debates at all? The answer is pure public relations: speeches are made in the hope that they will be reported by the media which, in turn, hopefully persuades the general public that something is being done on its behalf. If the speech is not picked up by the national press or television, an MP simply tears the report out of *Hansard* the following day and passes it on to his local newspaper. The paper, grateful for a free news item, will normally note the event under a headline like: 'Local MP Demands ...' It's good stuff for the punters back in the constituency, but it has nil effect on government policy.

The ultimate cynicism of the Parliamentary PR speech is reached when an MP, satisfied that his attack or defence on any particular issue has warranted the optimum amount of publicity, walks sheepishly into the lobbies to vote on party lines in total opposition to the speech he has just made. His speech will be reported, but his self-contradictory vote will not. He can have his cake and eat it, too, satisfying the opposing demands of his constituents and his party paymasters. In other walks of life there is a simple word for it: deception!

There are other ways of drawing the attention of the media to an issue, in the sure knowledge that they will never invoke the need for Parliamentary action. A member can put down an Early Day Motion, a proposal which appears on the printed order paper outlining the day's Parliamentary business. The House has no intention of debating these motions, and the mover has no intention of their being debated, but there is the hope that they will catch the eye of the newspapers. If this happens, the MP will be asked a few brief questions by a lobby correspondent and, with luck, the member will be reported as having raised the matter in Parliament. Again, the punters will be happy because their elected representative has raised *something* in Parliament. They are not to know that this is as far as the matter goes. An Early Day Motion is raised purely to be forgotten.

The reason why these motions – and even Bills – can be launched and sunk without trace, lies in the rigidity of Parliamentary procedure, which is in itself a by-product of the two-party system. One of the most frustrating questions asked of a back-bench MP is: 'Why don't you get it discussed in Parliament?' The answer, which many MPs decline to offer, is that it is almost impossible for anyone except a member of the government or the Leader of the Opposition to get *anything* discussed. Before the Queen's Speech is even delivered, the Cabinet has decided the vast majority of the Parliamentary programme for the coming twelve months. The Leader of the Opposition is allowed, grudgingly, to nominate motions for debate on the days which remain. Issues are allocated the Parliamentary time they are considered worthy of – most of the time is far too short, but on occasion far too long – and the chances of a mere back-bencher forcing in a debate on a vital issue of the day are virtually nil. Without being flippant, I often wanted to raise in Parliament the matter of why I am not allowed to raise things in Parliament but, of course, I was never allowed the Parliamentary time.

The men who wield the terrifying instrument which emasculates the House of Commons are the Whips of the Labour and Conservative parties. The word Whip has, in itself, a sort of archaic significance which is lost on most people (and I talk as a former Chief Whip of the Liberal Party). It is meant to conjure the vision of a small band of dedicated men 'whipping' disgruntled and potentially rebellious members into the Division Lobbies to support legislation important to the government but opposed by the free-thinking MPs. In other words, their job is to 'whip-up' support among the doubtful. The word is now an anachronism because there are no longer any doubtful MPs – or rather, there are no longer any MPs in the major parties willing to register their doubts by an 'anti' vote. The word 'whip' should now be replaced by the word 'noose', and Party Whips – Labour and Tory, anyway – would be better described as Party Hangmen. Make no mistake, a member of either of these two parties would be stepping onto the political gallows if he or she opposed the party line in any way that seriously mattered.

That chilling phrase, a 'three-line Whip' which one reads too often in the newspapers these days, is announced by the three lines which underscore voting times issued on printed forms by the Whips' offices each week. A vote underlined three times is a direct, unquestionable order to members to vote on party lines. It is incontrovertible, for, in the case of a three-line Government Whip, the very survival of the government is believed to be at stake. A two-line Whip means the vote is underlined twice, denoting a vote which would not force a government resignation, if lost – because the 'confidence' of the government is not judged to be at stake; in these cases, 'pairing' is allowed. If there is a single-line Whip, well, it's hardly worth attending to vote at all, unless there is a particular constituency interest at stake in the matter under discussion.

In effect, all the major legislation introduced in Parliament is backed, not by carefully indexed lists of facts or carefully worded argument or by carefully outlined pros and cons, but by three black lines. Once the Whips have decided in consultation with the party leadership to draw those lines, all possibility of further consideration, of the exercise of a free choice, is lost. If it is a government three-liner, those lines in fact create the

'THE LONGEST RUNNING FARCE IN THE WEST END'

legislation, for in these days of the lobby-fodder MP all that follows is pure theatre: interesting, entertaining perhaps, but still make-believe; the debate and the vote have been decreed on high. The tablets have come down from the mountain.

Winston Churchill was once bitterly criticised by a colleague after he walked into the 'wrong' lobby and voted against his party. He replied tartly: 'I was sent to this place to vote with my head, not with my feet!' There are no men of Sir Winston Churchill's stature in Parliament today – neither for that matter are there any Aneurin Bevans or Lloyd Georges – and the economy being what it is, one can only hope that British shoe manufacturers gain some benefit from our Parliamentary votes. How I long for the day when the Speaker of the House of Commons cries 'The Shoes Have It.'

I will now assuredly be accused of painting too black a picture of Parliamentary impotence. I will certainly be criticised privately for rocking the Westminster boat, but it is of some comfort to know that I am not crying alone in the wilderness. In the very week that I am writing this chapter, similar views have been expressed from such diverse and unlikely sources as Lord Hailsham and Lord George-Brown.

Lord Hailsham called his Richard Dimbleby Lecture on BBC television the 'Elective Dictatorship', and rasped: 'Until recently, debate and argument dominated the Parliamentary scene. Now it is the Whips and the party caucus. More and more debate, where it is not actually curtailed, is becoming a ritual dance, interspersed with cat calls.'

In the very same week, Lord George-Brown led a revolt in the House of Lords against Jim Callaghan's Docks Bill which would have given dockers the monopoly of cargo-handling within five miles of every port and waterway thus bringing the ultimate dream of a Trotskyist utopia a long stride closer. George-Brown, himself a lifelong trade unionist, argued that Parliament was no longer acting in the interest of the British people. He declared: 'I am not a trade union hack, I believe many things are better done publicly owned than privately owned, but I want to be shown that they are done in the interests of the public, all of us, the rest of us, and not just done in the interests of the Transport and General Workers' Union.'

Lord George-Brown, a former Foreign Secretary and Deputy

Prime Minister, was no longer a member of the Labour party, having resigned in disgust. Where are the others, now, who once stood up against the party caucus? Dick Taverne voted against his local Labour bosses in Lincoln because he refused to alter his lifelong pro-European convictions. He was ejected from the party and, although he won his seat for one brief session as an Independent, he is now *out*. Eddie Milne, MP for Blyth, upset the Labour monolith by demanding an inquiry into widespread corruption in North-Eastern politics. He is *out*. Reg Prentice, a Labour Cabinet Minister who has always voted on party lines, nevertheless upset his constituency party in Newham, London, because of his calls for moderation. He is *out* as the official Labour party candidate – and can he ever get back into Parliament as an Independent? The odds against are very high, although that is a bet I would dearly love to lose.

Any British voter who still believes that his MP is free to act out of conscience (unless he is a member of a minority party) is either grossly deluded or certifiably insane. Conservative or Labour MPs go to Westminster to represent the interests of the party, not the people. There are something like four hundred 'safe seats' in our electoral system, where little short of revolution could shake the sitting member. The voters of these constituencies probably feel *they* choose their MPs with their votes, but that is a well-disguised nonsense. The selection committee of the controlling party in fact make the choice, for any candidate they put forward will assuredly win. Who influences the local selection committee? The national party organisation! And who advises the national organisers? The party Whips, of course, because it is their duty to ensure that any prospective member will dutifully toe the line. The noose is pulled tight, and individual conscience is throttled and dies. The day of the party hack, controlled by the party hangman, is upon us!

If, then, an MP, as a back-bencher rather than a member of a government, is a political eunuch, what useful purpose does he serve at all? The simple answer is, very little! There are, however, a few occasions when his 'nuisance value' can win minor triumphs – so long as no party lines are transgressed. Yet even these rare occasions are dealt out by the luck of the draw! I am sure that the people of Britain would be – and should be – quite aghast if they knew that the lucky dip is an integral part of our Parliamentary system, and that an ordinary raffle ticket is one of the most prized Parliamentary 'documents'. It may sound amazing, but it is true. There are four methods by which a solitary MP can exert reasonably effective pressure on the government, and three of them are decided by the luck of the draw. They are: Questions to the Prime Minister, the Ten Minute Bill, the Private Member's Bill, and the Adjournment Debate, which I have already discussed.

When I say that a Question to the Prime Minister applies 'reasonably effective' pressure on the government, I do not mean that it can hope to sway a government decision — that would be asking too much. But because it causes the Prime Minister to 'do his homework', by asking his top civil servants to research a problem raised in a question, it causes a shockwave which passes down the civil service hierarchy with ever-growing reverberations, clearing blockages in the system which would normally take months to budge.

One of the first favourable impressions of Westminster was that I, an ordinary enough sort of fellow from a very ordinary town, could stand on my feet and quiz the Prime Minister of the land under the eyes, not only of Parliament, but also of the nation's press. There was a correctness about this, a democratic justness which I found highly satisfying. Then I began to discover the obstacles put in my way to make the process all but impossible.

Prime Minister's Questions are held on Tuesday and Thursday afternoons, and last for all of fifteen minutes, a time-limit which in itself offers little scope for anything more than the briefest encounter. To get a question down at all calls for a combination of skill and luck. First, you have to phrase a question in such a way as to bamboozle the Table Office, the civil service department which judges such matters and which seems determined to protect the PM from all-comers.

Should I wish to arouse a PM's interest in the state of the Lancashire textile industry for instance, it would be pointless to lodge a question containing the word 'textiles'. That word would merely ensure that the matter was referred to the Department of Trade and Industry. In fact, I would use the standard 'dodge' and simply ask: 'Does the Prime Minister intend to visit the county of Lancashire in the coming year?' This being something only the PM can answer, the question would be put. If he replied. 'Yes,' I could then ask: 'In that case, would he consider visiting the borough of Rochdale to see local textile manufacturers and discuss the growing distress of their industry.'

The farcical side of this circuitous exercise is that, having finally manœuvred the question onto the Order Sheet, I would have telephoned Number Ten a few hours earlier to warn the PM's staff of my intentions in order to set the civil service ball rolling.

That is the skilful side of Prime Minister's Questions, the use of cunning to outflank the Table Office. The lucky side is much more straightforward. The questions to be put are drawn out of a box by the Government Printer as he lays out the Order Paper. The first five out of the hat stand some chance of getting answered – again, if the questioner is lucky. In my early days, when Ted Heath was Prime Minister and Harold Wilson his regular and vituperative critic, Question Time regularly passed in a schoolboyish battle of political wits. The Leader of the Opposition can always ask the first question – and several supplementary questions if so desired. I was just one of many backbenchers who sat seething as our precious fifteen minutes slipped away during the Ted and Harold Punch and Judy show.

The Ten Minute Rule Bill is used to allow a member to introduce any piece of legislation he thinks fit. Who says what is decided by who gets in the queue first in the morning. The lucky member is then given the right to speak for ten minutes. Another MP can, if he wishes, take ten minutes to oppose the resolution. I have to relate, however, that this is yet another way of tricking the public into believing that words are being turned into deeds. Although ten minutes to address the House on an issue of burning concern is an opportunity not to be wasted – one can often air in public matters which only too often are discussed behind locked doors – the chances of getting a Ten Minute Bill passed as legislation are virtually nil. The ten minute speech is in effect a First Reading. To get a Second Reading, the House – in fact the Cabinet – would have to vote it further Parliamentary time. In my four years, perhaps five Ten Minute Bills have reached fruition – and only because the government of the day thought them good enough to be 'pinched' and made part of official policy.

'THE LONGEST RUNNING FARCE IN THE WEST END'

The absolute pearl of the back-bencher's all too meagre lawmaker's treasury is the Private Member's Bill. Over the years private Bills have introduced some of our greatest reforms. Hanging was abolished on a private Bill promoted by the late and greatly missed Sidney Silverman. David Steel brought about a reform of the abortion laws. Private members have tried to rid the country of the obscenity of hare-coursing and change our ridiculous licensing-laws, although the last two failed for reasons I'll discuss later. Yet these reforms and attempted reforms arose, not from the creative vision of gifted Parliamentarians, but by sheer luck – the luck of the draw. The great Private Member's Bill tombola, held at the beginning of each session, is the most enthusiastically followed raffle I have ever experienced, and I have organised a few in my time. It is – yes, it really is – decided by a plain, straightforward raffle ticket, torn from the sort of book waved under a million noses in dance halls and social clubs and pubs every night of the year. Anxious members repair to the Chamber of the House of Commons, where the Right Honourable Speaker – bewigged, begowned and, in my opinion in this case, belittled – draws the numbers from the box. It is perhaps the most tense moment of the Parliamentary session. It is perhaps also the most idiotic. On the floor, the lucky MPs – twenty at the most – are overjoyed. Up in the public galleries, the visitors from all corners of the world – wise old faces, eager young faces, smart suits, flowing gowns, gay silk saris and blue jeans – watch the ceremony with stunned wonderment. Is this how the Mother of Parliament governs the world's oldest democracy? By raffle?

Surely the MPs of all parties have enough wit and wisdom between them to meet, at the beginning of each session, and simply decide on some of the more important reforms the country cries out for? Surely all issues need not be decided on party political lines? What difference does being a Tory or a Socialist, a Liberal or a Nationalist, make, when the majority of people want to ban hare-coursing, give pensioners a free television licence, or simply update our antiquated licensing laws?

The ultimate tragedy of the Private Member's Bill is that it is inevitably the first to fall to the Commons' greatest enemy – Time – which, the general public is continuously led to believe, is precious beyond the dreams of man. That is, in fact, yet another carefully nurtured myth, for Parliament squanders time like a drunken sailor squandering his pay. The 'appointed hour' voting system means that many debates have to be stretched out endlessly until it is time to ring the division bell. As I said in the first pages of this book, one of my first shocks on entering Parliament was to see the party Whips going round the bars and restaurants of Westminster, wheedling MPs to enter the chamber and speak in debates which were progressing *too quickly*. The talking has to be kept going, however inanely, until the set time otherwise the system would collapse: to ring a division bell thirty minutes early could catch several dozen MPs unawares. They might still be out in the West End restaurants, or the theatres, or the bars – at the dog track, for all I know. An early vote could upset the mathematical calculations and the government might lose the division – absolutely unthinkable!

While all this Parliamentary time is being squandered, the vulnerable Private Member's Bill is invariably debated on a Friday, the shortest day of the working week, when the House rises at four pm. To stop a Private Bill doesn't even need the might of a combined party opposition. One crank with minority views – a blood-sport supporter, perhaps, or a non-drinker who believes that licensing laws should be drastically reduced, rather than extended – can, virtually unaided, 'talk out' a reforming piece of legislation. It does not need a spectacular 'Fillibuster' to take a debate to four pm, but once that time is reached, a Private Bill dies. It is technically 'referred' for further consideration – but in fact, is rarely heard of again.

The unfortunate member who launched the Bill, and who has spent months of hard and difficult work in the hope of steering it through, is expected wearily to accept the situation. Perhaps at the next sessions (if he hasn't lost his seat in the meantime) he might get another chance (if he wins the raffle again) to get his legislation through (if it isn't talked out again). Backing a Private Bill tends to bring out the very best in an MP, a too rare opportunity to act out of conscience in the simple human interests of the British people. One has to see the desolation on the face of a man whose Bill has been talked out to understand, in many cases, that a lifetime's dream has been shattered, the crowning ambition of a life's work trampled cynically underfoot.

For ten months I watched the stifling of deeply held convictions by the party machines, the deadening blanket of procedure at work. I could hold my peace no longer. In July 1973, I told foreign pressmen: 'This place is the longest running farce in the West End.'

The remark was, of course, very widely reported in Britain, and drew the reaction from my fellow MPs that I had come to expect. I was still wet behind my Parliamentary ears, said one. Why didn't I connect my brain before opening my mouth, sneered another. If the system had been good enough for Pitt, Disraeli and Gladstone, for Lloyd George and Churchill, why wasn't it good enough for loudmouthed Cyril Smith?

The answer to that is that Pitt, Disraeli and Gladstone, Lloyd George and Churchill, fired the House of Commons with life. The present incumbents, it seems to me, are capable only of the kiss of death.

CHAPTER NINE

Gains and Losses

The 'experts' dismissed my by-election win in October 1972 as a 'personal victory' brought about by my own popularity in Rochdale, rather than by any widespread desire to support the Liberal cause. While I agree that there is much truth in this theory if the by-election were studied purely from a local viewpoint, I believe strongly that to dismiss the win's national significance would be a major error on behalf of the party. My point is that, although I might have had a particularly strong local following, this was a fact only appreciated fully in Rochdale and a few of the surrounding Lancashire towns. As far as the remainder of the nation was concerned, the Liberal *party* had won a famous victory, and that was a major boost to our credibility. We were back to my theory that vast numbers of people in Britain would be prepared to vote Liberal if they were satisfied that their vote would not be wasted, that a Liberal vote would not let the Tories in (the concern of an anti-Tory voter) or give Labour the seat (the concern of an anti-Socialist). It was the Liberal party's classic dilemma: before we won, we had first to prove that we were capable of winning!

Fortunately, the Rochdale victory came at a time when the Old Guard of the party were under attack from other directions. A new type of Liberal radical was emerging, typified perhaps by Trevor 'Jones the Vote' whose formidable 'community politics' machine in Liverpool was on the verge of grasping control of the city Corporation although, a mere four years previously, the party had held only one of the city's one hundred and fourteen seats. Trevor, a tough, no-nonsense campaigner only too happy to get involved in the nitty-gritty of politics, was very much a man after my own heart. At the party's autumn conference in Margate that year, Jones won the party presidency, despite considerable opposition from the leadership, which was still very much in the hands of the Old Guard. Were we really seeing the birth of the Liberal revival, so long anticipated, so often crushed in a welter of disappointment and bitterness?

It was a time when the electorate were obviously tiring of Ted Heath's administration, but were not swinging their support behind the Socialists, whose extreme Left wing were becoming more and more vocal after years of hiding their real intentions, like creepy-crawly things, under rocks. There had probably never been a better time, certainly since the last war and possibly since the 1920s, for the Liberals to stage their long-awaited breakthrough. The opportunity to do so had already presented itself, the Sutton and Cheam by-election due on 7 December. The problem was: how to persuade the Old Guard of the party, still convinced that Rochdale had been a flash-in-the-pan result, that we could win Sutton – if only we tried, and tried extremely hard.

I think it is now clear that I thoroughly enjoy electioneering. I enjoy the excitement, the tension. I revel in the enthusiasm engendered. I even thrive on the hard, time-consuming graft of canvassing, writing pamphlets, posting thousands of letters. But there is only one word that can catch the spirit of a self-confident election bandwagon gathering momentum, and that is 'euphoric'. It is a spirit that can sweep through an election team, to be caught in the eagerness of the chatter in party headquarters, in the smile on the face of a canvasser on the doorstep. It is a mood that can infect the voters themselves. I set about, as the newest MP in the land, to push my colleagues to accept that, whilst Rochdale was the beginning of the great campaign, Sutton and Cheam was where the euphoria would be born.

We were, of course, desperately short of money, and Lord 'Tim' Beaumont, former party president, came to our aid by privately financing an opinion poll in the constituency. The result was quite startling: no less than forty-eight per cent of the electorate said they would vote Liberal if they thought our candidate, young Graham Tope, had a real chance of victory. Graham, not yet thirty, a local lad with a fine record in the constituency, needed all the help we could muster to prove that not only *could* he win, but also that we *would* win. For the first time in my experience, the Liberal party went into all-out attack. Jeremy Thorpe threw in every ounce of his heavyweight campaigning skills, and our six other MPs provided extra muscle. My own contribution to the campaign was an idea I had read about from America: the telephone talk-in. I persuaded our MPs and several Liberal Lords to sit down and telephone the chairmen and secretaries of every constituency Liberal party within one hundred miles of Sutton, some four hundred phone calls in all. The message was simple: we desperately need voluntary workers. It was, I admit, a campaign of flattery: it pleases people to receive personal calls from MPs or peers. And it worked – the troops came pouring into town in unbelievable numbers. The euphoria was beginning to take hold.

The night of 7 December 1972, will remain with me for the rest of my days. I had been invited, with my mother, to a Liberal party ball at, of all places, the Savoy Hotel in the Strand. Jeremy Thorpe and Jo Grimond were there, so were scores of Liberal peers and celebrities like Norman Hartnell, Derek Nimmo and Nicholas Parsons. Mother and I seemed to be among the star attractions, two unknowns from Lancashire being fêted by the cream of London society. If I were overawed, my mother certainly was not. 'Who are you, then?' she demanded of Derek Nimmo, producing one of the bigger laughs of the evening. She topped this by asking Norman Hartnell 'Can you run me something up in the five-guinea range?' This caused such a reaction that some of the guests held an immediate whip-round and Norman agreed to make a dress for my mother. She still has it now, the prize of her wardrobe. We never did find out how much it cost ... but I think it would be a fair bet to say that it was considerably more than five guineas.

Behind all the hilarity, however, we were tense, for this was the night of the declaration of the Sutton and Cheam vote.

I went off, by taxi, to the BBC studios halfway through the evening, for I had been asked to be the Liberal commentator in a programme covering the announcement of the by-election result. If there was any doubt left about a growing Liberal euphoria, it must have been dispelled that night by the beam on my face when the figures came in. Graham Tope had overturned a massive Conservative majority to win by seven thousand four hundred and seventeen votes. The immensity of the breakthrough can be judged by the fact that in the General Election two years previously, the Liberals had only managed to take third place in the poll, more than five thousand behind Labour and an unthinkable seventeen thousand nine hundred and thirty-four behind the Tory victor. It was a victory which overshadowed even Eric Lubbock's almost legendary win at Orpington. When I got back to the Savoy, the revellers were standing in a crowd in the centre of the ballroom, singing *Land of Hope and Glory* to an accompaniment of popping champagne corks. Was this really it? After all the years of trampled hopes, were the Liberals finally on their way?

The months which followed seemed to suggest that this was true. The Liberal challenge was at last being taken seriously, not only by the media, but by politicians in other parties and the people on the street. Acres of newspaper space, hours of broadcasting time, were devoted to the discussion of the rebirth of middle-of-the-road politics in Britain. Serious commentators raised the question of possible splits in the Labour and Tory ranks, with the moderate wings of those two parties joining in a 'centrist' third force. And the by-election results continued to swing our way ...

On 27 July 1973, I was driving my car along the motorway between Oldham and Rochdale, listening to the radio. Then came the results of the previous day's two by-elections: Clement Freud had won the Isle of Ely from the Tories, and – a result which verged on the miraculous – David Austick had overturned one of the largest Conservative majorities in the country to win Ripon by nine hundred and forty-six votes.

I had helped in both campaigns (in fact, as I write this, I have spoken at every by-election in Britain since 1972!) and liked both men, although they are of vastly different character. Clement, shrewd, very quick to learn, always ready to seize any half-chance that presents itself, had taken me back to a restaurant in Ely and ordered me a gourmet meal complete with champagne. David, quiet, serious, deeply committed to helping the needy, took my mother and I to a fish and chip shop in Otley. Without wishing to offend Clement, who is a superb cook, I think I preferred those fish and chips.

Food, however, was not on my mind after I heard those results on my car radio. I burst into song, began banging a triumphant tatoo on the roof with my free hand and climaxed my lonely celebration with a prolonged root-a-toot on the car horn. I was overtaking a foreign lorry at the time – French, I believe – which drew up on my offside as we approached a traffic island on the outskirts of Rochdale. The driver, on the left-hand side of the cab, of course, wound down his window and, shaking his head, waved a forefinger in the classic circular motion by his temple – the international gesture for madness. I responded with a V sign combined with a broad grin. The last I saw of him in the mirror as I drove away, he was shaking his head even more vigorously.

The final by-election triumph, at Berwick-on-Tweed, symbolised my personal attitude to electioneering – and also signalled the end of the road for the Liberal euphoria wagon. The seat became vacant, it will be remembered, because Lord Lambton, the Tory, resigned after being involved in a tawdry affair with London prostitutes. The morality issue was, however, never raised by the Liberals in the campaign, as far as I am aware, and when I spoke there I was determined to ignore it: I do not believe in the politics of the smear. A man's private life is his own affair. Yet only a few months earlier, I had been brought under a vicious attack from the Labour party for alleged 'smear' tactics.

It had happened during one of the most significant campaigns of the 1973 by-elections, at Chester-le-Street, County Durham, an area which had been under Labour party control for so long as to be virtually a one-party mini-state. I made the opening speech of that campaign and in it I deliberately, if obliquely, raised the matter of corruption. The T. Dan Smith affair was at its height, and every day was bringing new allegations of corruption among the Labour councillors in the North-East. One of the leading figures in the case – who actually went to prison – lived in Chester-le-Street. As far as I was concerned, this was legitimate political meat – and the Liberal party sank its teeth into it with relish.

This line of attack brought frenzied protests from the Labour ranks. 'Foul', they cried. 'Dirty tricks', and 'smear'. I did not apologise then, and I do not apologise now. So Lord Lambton dallied with a couple of floozies. So what? What effect did that have on the government of Britain? But the matter of deep and widespread corruption in the Labour party's North-East political machine was a far different matter. If a voter can expect nothing else, surely he can expect his elected representatives to be honest? I am sure this viewpoint is shared by every intelligent voter in Britain – if not by some members of the Labour party, who went on to hound Eddie Milne out of his Northumberland seat because he spoke up against corruption.

We won the Berwick seat, and its victor, Alan Beith, is arguably the best Parliamentarian at Westminster. We lost Chester-le-Street, but only after hammering the Labour majority down from twenty thousand three hundred and thirty-one to seven thousand and sixty-six. Although this was a tremendous achievement in a dye-in-the-wool Labour area, it did expose one trend that was worrying me: we were having our major triumphs in Tory seats and – apart from my own win in Rochdale, were having little *real* effect in Labour strongholds.

It was a lesson not lost on the formidable Conservative party machine which, as well as being the richest in the country, is also perhaps the most ruthless. By the time the Berwick by-election arrived, the Tories were taking our gains seriously. They flooded the small border town with supporters, and trained their biggest guns fairly and squarely on the Liberals. Although by tradition a serving Prime Minister never takes part in by-election campaigns, Ted Heath managed to find an excuse for attending. He toured, of all things, a local kipper factory, a visit, it was claimed, that had been arranged long before the by-election. To me, this visit certainly *did* smell fishy!

Our victory was a near thing. As polling day approached, the massive effort of the Tories was beginning to eat away at our earlier gains. It was a time for concern because I was convinced, had the by-election been just two weeks later, we would not have won. The time had come for the Liberal party to show that it could do other things than just win by-elections. It was time to translate our newfound support in the country into effective political action. It was time, fate decided, for me to have my first brush with Jeremy Thorpe.

Even with our little Parliamentary group almost doubled in

number to eleven, the Liberals were still forced to live very much in each other's pockets. This had its advantages, like the ease with which the whole group could discuss opinions and contribute to decisions almost as a family. Each one of us was, by the simple fact of small number, very close to the central policy-making processes. There were disadvantages, too, for like all families, there were disagreements during which it was impossible to hide in the crowd: one had to take sides, to stand up and be counted. As the dreadful political winter of 1973-4 came upon us, the glories of the preceding summer were all too easy to forget.

I don't suppose anyone old enough to read will ever forget that winter. The Heath government had put the economy into top gear, printing money like confetti, only to be struck down by the Arab oil sheiks who had finally decided to challenge the smug superiority of the industrialised world. At home, the miners had decided to tackle the Heath administration, and the nation was as divided as it had ever been since 1926. It was a time that cried out for adventurous political action, a time when a small group of Liberal MPs believed we could use our position between the country's two social wings to useful and effective ends. My annoyance was not lessened when Jeremy flew off on a previously arranged foreign trip.

For some months, I had been simmering with impatience, waiting for Jeremy to take advantage of our new political weight, backed, not by actual seats in Parliament, but by our growing support throughout the country. His decision to go abroad while the country was facing the miseries of the three-day week was the last straw.

I was, by this time, party spokesman on employment affairs and I wrote an angry letter to him, demanding that he should 'come down off the fence'. To strengthen my case, I released the text of the letter to the press. The letter demanded. 'When the hell are we going to do something?' and Fleet Street had a field day. I told reporters who interviewed me after they had read the letter: 'This letter is meant to be critical of Mr Thorpe. I am tired of letters between Heath and Wedgwood Benn. The people are sick of party politics.

'I want Mr Thorpe to take the initiative and meet Mr Heath and Mr Wilson. This is a national issue and it's not funny any

Me in the House of Commons, sat on the benches. It was the morning of the State Opening.

I met Lord Thompson of Fleet, with Jeremy Thorpe, PC, MP.

Princess Anne and me enjoying a joke. Is it any wonder I'm a great fan of hers? She visited Rochdale Youth Music Festival.

I chat with HRH the Duke of Edinburgh, during his 1976 visit to Rochdale.

I was introduced to HRH the Queen Mother in 1973, when she received purses for the Family Service Unit.

I am invested in 1975, by Lord Caccia, the Lord Prior, as a Serving Brother of the Order of St John. I have been President of Rochdale St John Cadets for nearly twenty years.

Mr Waldron West, with the portrait of me which he painted and presented to Rochdale Art Gallery, where it now hangs.

Centre: My mother and I arrive at Covent Garden for the wedding reception of Jeremy and Marion Thorpe.

Bottom left: My mother and I arrive at 10 Downing Street for the reception given by the Prime Minister (Sir Harold Wilson) for Pierre Trudeau, the Prime Minister of Canada. I liked the place!

Bottom right: The night I won – 26 October 1972. Here I am, victorious, with my mother, my sister Eunice and my brother Norman in Rochdale town hall.

In 1974 I attended 'Burns' Night' in Rochdale town hall, with Ronnie Corbe This shows my good friend and dresser, Mrs Wilson, 'fitting the kilt'.

In my 'T'-shirt outside the House of Commons. I wanted all the Liberal MPs to wear one for the State Opening of Parliament.

My favourite election photograph taken in 1974 by Brian Duff, the chief photographer of the *Daily Express*. It's so self-explanatory!

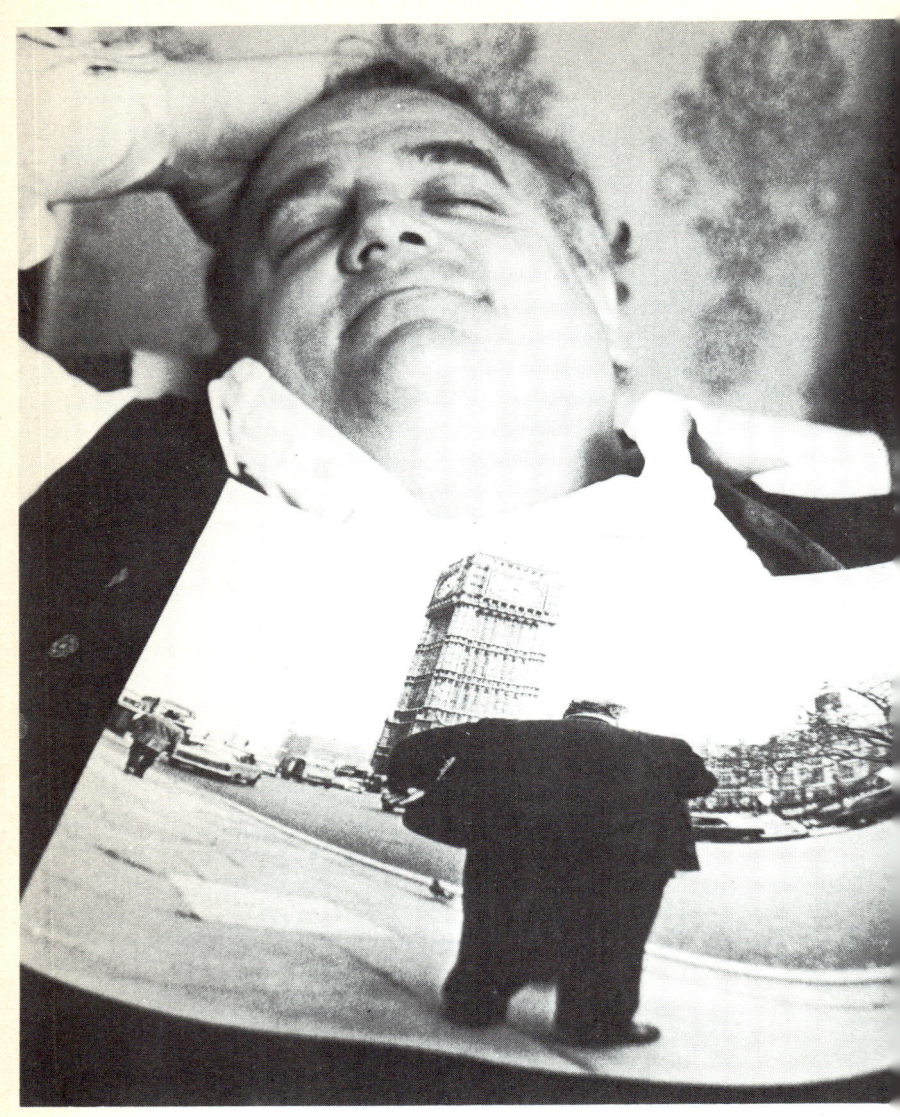

Democracy rests on me, and my mind is at ease.

more. We need an all-party approach to the miners and the TUC to find a way out of this impasse.'

I added – and I meant it: 'Jeremy Thorpe is still the best political leader in this country, but he has sat on the fence on this issue.'

Even to write such a critical letter was considered, by some members of the party, to be discourteous. To issue it to the press, and to meet reporters to discuss it, was branded as intolerable. There is still a feeling that I provoked the entire issue myself, and that I was launching a one-man attack on Jeremy, but that is not true. The rank-and-file Liberals in Manchester had already passed a strong demand for some sort of Liberal initiative on the industrial crisis. I was supported by other MPs, one of whom, David Austick, also commented to the press: 'I agree with Cyril Smith. There is a feeling within the party that we should have said more on this issue.'

Jeremy was still reeling under the blow from the London and County fringe bank débâcle. The firm, of which he had been a director, collapsed leaving debts in the millions and was under investigation by the Department of Trade. As a result, Jeremy had resigned all his company directorships and planned to concentrate on Liberal party matters. My letter and my remarks to the press were taken as a personal attack, and even worse, kicking the man while he was down. I did not, and do not, see it that way: the affair was behind us, a thing of the past. Jeremy had promised to devote all his time to leading the party and, in my view, it was time he got on with the job. After all, wasn't the nation facing the biggest industrial crisis since the General Strike?

I didn't expect that my actions would make me over-popular with Jeremy, but I was a little unprepared for his reaction. The next day, he went on BBC radio to say: 'I think Cyril has made rather an ass of himself. But this, of course, is the disadvantage of sending people letters, releasing them to the press, and not waiting for an answer.' The papers picked on this, of course, and the headlines read, 'Cyril is an ass, says Thorpe.'

I was incensed by the remark but not, as many people thought at the time, because I had been called an ass. I had been called many things in my time, a clown, a big mouth, a buffoon, and one more insult added to the long list did not unduly concern me. What, however, did infuriate me was the possibility that Jeremy intended the matter to rest there, that by a fairly innocuous jibe he could fend off the real purpose of my letter – to force him to take an active stand in the industrial crisis. From that day on, my relationship with Jeremy, a man for whom I had held the greatest admiration, went into decline. We would continue to work together as professional politicians, but our former friendship was never restored. Sadly, my intervention came too late to make any impact on the political drama – to call it a tragedy would not be an undue exaggeration – which was about to unfold.

It was at this time that the eleven Liberal MPs sat down round a table for our weekly meeting to discuss our policy for the immediate future. Jeremy, as chairman, went round each member one by one, asking what view we should take re the miners' pay claim which was being opposed too stubbornly by Ted Heath. When it came to my turn, I said: 'Whatever our view towards the miners should be, I think we should decide our attitude towards the next General Election.'

There was silence, a few nervous laughs. No one believed that there was any danger of Heath going to the country. He had a safe majority – he would be foolish to risk it. But while I do not pretend to be a political prophet, I could sense a confrontation building up. It was, I knew, a confrontation which Heath would lose because at that time, and this is not necessarily true today, there were two sections of the working class which held the great emotional sympathy of the general public, the miners and the seamen. Why this was so was not sure, for there are in fact many jobs which are just as arduous and some a good deal more dangerous. Yet the miners and the seamen – particularly the trawlermen – held a strong and central part of the nation's conscience.

If Heath were to attack the miners head on, I said to that meeting, the Tories stood to lose even more votes in a General Election – and they were votes the Liberals should be ready to catch.

I do not think that Jeremy, or any other of my colleagues, had anticipated this possibility. Now I had raised it, however, the thought clearly enthused him. His eyes shone at the prospect of another great campaign, a campaign in which, for the first time in a lifetime, the Liberals had a chance of winning real power. In the meantime, what to do? After all, we were only guessing – and it was perhaps only a pipe dream? I suggested, as I had done in my letter, that the Liberals might intervene in the miners' dispute. Jeremy was doubtful. 'I don't think they would agree to see me,' he said, revealing for the first time the reason for his hesitancy. He was afraid, like all of us, of rejection.

'If I fix up a meeting will you come?' I asked.

'All right, we'll give it a try,' he said, still a little uncertain.

I can understand his reticence, for it was new territory to him. A magnificent operator as an electioneer, a smooth, entertaining and accomplished speaker at a public function, a man happy rubbing shoulders with world leaders, Jeremy was nervous to dive into the cold turbulent current of industrial affairs. What he didn't realise was that I had known Joe Gormley, the miners' leader, for years, and considered him, not only a friend, but as a man open to new ideas from any quarter. I telephoned Joe and arranged a meeting for the following day.

Jeremy, John Pardoe and myself were our party. We were met by Joe, Len Daly and Mike McGahey, the miners' formidable negotiation team. News of the meeting had attracted widespread interest, and the press and TV cameras were outside NUM headquarters. I could see Jeremy's tensions evaporate as he realised just what a reasonable man Joe Gormley was. The nervousness was replaced by his normal outgoing confidence as Joe pointed out that the union had no wish for a head-on collision with the Conservative government. If only Ted Heath could be persuaded to make some compromise in his stance on the miners' pay claim, he said, the union was sure that an amicable solution could be reached.

Suddenly, Jeremy realised that here was a real opportunity for a major political coup – something I had been telling him for weeks. In a fever of excitement, he telephoned Campbell Adamson, the Director General of the Confederation of British Industry, demanding an immediate appointment. It was difficult, said Campbell, he was involved in an important conference. This was a matter of the gravest national importance, replied Jeremy, and off we went in a taxi to the CBI.

Campbell, the man who was later to be accused of losing

Heath the election by a speech in which he pointed out that the government had got its sums wrong over the cost of the miners' pay demand, met us with apparent reluctance. On hearing of our talks with Joe Gormley, however, he became fired by Jeremy's enthusiasm. He revealed that the CBI too had been pressing the Prime Minister to come to some compromise with the miners.

'We have been asking him for three days to change his stance, but he won't budge,' this elegant, articulate man confided. 'If you can do anything to soften him up, we might still be able to avert a disaster.'

This news came as a complete surprise to our party, and we asked why the CBI had not made its attitude known.

'There are rumours of a General Election coming up,' Campbell Adamson replied. 'We can't say anything which would undermine the Conservatives' chances.'

When the implications of this sank in, we three Liberals realised that we had in our grasp the greatest opportunity offered to the party since the last war. With the NUM and the CBI in virtual agreement, and Jeremy Thorpe acting as a political mediator, we might even be able to settle the dispute! As we pondered the enormous implications, a secretary came into the room and announced, 'Mr Adamson, there is to be a important news flash on the television in a couple of minutes. Perhaps you would like to watch it ... ?'

With Adamson and senior members of his staff, we filed into another room where a television set was already switched on. The announcement came within seconds ... Ted Heath had called a General Election!

The feeling of desperation was overwhelming. We had been so near and yet so far. We stood in dumbfounded silence. It was Jeremy, exhibiting his tremendous resilience, who eventually spoke: 'Well, chaps, we've lost a battle, but now we've got a war to fight. Let's get on with it ...'

We returned to the House of Commons in a curious mood, a mixture of high excitement over the fight to come, and bitter disappointment that we had already lost the first round before the bell had even rung. If only Jeremy had agreed to step into the industrial arena a few days earlier, we may even have solved the dispute with a tremendous bonus of goodwill for the Liberal party. Even if we had failed, our efforts would have given us a new active image as a party willing and ready to become involved in the great issues of the day. It was a great loss for the Liberal party and, I sincerely believe, a great loss for the people of Britain. If it is possible to trace the country's present sorry state back to any one single incident, it must be the miners' strike and the pathetic General Election that it spawned.

We had no time, of course, to dwell on these sombre thoughts. A General Election was upon us, and we were at the height of the greatest upswell in our popularity for half a century. It was time for an all-out attack, a time which could – and possibly did – settle the fate of Liberalism in Great Britain for all time. We decided to field the greatest number of candidates this century – five hundred and seventeen – and we were going for *power*. The euphoria wagon was not only dragged out of its stable, but was pushed off on a tearing, whooping, cheering downhill charge. Life aboard the wagon, in February 1974, was the most exhilarating period of my life.

For me it was the beginning of a flat-out, exhausting time of seventeen-hour days, seven-day weeks, often with five speeches a day and many a town in between those speeches. Jeremy, defending a smallish majority in North Devon, decided rightly to stay in his constituency and keep his seat at all costs. As one of the party's newest flag-bearers – and the only member to have won a Labour seat – I was judged as one of the stars of the rolling Liberal show, and speeches were planned for me in all parts of the country. One speech I made, entirely unrehearsed and completely unintentional, proved that my lucky political star was still shining down on me.

I was booked for a speaking tour in Kent and, my travelling schedule being so tight, it was arranged that a small private aircraft would fly me from Manchester. Because of the lack of civilian airports in the area, the Royal Air Force had agreed that the plane would be allowed to land at RAF Manston, Kent. What I did not know, as the tiny five-seater winged its way south, was that some stuffed-shirt in a sky-blue uniform had decided that the RAF must make a great show of its political neutrality. An RAF base was not to be used for common electioneering and at the very time I was sitting in the plane, airmen were going round asking my small band of supporters waiting in welcome to take off their Liberal party rosettes. They even forced a young mother to unpin the rosette from the 'noddy-hat' of her young daughter sitting in a perambulator.

Now this is exactly the sort of mind-crushing red-tape which is calculated to make me blow my top. As the tiny aircraft taxied to a stop, and I climbed inelegantly out onto the wing – there was no way in which I could perform that manœuvre elegantly – one of my supporters shouted sardonically: 'The Royal Air Force says you must take off your rosette, Cyril.'

My reply, I think, was quite justified in the circumstances. I roared back: 'You can tell them to get stuffed!'

Now while I had seen the press photographers in the crowd, I had not noticed the television cameras. Neither did I know that boom microphones – capable of picking up sound at long distances – were trained on me. Had I known this, my reply may have been a little more restrained. As it was, I watched the incident on television that night and allowed myself a shudder. After all, it was hardly Parliamentary language or, more accurately, the language Parliamentarians normally use when faced by a microphone. But, as I said, my lucky star was still shining down. I received literally hundreds of letters from people with messages like: 'I am going to vote Liberal now because you have proved to me that your party understands the feelings and talks the language of ordinary people ...' Yes, there were literally hundreds of letters. It was a lucky but important guide to the feelings of the general public: they were tired of the standard political gabble, the long words which said nothing. 'Get stuffed', may have lost the Liberal party a few hundred votes from old ladies shocked over the rims of their china tea cups, but I am convinced it picked up many thousands in the pubs and working men's clubs where people value a straight answer.

That was the funny highlight of my campaign, the first I had fought as a Liberal MP. There were many, many more serious meetings, speeches and discussions, and at the centre of them there was always that magical figure: twenty-three per cent. If ancient religions were built round the mystical properties of a number, the Liberal campaign in February 1974 centred round the number twenty-three. The reason for the importance of this apparently arbitrary sum lies in the appalling injustices of our electoral system.

GAINS AND LOSSES

Because our elections are fought on the basis of rigidly fixed, geographical constituencies – which can vary in size by many tens of thousands of voters – it is quite normal for control of our Parliament to go to a party on a minority vote. A system of proportional representation based on the total number of votes cast throughout the country would automatically give minority parties a large number of seats in Westminster. That is why 'PR' has been opposed so strongly by the two major parties – Labour and Conservative – who stand to lose most, and supported so passionately by the minority parties, who stand to gain most. As by far the biggest of the minorities – in England, at least – a 'PR' system would automatically give the Liberals a very substantial hold in the House of Commons.

By 1974, however, Liberals were tired of their years of crying in the 'PR' desert. We were convinced we could break through under the existing, inequitable system, and that meant topping the magic twenty-three per cent figure. The statistical side, which I do not propose to explore at length for better minds than mine have already done so, demonstrates just how *un*democratic our so-called democracy actually is. With eighteen per cent of the vote, Liberals tend to win a dozen or so seats. If that can be increased by a mere five per cent, the gain in seats is quite phenomenal – as many as fifty or even more. Although many of my more starry-eyed colleagues in that February were talking in terms of winning an actual majority in the House – calling for a vote well up in the late thirties in percentage – I was more realistic. Our opinion polls had once shown a support going into the thirties, but by the time polling day arrived, we were back in the low twenties. I had no illusions that we were about to take absolute power, but I did have the strongly held belief that we would beat the twenty-three per cent barrier.

On the night of 28 February I drove off to Rochdale Town Hall to hear the result of my own count, sure in my mind that within the next twenty-four hours I would have forty or more colleagues in the House of Commons.

My own result was a personal triumph. I almost doubled my by-election majority to eight thousand nine hundred and ninety-nine, whereas the majority of by-election victors – in safe seats, at least – dropped votes. But my election was dimmed by the news as I arrived back at my headquarters in Drake Street.

Something had gone wrong. At the very last minute, the public had deserted us.

Later that night, Jeremy Thorpe telephoned me at home. He, too, had won a major personal success, increasing his tiny North Devon majority to a handsome eleven thousand and seventy-two. But the breakthrough hadn't come, the early results proved it. The Liberals were in second place in scores of seats ... but second place is not a victory, but a defeat. As I have said many times, I prefer my opponents to have the moral victories.

'Don't give up hope, yet,' said Jeremy. 'There are still many of the rural seats to come in ...'

Even Jeremy Thorpe, the most forceful and energetic electioneer I have ever known, couldn't put any conviction into the statement ...

When the last results finally trickled in, the full extent of the disaster became known. The Liberal Party had polled 6,063,470 votes – 18.3 per cent of the total. If there were any real justice in our political world, we would have won a hundred and twenty seats in the House of Commons. Because of the damnable iniquity of the system, our total was fourteen, a baker's dozen, plus one.

How the British people will tolerate an electoral arrangement which gives a moderate and honourable party little more than a tenth of its rightful rewards, I do not know. Nor will I ever know why the British public, in which I have such inordinate faith, deserted us when we were within inches of a democratic revolution. Was it the very fear of fundamental change, the smashing of the two-party system with all its evils, that caused them to back away from the doorway which had been opened? I do not know.

What I do know – and history will prove me right – is that February 1974 was a black month for democracy.

CHAPTER TEN

Coalition... and Bribery

During the first weekend in March 1974, Britain lay uneasy in a new and worrying state of political limbo. Across a chasm of personal dislike and political discord, two very different men faced each other in implacable confrontation. Ted Heath and Harold Wilson were, at the best of times bad losers. That weekend, the British public believed both had lost. As is the way in these things, however, both thought they had won.

The British electoral system is 'rigged' in such a way that it traditionally produces a clear-cut, but usually unjust, division of power. Its most ardent supporters can produce only this single historical fact in its defence. On 28 February 1974, even this objective had not been reached, reflecting the growing disillusion of the electorate. Harold Wilson, whose party had won only thirty-seven per cent of the vote, claimed he was the winner with three hundred and one parliamentary seats. Yet Ted Heath, with two hundred and ninety-six seats, was not going to resign as Prime Minister without a fight.

The key to the future lay with thirty-seven 'minority' MPs, the various Ulster Unionists, the Nationalists from Scotland and Wales and, of course, the Liberals. As the leader of fourteen Liberals – our disgraceful reward for gaining a fifth of the vote – Jeremy Thorpe became, for the first time in his political life and for a very brief period at that, a figure of true national importance. Different again in style and personality from Heath and Wilson, he was to be the 'Third Man' who, like Harry Lime in the sewers of Vienna, was to pick his way through our political underground that weekend in negotiations which, without being over-dramatic, were to decide the fate of the nation.

The characters of these three men were startlingly diverse. Heath, still the serving Prime Minister, was displaying all his deep-lying stubbornness by refusing to resign, yet I do not believe he was the paranoid Right wing extremist that history seems to depict. He is a very human man – the deep sorrows he later suffered showed with painful clarity his susceptibility to personal betrayal. As a Prime Minister, he was far more moderate than he has been given credit for – in fact some of his policies could have been taken straight from the Liberal party manifesto. He had, also, as an ex-grammar schoolboy from a middle-class background, taken the Conservative party out of the hands of the Grouse Moor set.

There were two flaws, however, both of which did him political harm, one of them quite unnecessarily so. He suffers from great personal shyness, both publicly and in private. On television, in particular, this shyness came over as aloofness and unfairly alienated him in the eyes of the viewers. The second flaw, a serious one in a man practising the art of the possible, was more dangerous – his deep distrust for compromise. His confrontation with the miners at a time when they claimed great public sympathy was a major political miscalculation, but he felt himself unable to compromise – or, as I am sure he would have described it, to 'back down'. Later, when he was ousted by Maggie Thatcher, the same trait shone through.

I find it difficult to be so charitable towards Harold Wilson, a man whom I once admired as the definitive political 'pro'. There was never any doubt that he had a magnificent brain, but in his latter years as Prime Minister the question was: to what ends was he putting that brain to work? He was a difficult man to judge objectively, because he was as slippery as an eel wriggling through a pond. I think he wanted to be liked but, quite frankly, I did not find him a likeable man: one could never judge, when he turned on the charm, whether he was talking from his heart or from a cold and calculating mind. His later appearances on television with David Frost sickened me with their treacly self-justifications. I suppose he wanted to go down in history as a great Prime Minister, but I am afraid he will have failed. He might be recorded as a great leader of the Labour party, which he assuredly was, but one wonders how often the interests of the Labour party and the interests of Britain have coincided in recent years. Wilson may well have been the longest serving Prime Minister of this century. Was it coincidence that his period also saw the greatest decline in the fortunes of Britain since the days of the Tudors? Was it an historical inevitability, or did Wilson accelerate the process? That point will no doubt be argued for generations. I know my view: when the many crunches came – and there were so very many – and the interests of a united Labour party and the interests of the United Kingdom were at variance, it was the Labour party that won.

The personal hostility between Heath and Wilson reached its peak at the beginning of March 1974, and it was at this point that Jeremy Thorpe strode jauntily onto the stage. Compared with the other two wily old birds, he was a veritable kingfisher, nattily dressed, his gold watch-chain swinging from his double-breasted waistcoat, his trilby at a jaunty angle. He had led a magnificent election campaign, only to be robbed by the system. He was alternately filled with a bursting enthusiasm fed by our six million votes, and a brooding disillusion with the futility of it all. He wanted, like all politicians, power and influence. A fifth of the country wanted him to have it also. The *system* had robbed him of natural justice, but there was still a backdoor chance half-open. There was talk of coalition in the air ...

I was at home in Rochdale on the Friday evening after the poll, answering a continuous stream of calls from members of the Liberal party demanding that we should not become involved in a coalition with Ted Heath. 'I did not vote Liberal to keep the Tories in,' was the constant theme of the calls. Many came from Liberal candidates who had just fought – and narrowly lost – Parliamentary seats, and some were prepared to go as far as public resignation from the party if we did join the Conservatives. My own views were less extreme. While being no ardent supporter of coalition government, I was in favour – in view of the obvious public demand for something less partisan than the traditional system – of some form of loosely based government of national unity, at least until the then current industrial crisis was solved. I also saw a strong political possibility of using the Liberal position to achieve our long-sought demand for electoral reform. We were in a stronger bargaining situation than we had known for many years, and I believed we should use it. If that thought brings the charge of 'party politicking' down on my ears, I should point out that on this occasion, the interests of the Liberal party were very much the interest of the country. Our huge vote had demonstrated the longing in the country for a Third Force in Parliament. It was time for the Liberals to use their moderating influence in some sort of alliance. Whether that alliance was with Heath or Wilson did not unduly concern me.

Watching television on that night, I heard that Jeremy Thorpe was to visit Heath at Number 10 the following day. The momentum was quickening. I tried to contact Thorpe and David Steel, our Chief Whip, by telephone, but was unable to raise either. What was happening? Were they cloistered away somewhere, cutting and drying, without consulting the rest of the party? My anxiety increased the following day as I was still unable to extract any official news from the party machine. Like everyone else in the country, I was to discover from television on the Saturday evening that Thorpe had met the Prime Minister and that he was having lunch the following day with a group of Liberal *peers*. What about the MPs? My fears were bordering on alarm for, if Thorpe had one major fault, it was a leaning towards the traditionalists in the Liberal party, the dinner-party politics practised with great charm but to little concrete result. Surely Thorpe wasn't going to decide the coalition issue with members of the Upper Chamber? What would that mean in the eyes of the six million men and women who had willed us power in the Commons? After all our work, were the political dilettantes back in the Liberal saddle?

The situation was preposterous. I was still unable to contact Thorpe or Steel. I telephoned Emlyn Hooson. Had he heard any official news? No! I telephoned Russell Johnston, MP for Inverness. Had the Scottish Liberal party heard any news? No! We discussed the matter urgently and it was decided I should contact the President of the party, Lord Lloyd of Kilgerran – Rhys Gerran Lloyd, the Liberal life peer and one of Thorpe's inner circle – who was due to attend the Sunday lunch.

I was in no mood for pleasantries when I told him: 'The future of the Liberal party will be decided by today's men, and not by yesterday's.'

He was clearly offended, and considered his words carefully before replying, 'You must remember, Cyril, that I hold in my hand the conscience of the Liberal party.'

I exploded: 'Don't come at me with your fine words. You can make as many pretty speeches as you wish, and eat as many fine lunches as you wish, but make no mistake this time: no policy decision must be taken on behalf of this party without the consent of its *elected* representatives.' With that, I slammed down the receiver.

Finally, on the Sunday, David Steel telephoned with the news that Heath had offered the Liberals a full-blooded coalition. What were my views? I told him of all the anti-coalition views I had heard and said I would prefer a less formal arrangement. There was, however, one inducement which, I thought, would make joining with the Tories worthwhile – a firm promise of the electoral system to give us proportional representation. David listened quietly, and then rang off to take the views of other MPs.

When we did eventually meet, at the House of Commons on the Monday morning, it was a solemn affair. Only Jo Grimond supported an all-out coalition, and I gave him his only support – conditional on the offer of 'PR'. Jeremy Thorpe, that morning, set an example of real statesmanship. Although we all knew he had a terrible longing for power – and that agreement with Heath would automatically have given him a senior post in the Cabinet – he accepted that the majority of Liberal supporters were against the idea and, therefore, he advised us to reject the offer. It was, possibly, the most crucial decision of his life up to that point. Wilson had already indicated that he would reject an offer of Liberal support on a moderate economic package. Heath's offer to Jeremy represented a last chance...

The letter arrived from Number 10 during that meeting. Addressed to 'Dear Jeremy' and signed, 'Edward Heath', it was a letter which set the seal on the immediate government of this country – and sowed the seeds of the economic disaster we have been reaping in a long and bitter harvest ever since. Because of its importance, I will quote the letter in full.

10, Downing Street,
Whitehall,
4 March, 1974.

Dear Jeremy,

When we met on Saturday afternoon, we agreed that, in the situation created by a General Election which left neither of the two major parties able to command an overall majority in the House of Commons, and with only a small difference in the number of seats held by each of them, the essential and urgent need was that an Administration should be formed which would have sufficient support in the New House of Commons to carry on the Queen's Government, and in particular to command the degree of confidence at home and overseas necessary to take the measures required to deal with the economic crisis – something which both of us believe must take highest priority. We noted that the Leader of the Labour Party had issued a statement which made it clear that he would be prepared to form a minority government but not to enter into any coalition or understanding with other parties in the House. In that situation it was my duty, as Prime Minister, to see whether the basis existed for an arrangement between the Conservative and Liberal Parties, two parties which had most in common, which would ensure the necessary support to enable a Government to deal effectively with the overriding needs of the economic situation.

I recognised that the programmes of our two parties differed in a number of respects. Any such arrangement would involve decisions on either side to postpone policies and measures which in other circumstances we might have wanted to carry out but which did not have immediate priority in relation to the overriding requirements of the economic situation. But there was much we had in common. In two major respects in particular, the policies of our two parties are both alike and both different from the Labour Party. Both of us are committed in present circumstances to policies for countering inflation which deal with pay as well as prices with statutory backing. And both of us are committed to British membership of the European Community, subject to changes and improvements in Community arrangements where these could be agreed with our Community partners but not subject to any re-negotiation of the terms of British entry. I made it clear in my belief that it would be possible to construct a programme for the Queen's Speech on the Opening of Parliament which both the Conservative and Liberal Parties could honourably and in good conscience support.

When we met on Saturday, we considered various possible arrangements, and in particular an undertaking by your Party to support and vote for a definitive programme of policies and measures to be incorporated in the Queen's Speech which would naturally have to be drafted in consultation with you, or a coalition arrangement under which you, as leader of the Liberal Party, would be offered a seat in the Cabinet with Ministerial appointments for some other members of your Party.

On this latter basis, of course, you as a member of the Government would have a voice in all the Government's decisions. At the same time your Party would be committed to support the Government in the House of Commons.

I told you on Saturday that I thought from the point of view of the stability and confidence of a new Administration, full Liberal participation in Government was preferable to other possible arrangements. Since we met, I have had an opportunity of discussing this further with my colleagues. We are now convinced that full Liberal participation in Government, and thus in all the decisions of Government, will be essential if we are to ensure a stable Administration, able to take the measures required by the economic situation, and able to command confidence at home and overseas. We do not think that, on its own, an arrangement for Liberal support would be sufficient to provide the stability and command the confidence necessary in present circumstances.

When we met, you drew my attention to the fact that, though your party had polled nearly six million votes in the Election, it had won only fourteen seats. You said that this outcome had given rise to deep dissatisfaction among your colleagues and Liberal voters, and had underlined the need for electoral reform. You asked what were my views on this subject, and I told you that I should have to consult my colleagues. I have now done so.

Electoral reform has always been a matter for Parliament itself, expressing its views by means of free votes on recommendations by a Speaker's Conference. My colleagues and I cannot commit Parliament, or indeed our Party as a whole. But I am authorised to tell you that my colleagues and I in the present Cabinet would be prepared to support the setting up of a Speaker's Conference to consider the desirability and possibility of a change in our electoral arrangements. This would ensure that the whole matter was fully ventilated by Parliamentary and public opinion. We would then be ready to co-operate in seeing that the conclusions and recommendations of the Conference were put to Parliament in the customary way.

Yours sincerely,
EDWARD HEATH.

The letter was received by the tiny gathering of Liberal MPs without elation. Those of us who knew just how proud and stubborn a man Heath was knew the pain he must have suffered in writing it. Much of it made good sense – we were united in a desire to fight pay as well as price inflation, in our determination to join the Common Market. Many of us felt that a Liberal presence in the government would buffer the effects of the collision between Heath and the trade unions, allowing an honourable settlement of differences by both sides. The first part of the letter also seemed to be a genuine expression of the Prime Minister's desire to push party differences aside in an effort to do battle against the ever-growing economic crisis.

But the final two paragraphs had the all-too-familiar smell of party machinations. He had consulted his colleagues, he said, and they were prepared to offer a Speaker's Conference. Using procedural loopholes, he then pointed out that the matter would have to be decided on a free vote of Parliament. That, we knew, would mean the death of any prospect of reform.

Heath knew very well that a system of proportional representation would automatically give the Liberals a very substantial block of MPs in the House, as many as a hundred and twenty at that particular time. A publicly acceptable performance by a group that large could eventually lead to an even greater representation and – as we had been taking the majority of our votes from the Tories in previous elections – the real possibility of the Liberals replacing the Conservatives as one of the major parties. We knew, too, that the growing tide of nationalism, particularly in Scotland, would disastrously harm the Labour party if it were allowed to express itself through proportional voting. We knew, to a man, that even if we had a Speaker's Conference, we had no hope of winning a free vote in an unrepresentative Commons.

To be fair we, too, had our own particular party attitudes to consider. The rising crescendo of anti-coalition feeling in our own ranks was something we had to take seriously, for to ignore it would have harmed the Liberal party and its hopes of forcing Liberal ideas and policies into our public life.

Eventually, Jeremy sent the following letter to Ted Heath:

4 March, 1974.

Dear Prime Minister,

Thank you for your letter of this morning. You will recall that our meeting on Saturday was at your invitation when you indicated that if possible it was your intention to carry on in Government. As I made clear then, and subsequently in public, no commitment of any sort was entered into by me, save that I would report our discussions to my colleagues and seek their views. This I did.

Subsequently, a second meeting took place at your request on Sunday night, to which your letter does not allude, in which I made it clear that in my view, after preliminary soundings, there was no possibility of a Liberal–Conservative Coalition proving acceptable, but that we might give consideration to offering support from the opposition benches to any minority government on an agreed, but, limited programme. This you have now explicitly rejected.

After meeting my Parliamentary colleagues in the Commons this morning this attitude was confirmed. In recognizing the grave and immediate economic problems which this country faces the initial necessity for an early settlement to the miners' dispute and the restoration of a full working week, we believe that the only way in which the maximum degree of national co-operation can be achieved is for a government of national unity to be formed to include members of all parties to carry out a limited programme on those matters of overriding priority. At this stage I do not think it would be helpful to comment on the assumptions that you have made concerning policy save to say that in the present economic emergency I think that sufficient common ground and good will could be found between all Parties to sustain a national government. As the enclosed Press Statement indicates, this would have our enthusiastic support. I would urge you immediately to approach party leaders for this purpose.

Accordingly, I do not believe that a Liberal presence in the Cabinet, designed to sustain your government would prove acceptable.

I am glad to note your support for a reference to a Speaker's Conference, to examine the unfairness of our present electoral system. I am sure that this should take place at an appropriate time.

In the Press Statement issued that day, Jeremy wrote:

> *The Parliamentary Liberal Party this morning received a report from Mr Thorpe on the arrangements proposed by the Prime Minister. A reply has been sent to 10, Downing Street this afternoon, indicating that these are not in the national interest.*
>
> *The outcome of the Election clearly shows that the electorate is not prepared to give either a Conservative or a Labour administration a mandate to pursue their conventional policies. The six million people, whom we represent, voted for policies of moderation. In the present situation we are convinced that such policies can only be carried out effectively by a government of national unity consisting of members of all parties, committed to a limited programme for an agreed period. This would give overriding priority to those policies required to be implemented in the national interest. The gravity of the country's economic plight is such that party conflict must be subordinated to the country's need.*
>
> *It is now the duty of the other parties to enter into immediate discussion with a view to achieving this. To this end we have urged the Prime Minister to convene an immediate meeting of the party leaders.*

Ted Heath resigned as Prime Minister as soon as he received our reply. The Queen called for Harold Wilson.

Looking back now, I think the Liberal MPs were right in their decision at the time, given the circumstances which then existed. If we had been able to predict the changes which were imminent, we would have been wrong – but the political crystal ball is a fickle instrument. Speaking with all the benefit of hindsight, I think we should have entered into coalition that day and I believe most Liberals, even the ones in such voracious opposition then, would agree with me now. We have only one excuse: we were totally unprepared for the way in which Harold Wilson was to set out cynically and recklessly to buy the British electorate with its own money. Election by bribery is not new, but I doubt if any modern leader has pursued such a policy with such abandon as did Harold Wilson in eight months of 1974.

To be fair to Labour, they have no monopoly on this practice: the famous 'Stop-Go' era of the fifties, under the Tories, meant 'go' just before an election, and 'stop' immediately afterwards. The economy was deliberately boosted to produce a peak as the country was going to the polls, totally ignoring the basic need of industry for steady, sustained growth. Heath himself was equally guilty, and his last Chancellor of the Exchequer, Anthony Barber, is probably to blame for at least fifty per cent of the country's present financial ills. In his last budget, Barber totally misread the public's willingness to accept a measure of austerity to avert the economic smash-up. It was obvious even to the man in the street that severe measures were necessary. Barber, perhaps with his eye on a coming election, kept his foot on the throttle.

It was largely due to Barber's lack of action that the nation was in such a precarious state when Harold Wilson went to Buckingham Palace in March 1974. Inflation was soaring, industry was in a turmoil of doubt about the future and, overseas, the foreign bankers were getting edgy. It was a bad time for a minority government but – thought many people, including myself – Wilson's sheer political cunning might just pull us through.

My disgust was that much stronger when Wilson announced his Cabinet and it became obvious that even the wily Wilson had sold out to his Left wing. The three appointments which particularly shocked me, and I believe the majority of the nation, were Tony Wedgwood Benn as Secretary of State for Industry, Peter Shore as Secretary of State for Trade, and Michael Foot as Secretary of State for Employment. Although there was a certain style about Foot's appointment – after all, his first job was to settle the miners' strike – the trio as a whole represented a tremendous slap in the face for industry. The country's manufacturers, and, therefore, the economy itself, were crying out for reassurance. Instead, they had been delivered into the hands of the Left. In the financial capitals of the world, confidence in Britain went into a power dive which has still to level out.

What to do? Here we had a Prime Minister who had no real mandate, but was determined, nevertheless, to ignore the clearly expressed wishes of the majority of the people. I began studying the books on the constitution, and found that Wilson was acting within his rights. There was no need, by any precedent, once the Queen had sent for him, to submit himself or his controversial Cabinet to the approval of Parliament. We, the country's elected representatives, had no power to tell him: we don't like your government, so go away and form one we can accept. We had only one choice of action, and a drastic one at that: we had to bring the government down. Our first opportunity to do so would be to vote against the Queen's Speech.

We set about to put down an amendment to the Speech which would have meant Wilson's immediate resignation if approved by the House. When news of the plan leaked out, the fury of the press came down on my shoulders for the first time. The *Sun*, of all papers, carried a leader, under the headline, 'Belt Up, Cyril', and it was generally accepted in the media that I was trying to force another General Election on the country. This was far from my intention, but perhaps I had expressed myself badly and, if that were so, I was at fault.

What I was trying to achieve was a form of national government, but I was aware that under our hazy constitutional procedures, the only person capable of bringing that about was the Queen. I knew I was entering a minefield in appearing to bring Her Majesty into the political arena, but I failed to anticipate just how loud the explosion would be. Throughout the land, people accused me of trying to tarnish the Queen's impeccable constitutional record, of tarring her with the brush of party politics. In all honesty, this was just not so. It was a time of constitutional vacuum and the only person who could fill it was Her Majesty.

She has two important constitutional functions: she alone can dissolve Parliament, and she alone can invite a man or a woman to form a government. In normal times, when one party has a clear majority in the Commons, her choice of actions are automatic. She dissolves Parliament at the request of the serving Prime Minister – or when the legal life of the Parliament has reached its end – and after the elections which ensue, she calls for the leader of the majority party.

But her choices were far from clear in the spring of 1974. I believed that if we defeated the Wilson administration on the Queen's Speech, she would not dissolve Parliament. Instead, I felt she would call for a second man and invite him to form a government acceptable to the House of Commons. To enter the realm of pure speculation, I believe she would first have asked James Callaghan, who would, I think, have refused to enter into any alliance. Her third choice would surely have lain between Roy Jenkins and Willie Whitelaw and – who knows? – one of these two might have picked up the gauntlet.

Either of these last two choices would have given the country exactly what it had voted for less than a month previously – a government working in the interests of the nation as a whole, its back firmly turned on the narrow sectionalised interests of the extremists of all parties. I do not think such a situation would have left the Monarch open to attack. It would have brought forward by twenty years – I will discuss this at length later – the inevitable rearrangement of the centrist forces in Parliament. It would also have brought about great benefits for the United Kingdom – and avoided the disasters which were to follow.

Could Queen Elizabeth possibly have suffered any historical blame for such an action?

Sadly, the plan was never put to the test. The spectre of procedural hocus-pocus raised its head again, and the Liberal party's amendment to the Queen's Speech was never called. Why? By tradition, only one amendment was allowed to the Speech and the right to put it down went to the majority Opposition party. The Tories did, in fact, place an amendment but – for internal party reasons I never discovered – they withdrew it at the last minute. The Speaker, Selwyn Lloyd, refused to take the Liberal amendment, and Harold Wilson's Leftwing plans were read unopposed.

I was livid. I wrote an angry letter to the Speaker, accusing him of inexcusable Parliamentary bias. It was another mistake. Selwyn, much to my surprise, simply refused to accept the letter. He handed it to David Steel, who brought it into my office holding it between two fingers like a hot, wet cloth just stripped from a steak-and-kidney pudding.

'You really will have to apologise this time, Cyril,' he said.

'I won't,' I said.

'You will. You see, Selwyn had no alternative – Commons procedure forbids the taking of two amendments on the Queen's Speech!'

That time I did apologise. I wrote a letter to Selwyn, completely withdrawing any of the personal criticism. I did add, however, that I was still deeply opposed to the procedure which forbade our amendment. It gives me some satisfaction to record that this procedure has now been changed.

The change came too late, however, to prevent Harold Wilson setting off on his blatant bribery of the British voter. Knowing full well that he would be forced to call another election within a year, and ignoring the dire needs of the economy, he opened the floodgates to the biggest round of pay claims the country has ever seen. Millions of workers – many of them in nationalised industries or local government – rode on the backs of the miners to pay increases which, temporarily, disguised the economy's critical weakness. Some of the rises were huge: National Coal Board doctors, for instance, using the political weight of the coal-face workers, asked for and were given thirty pounds a week. The money printing presses were wound up to full speed, and the fuse was lit under the rocket which was soon to take the inflation rate soaring towards the thirty per cent stratosphere.

Any old-age pensioner struggling today to buy half a pound of butter, any householder worrying today where the rates money is coming from, any worker drawing his dole today because his firm went bankrupt, should look back and remember the summer of 1974, when Harold Wilson set out to buy himself another term of office.

Unforgivably, Wilson went on his spending spree virtually unopposed. The Conservatives, having decided they did not want another General Election, spent the early summer avoiding votes which would bring the government down. Parliament which, for once, could have exercised a truly democratic control over the administration, shirked its duties for three vital months. Parliamentary business was so pointless that I began to turn my mind to electioneering ...

It was apparent to everyone that another election was just over the horizon, and it was apparent to me that the Liberal party was not doing enough to consolidate our six million votes. We were a bit too *respectable*, a trifle too *smooth*. The image went down well in the suburbs among the young-marrieds, but had made no inroads on the council estates and the terraced streets of the great industrial areas. We needed, I thought, to be more *abrasive*.

This led to one of my more hilarious experiences in the House, planned as a joke with a sting in the tail. As the Tories were manifestly failing in their duties to oppose, I suggested that the Liberals, the most vocal of the opposition groups, should by right have the Opposition Front Bench. The Great Invasion was planned, I admit, with all the giggling temerity of a bunch of school kids launching a raid on an orchard.

'Come on, let's do it now,' I whispered in the House one night as the Tory bench was voting in a division.

'You go first,' said someone in a choirboy voice.

So I did. I got up, strode past the Mace, winked at the Speaker, and plumped myself down. There was a silence, followed by a buzz and whispering, then a few half-smothered laughs. In the corridors of power, news of the 'invasion' spread like wildfire.

In strode Maurice Macmillan, son of the former Prime Minister and a Tory shadow spokesman. 'Will you please move from there?' he asked.

'No,' I said.

To widespread hilarity, he began trying to push me off the bench.

'Gerroff, lad,' I laughed. 'I'm twenty-seven stone – you'll never budge me without an army.'

At this point, John Pardoe and Richard Wainwright joined me from the Liberal benches to be followed by more. The Tories gathered round us, arguing and angry. Some walked out, disgusted by such a scene on the floor of the House of Commons. We sat there for ten minutes and then trooped back, hoping we had made our point. Even if we didn't, we had a bit of a laugh – and laughter's a rare commodity in Westminster.

In an attempt to take our electioneering to the country, I put forward the suggestion that we should hire a bus and take the whole Parliamentary party on a barn-storming tour, saturating key areas with our MPs and followers. This idea, too, was rejected, although a newspaper offered to pay for the hire of the coach in return for exclusive rights to send a reporter and photographer along with us. Jeremy had another idea: his now infamous hovercraft tour of the summer holiday resorts.

It was a good idea, but much of the publicity went wrong, largely due to the fact that the hovercraft kept breaking down, much to the hilarity of the media. I, too, was cajoled aboard a hovercraft one rainy day on Southport sands. The craft, of course, stubbornly failed to move. There I was, soaked to the skin, stranded on a beach surrounded by hordes of laughing children. The press, of course, found it irresistible and had another field-day.

Suddenly, in the middle of that summer, Parliament turned serious. The Tories decided it was time to *oppose* and a rare excitement swept through Westminster. Democracy came alive as we, the humble back-benchers, took the power that the people had willed us. Bill after Bill was amended, controversial legislation was chopped and changed, to the ever-growing chorus of hate from Labour's Left wing. It was their pet projects – like the introduction of the legally imposed closed-shop in industry – that fell like ninepins. The extremists, the apparently irresistible demands of the trade unions, were suddenly resistible. Power was back where it belonged, on the floor of the House of Commons, and each vote became an occasion for tense anticipation. Members no longer strolled through the lobbies and went home, without waiting for the inevitable result. Instead, they stayed round in their hundreds, gossiping, arguing, chattering until the Speaker read out the count. The boos, the cheers, which followed were genuine expressions of emotion, not theatrical tinsel.

In short, Parliament was a Parliament once more.

It was by far the most stimulating period of my brief Parliamentary life. It was also, to my intense regret, shortlived. The summer recess was soon upon us, and it was time – Harold Wilson decided – for the country to be dragged reluctantly back to the polls.

The Liberal party Conference in Brighton that year should have been a great occasion. We had the backing of a huge section of the country, and unheard-of things were happening. Christopher Mayhew, former Labour Minister of the Navy, had crossed the floor to our benches, sickened by the growing Marxist element in Wilson's ranks. There were rumours of more defections to our side – one of them, I can now reveal, which we were very lucky to avoid. The appalling John Stonehouse had launched preliminary talks with David Steel. They were, thank God, indecisive, and Stonehouse flew off to Miami the following day to start one of the strangest interludes in British political history.

Despite the arrival of Mayhew, despite our tremendous public backing, that Brighton conference was bungled. The coalition problem, still at the forefront of our minds, raised more rancour. By this time, most of our MPs had decided that we must accept coalition if we were offered it again. There was, however, great opposition in the rank and file, particularly among the militants of the Young Liberals and the Left wing group calling themselves the Radicals. Jeremy Thorpe discussed the matter with us, the MPs, and we decided, wrongly, not to force the issue. So the Liberal party sat on the fence on coalition... and within a week, Harold Wilson called the year's second election.

What happened then is a simple matter of record. We put forward another hundred candidates – at six hundred and nineteen the greatest number of Liberals to stand at a General Election this century – and despite that, dropped seven hundred thousand votes. Wilson's pay bonanza had improved his own support. The Tories, who throughout the campaign attacked the Liberals with an unprecedented and often malicious ferocity – made little headway. The march of the Nationalists went on...

Two million people who had voted Liberal in February changed their minds (but for our extra hundred candidates, our vote would have taken an enormous cut) and the chance of a powerful force for moderation slipped away once again.

The voting public, to use an Americanism, 'chickened-out'.

Was it our lack of campaigning zest? Our blurred stand on coalition? The Conservative attacks? Or merely Wilson's sweetening of the electorate? Probably a minor combination of the first three, added to the major effect of the latter. Wilson had put the rosy apples at the front of the stall. The rotten fruit was to come on view later – too late for the shoppers to take their custom elsewhere.

What is it about the British people that makes them reject coalition? Is it a fundamental fear of change? Do they still believe, after the last decade, that one-party government is still strong government? When will they realise that the Labour party they vote for today is a fraud, its ranks ever swelling with Marxists who intend to destroy our system, not improve it?

I do not know the answers to these questions. I do know that many of the most efficient governments of Western Europe are run by coalitions, or groups of minority parties which automatically impose a built-in brake on the wilder dreams of the extremists. West Germany, the country I suppose most similar to ours, has risen to once unthinkable heights of prosperity and world influence through coalition rule.

Is it not a matter for grave sadness that the democracy which fought tyranny at such horrendous cost, now seems bent on reversing those roles?

CHAPTER ELEVEN

Scandal

It was undoubtedly the ultimate irony of my career that I should become Chief Whip of the Liberal party.

There was, firstly, my deeply held and often expressed animosity towards the whip system itself, trampling, as it so often does, on Parliamentary freedom. There was also the unexpressed opposition of Jeremy Thorpe himself, who delayed the appointment by seven long months. Nevertheless, I took on the job hoping that I could overcome all objections from my party leader and my own conscience, believing that I could use it as a platform for launching a new vitality into the Liberals' political offensive. I hoped it would bring Jeremy Thorpe and I closer for the benefit of the party as a whole, combining his style and vitality with my own desire for a more abrasive combativeness. I laid no claims to great visions, but I saw a real opportunity of converting our nationwide support into effective political power.

The supreme irony, of course, is now a matter for history. Instead of Jeremy and I becoming closer, we were driven by events irreconcilably apart. Instead of welding together in a new Liberal dreadnought, we were to sail together into a horrendous shipwreck. It is still too early to say whether the Thorpe Affair – as it was to be known – sank the Liberal party for all time, but there is no doubt it set back the course of British politics for at least ten years. Perhaps Fleet Street, which fired the torpedoes, will reflect on this in the dark years to come – and make no mistake, I think Britain faces some very black years indeed.

All this, however, was in the future after the October 1974 General Election. The charges had been set ... but they were burning on a very long fuse.

The Chief Whip's post in the Liberal party is a unique position. For the Tories and Labour, the Chief Whip is a sort of disciplinary bully-boy, a glorified school prefect who carries out the headmaster's dirty work. The so-called 'leaders' of the major parties haven't the time to soil their hands settling squabbles in the ranks: if they are in power, they have Ministries to attend; in Opposition, they must do their Shadow Cabinet homework. The Liberals have no Shadow Cabinet. They do not even have a Deputy Leader. They have, in fact, just two Parliamentary posts – the Leader and the Chief Whip.

It is a job with lots of kicks and very few ha'pence. The Leader, rightly, gets the glory. The Chief Whip gets the work. He is responsible for the daily grind of party administration, the liaison work with Liberal associations throughout the country, and keeping an informed grip on the complex and often boring routine of Parliament. He is adviser-in-chief to the Leader, and should be his *confidant*. He is the fountainhead of much Parliamentary policy and – perhaps the trickiest job in politics – the party's main contact with the press. The job's only advantages are the dubious status of the Number Two role and the only decent suite of offices available to a Liberal at Westminster (if one largish office and a small ante-room complete with built-in staircase can be called a 'suite').

Even after the February 1974 General Election, David Steel was tiring of the Chief Whip's post. He asked to be allowed to resign then, but was persuaded to continue so that he could use the weight of his great tactical skills during the stresses of a period of minority government. After October 1974 he was determined to step down. The decision of his replacement could only be made by Jeremy Thorpe – who seemed very reluctant to make it.

The first months of that Parliament passed under a blanket of tedium and frustration. Harold Wilson, pandering to his own sense of injured pride as well as the baying of his Left wing, forced through a series of amendments to amendments. All the amendments to his sectarian legislation which had been imposed by the Opposition during those brief weeks of heady democracy in the summer were re-amended: the hounds of the Left were dutifully thrown their bone. While the majority of the country glowered and demanded action, the Opposition pouted and did nothing. Parliament was back to its own mindless, speechifying, impotent self. In the Liberal party, where the savour of recent success was quickly going sour, the bickering started.

When was Jeremy going to appoint the new Chief Whip? The question was being asked, not only in the lobbies, but in the newspapers. There was a crying need for a new impetus. In consultations among our small group, it became clear that I was the favourite for the job. Was this the reason for the delay?

I have never discussed with Jeremy why he took so long to appoint me, and he has never chosen to volunteer the information. There is no doubt, in my mind, however, that he faced the prospect with the greatest reluctance. Why, I do not know. We had been involved in a few minor brushes – he had, of course, called me a 'bit of an ass' in public – but to me these were the inevitabilities of daily political life. Perhaps he wanted David Steel to continue as Chief Whip, a wish I would not question. I tend to believe, however, that the real cause was a clash in *style*, in political method. Jeremy was the master of the subtle manœuvre, the delicate diplomat. His heart, I always thought, was too close to the Harrod's Liberals, the fine claret and Savile Row set. I, of course, had never shared a part of that world and, indeed, would never describe myself as a diplomat. I did, however, want to get things done. I wanted to grab the political world by the scruff of the neck and shake it – hard. I did not think our differences in upbringing and lifestyle made us incompatible. On the contrary, I thought they would give us increased strength, appealing, as we patently did, to different types of voter, searching for answers to some of society's problems from different levels. We would be a great team, I thought.

Jeremy, I suspect, did not share this view.

After two or three months of inactivity, plans for forcing Jeremy's hand were a matter of open discussion among Liberal MPs. Clement Freud floated the ingenious suggestion that all MPs but myself should sign a round-robin letter refusing to accept the Chief Whip's job. What happened to that one I do not know, but by March 1975 the matter had come to a head. It led to a blazing row over the table in a Westminster dining room.

It was a perfectly routine dinner engagement for the Parliamentary Liberal party, until John Pardoe rounded on Jeremy and demanded icily:

'When are you going to appoint a Chief Whip?'

Equally coolly, Jeremy replied: 'When I am ready.'

'That's just not good enough,' said John. 'The time has come when you should be ready. Either you make the announcement tomorrow, or we will.'

The threat of this sort of unilateral action obviously shook Jeremy, but he refused to back down. The argument raged for something like four hours, and still he would make no promise of an announcement. It was not until the following morning that he telephoned me to ask, almost as though the matter had just crossed his mind: 'Cyril, I would like you to be the new Chief Whip.'

I too, had something to say. I would not take the post, I pointed out, if I were expected to act like a House of Commons drill instructor. I would not – and I never did – issue three-line whips ordering my colleagues when they should vote and how they should vote. I took the view that Liberal MPs were grown men, quite able to decide the correctness of their own behaviour. I would inform, advise, but I would refuse to become judge and jury of party political misdemeanours, real or imagined. How prophetic those words sound now!

Jeremy agreed my terms quite readily and that, I thought, was that. The rearguard action was still under way, however. Although the offer had been made and accepted, no announcement was made. More useless, frustrating weeks passed, with me mooching round, anxious to get to grips with a job which no one knew was mine. Eventually, there was yet another row. John Pardoe threatened once more to make a press statement. I left London for the spring holiday recess, still ignorant of the future. On 9 June, I was officially appointed Chief Whip of the Liberal Parliamentary party. No one rang up to tell me. I read about it in my morning newspaper!

Here, at last, was a job of work I could get my teeth into. No longer would I have to dance meaningless Parliamentary waltzes. With great hopes for the future, I threw myself into the work with all my enthusiasm.

Recent reforms by Ted Short, then Leader of the House of

Commons, meant that minority parties were, for the first time, allowed a grant from public funds to assist their operations. The Liberals were entitled to some thirty thousand pounds and I spent it readily, appointing researchers and a fulltime public relations officer. I raised another three thousand to appoint a fulltime liaison officer to keep the regional groups informed of the activities of the Parliamentary party, hoping thereby to answer increasing numbers of complaints from the 'grass-roots' members that the MPs had grown too aloof. It was time, too, to sharpen the cutting edges of our political weapons.

The Conservative party, finally aware that the Liberals had become a major threat, began sniping at us, alleging that we were not attending divisions regularly. It was an underhand attack, based more on gossip than on fact, and its purpose, one presumes, was to rebuild the myth in the country that a Liberal vote was a wasted vote. I counter-attacked after making careful studies of the voting lists, and leaked stories to the press about the number of Tories missing from important divisions. I discovered the names of the Tory MPs who had been the leaders of this sniping campaign against us, and began writing letters to the newspapers in their constituencies, pointing out that their voting records left much to be desired. It was something new for these Conservatives – to be attacked on their home ground – and there were yelps of protest.

I remember one encounter particularly, a snide remark in the Lobby from William Van Straubenzee, the Tory from Wokingham. 'Fancy seeing you here, Cyril,' he said in a loud voice. 'We don't see much of you these days.'

I didn't reply, but after the division I went to my office and checked through the voting lists. There was the evidence in black and white – I had voted in something like fifty more divisions than the Honourable Member from Wokingham.

Later that night, I handed Van Straubenzee my research on a piece of paper.

'What is it?' he asked, puzzled.

'It will show you why you don't see much of me these days,' I replied, perhaps a little pompously. 'It's not because I am missing from the Lobbies – it's because you are!'

In the end, it was the Tories who called a halt to the attendance row. Bernard Weatherill, their Deputy Chief Whip, came to my office and said: 'It's about time we called a truce, Cyril. We should be fighting the Labour party, not each other.' There was some truth in that, of course, but on the attendance issue at least, Labour was at that time beyond reproach. As the government party with a slender majority, their MPs *had* to attend.

These minor skirmishes made few headlines, but were all part of my avowed policy of helping the Liberal party shed its 'nice guy' image. I wanted it to be known, inside Westminster, that the Liberals were not a party to be trifled with – that someone who decided to take us on had better first get his facts right and secondly, be prepared for a fight. Outside Westminster, I still held a grave concern that we were not making enough impact on the voting public. If we were to become accepted in the electorate's eyes as the new radical party, we had to choose radical methods. In this field, I was to meet a more determined resistance – from members of my own party.

The first example of this came in our preparations for the Queen's Speech at the opening of the new session in November 1975. Still smarting under the crippling injustice of our electoral system – will we ever get fair play, I wonder? – I had specially printed a batch of T-shirts emblazoned with the demand 'Electoral Reform Now'. My plan was that every Liberal MP should wear one as we trooped ceremonially from the Commons to the Lords to hear Her Majesty's Speech from the throne. The evening before the Speech, I put my plan forward at a dinner party at Jeremy Thorpe's home in Orme Square.

It met with almost total opposition. Only Richard Wainwright was prepared to join me in wearing one of the shirts. When I went on to suggest that, after the Speech – I stress, after the Speech – we should chant 'Electoral Reform Now', a barely muffled gasp of horror whistled through tight-stretched lips.

After much clearing of his throat, Lord Byers said sternly: 'I would take the gravest exception to anyone embarrassing me in front of the Queen in *my house*.'

The 'my house' meant, of course, the House of Lords. That evening, the Lords once again swayed the policy of the Liberal party. The T-shirt plan, I agree, was only a publicity stunt, but it was a stunt with a sting in its tail. It was direct action on the Liberal party's biggest single grievance, an action which would undoubtedly have led to a great deal of discussion in the media. The electorate would have been reminded once more, and it can never be reminded too often, that the electoral system of this country robs them of truly democratic representation.

I posed outside the House for photographs in my T-shirt, but the remainder were never worn. From that day onwards, I think, I lost hope that the Liberal party could ever be stirred into the kind of action which I believe is essential if it is ever to break through as the major radical force in this country. Politics is a bloody game and – as the Australians and West Indians have shown us at our national game of cricket – 'nice guys' do not win.

On other fronts, where the Liberals found the game played to more gentlemanly, if equally deadly, rules, we were meeting with some success. Another major blow was struck at the Conservative party by a series of meetings held at Orme Square between our MPs and industrialists. Our aim was to persuade the major companies to hold back their financial contributions to the Tories unless they agreed to a programme of electoral reform. The list of companies which took part reads like a roll-call from the Queen's Award to Industry. This was the 'smoke-filled room' type of politics at which Jeremy Thorpe excelled and, indeed, several great companies promised us their support. If any measures were guaranteed to throw the Conservatives into panic, these were the ones ...

We were making progress, too, in the minefield of press relations. I believed that it was essential for the party to get a fair hearing in the press, and one of my first moves as Chief Whip was to issue a standing invitation to all the Westminster lobby correspondents saying: 'My door is always open.' I began holding a series of weekly lunches, inviting political journalists in groups of six, for a sandwich, a glass of wine, and a chat. Although this had not led to a series of articles in praise of the Liberal party – which could and should never happen – these highly experienced journalists were beginning to take Liberal attitudes more seriously. At the same time, I was building up close personal friendships with many of them ...

That perhaps was to be the greatest irony of them all. The

fuse which, unknown to me, had been burning away for almost five years was about to reach the powder.

Of all living British politicians, few were to show so much promise as Jeremy Thorpe, and none was to be cut down more brutally. Son of a Conservative MP, grandson of a baronet, he could have converted the silver spoon he was born with into the highest honours this land has to offer – had he chosen to join the Tory party. Instead he decided to do it the hard way, joining a party which, although electorally decimated, permitted him to exploit his undoubted political charisma.

His background – educated in America and at Eton, Trinity College, Oxford and called to the Bar – offered him a fairy-tale route to success. Instead, he was to be dogged by bad luck, personal tragedy and appalling publicity. His first wife was killed in a car crash. His marriage to his second wife, Marion, the divorced Countess of Harewood, gave the gossip writers a fieldday. Yet the British voting public adored him.

Even before I became Chief Whip, a major scandal was hanging over his head like the Sword of Damocles, brought about by his association with the notorious London and County Securities fringe bank. As early as October 1973 questions had been asked in the House about the usurious rates of interest charged by the company on its second mortgages. In December that year, Jeremy bowed to pressure from his Liberal colleagues and resigned his directorships of London and Counties and five other companies. In February 1974 the bank collapsed with debts reported to run into millions of pounds.

A Board of Trade inquiry was ordered into the company's affairs, and by March 1975 the newspapers were saying that the report of the inquiry was causing apprehension in Liberal ranks, although, as the *Daily Mirror* pointed out, 'Mr Thorpe's conduct throughout the entire, unhappy business was immaculate.'

As the New Year of 1976 passed, I, as Chief Whip, was waiting with some trepidation for the Board of Trade report. I had forgotten entirely, although I was to recall it very abruptly later, a conversation between myself and Richard Wainwright during a car journey to Oxford in 1974.

'Did you know there was an inquiry about Jeremy in 1971?' he asked casually.

'No – what about?' I replied.

'Some fellow came to the House of Commons and claimed he once had a homosexual affair with Jeremy.'

'Really – what happened?'

'We had a meeting with Jeremy and decided there was nothing to it.'

My only reply was: 'Oh.'

The conversation ended there and, as I have already said, was quickly forgotten. The reason for my lack of interest was quite straightforward: anyone in public life must be prepared to suffer malicious attacks from mentally deranged people with highly developed persecution complexes. In these days of the nut-case and the odd-ball, when a single psychopath can kill an American President, these insinuations and slanders have become a lamentable but routine part of political life.

When Jeremy Thorpe came into my office early in January 1976, and said he wanted to talk to me, I was preoccupied with anxieties about the imminent publication of the London and Counties report. I was totally unprepared for the conversation that followed as Jeremy sat down on a small stool, crossed his legs, and asked:

'Have you heard about my hot head?'

'No', I said. 'What hot head?'

'I think I will have to tell you about it – it could lead to some publicity.'

Puzzled, but with my interest fully aroused, I listened as he went on:

'There's a man called Norman Scott who is going to appear in a court case in Devon as a witness because his dog was shot. He is going to allege that he had a homosexual affair with me and that I paid to have his dog shot as a warning to him to keep his mouth shut.'

For a second, I could only gaze at him in astonishment. It was a situation so beyond anything I had previously experienced that I did not know how to react. Eventually, I burst into laughter.

'Why should the newspapers want to publish rubbish like that?' I guffawed.

'I am not saying they *will* publish anything,' he answered

solemnly. 'All I am saying is that they *might*, and I thought it was only fair to warn you.'

After he left, I pondered on the meaning of the interview and decided – how wrong can a man possibly be? – that it was of little significance. The press, I was sure, would not publish such allegations and the matter, though unpleasant, would soon be forgotten. I continued, for a few days afterwards, to treat the matter as a joke. 'Shot any dogs, lately?' I would say when I saw Jeremy, hoping that a ribbing might help him throw off a mood of quiet desperation that seemed to have settled on him.

The joke – and how I regret making a joke out of it now – did not last long. Suddenly, the pressmen who were by now coming to my office regularly began dropping hints about documents which were being held by their offices, photo-copies of letters which they seemed to think had very serious portents for the Liberal party. Finally, at one of my press lunches, one of the best-known political commentators in the country warned me: 'Thorpe will not be the leader of the Liberal party by the end of February.'

I suppose I must confess that I had been particularly obtuse in this matter. I could still barely grasp the possibility that the word of a man like this strange male model Norman Scott could be taken seriously – but it finally dawned on me that there could be real trouble ahead. I began to make my own inquiries. David Steel told me about the 1971 discussions on the allegations, and said he was satisfied that Jeremy was 'in the clear'. He did add, however, that he lost many nights' sleep over the matter. Emlyn Hooson, whose experience as a QC allowed him to apply a brilliantly analytical mind to the subject, said that in 1971 there was not enough evidence to give the allegations any weight.

I spoke again to Jeremy, this time a great deal more seriously, and he assured me that Scott had a record of psychiatric trouble. Would I make sure that the police in Devon knew about this record, he asked? By now thoroughly concerned, I arranged a meeting with Roy Jenkins, then the Home Secretary, and went along with David Steel. Hesitantly, I asked Roy if he thought it would be proper to bring the psychiatric evidence to the attention of Devon police? Roy, a man of the highest possible integrity, said he would draw the attention of the police to Scott's background – but could not, of course, interfere any further.

We had done all we could. The visit to the Home Secretary was in no way an attempted cover-up, but a move prompted by genuine concern to ensure that the police had all the facts available. From then on, we could only sit and wait ...

With all the viciousness of what seemed a malign fate, both storms broke on the same day. Thursday, 29 January 1976, was the day when the destruction of Jeremy Thorpe began, the day when the Liberal party took its biggest public beating since the war, and the day that started, for me, eight weeks of nightmarish quality. Had I been able to foresee them, they would have prevented my standing for Parliament at all.

It began, ominously enough, with the publication of the Department of Trade report on the London and Counties bank, whose losses were finally estimated to be in the fifty million pounds region. The report was bad – for Jeremy and hence the party – but not bad enough to be disastrous. The report totally exonerated him of any blame for the collapse, but observed that it 'must remain a cautionary tale for any leading politician'. More seriously, when one considers that a man's judgement is his greatest political asset, the report outlined the role of a company director: 'Unless he is properly informed of the affairs of the company he joins, he cannot make his own judgement on the propriety of its transactions.'

Jeremy, I knew, was to issue a statement admitting he had made an error of judgement. This sort of honesty, I felt, would satisfy public concern and allow him to escape without too much damage to his reputation. As I sat alone in the Chief Whip's office later that day, I was in a mood of reasonable self-satisfaction. The London and Counties hurdle, which, I was still convinced, was the biggest the party had to clear, had not been so high after all. Then the phone rang.

'This is Bob Carvel of the *Evening Standard*,' said a voice. 'Is Jeremy going to issue any statement about what has been said in Barnstaple Court?'

To use the language of the detective novel, my blood froze. There was a distinct prickling in the hair at the back of my head. The feel of my hand on the receiver took on a distinct clamminess.

'Why?' I croaked. 'What has been said?'

It had started, and we were all caught unawares. We had been expecting Scott to make his allegations when he appeared as a witness in the dog shooting trial. Instead, he himself had been taken to court on a minor fraud charge involving social security payments, and had blurted out the remark: 'I am being hounded by people the whole time because of my sexual relationship with Jeremy Thorpe.'

'I don't know where Jeremy is at the moment,' I told Bob Carvel. 'I'll try to track him down.'

I walked up to Jeremy's office, but it was empty. By the time I returned to the Whip's office, bedlam had broken loose. The place was packed with reporters – hadn't I told them a few weeks before that my door was always open – and all the phones were ringing. Questions were fired at me left, right and centre, questions I couldn't answer because I didn't *have* any answers. In the midst of this chaos, I realised with sickening clarity that I had completely misjudged the situation: Scott's allegations were not to be ignored but, worse, they were to be taken up like some huntsman's tally-ho. The hounds were in full cry, and because no one could find the fox – I still didn't know where Jeremy was – I was to be the substitute quarry.

I think now is the time to make my attitude clear towards the Thorpe Affair. I believe to the depth of my soul that a politician's private life is his own affair, and should remain so unless private behaviour jeopardises his political role. I suspect that most men and women in this country have a skeleton rattling away in a cupboard, and I think it should be allowed to stay there unless it can be proved that its exposure can right some injustice to another individual. That does not mean I believe Jeremy Thorpe did have an affair with the unspeakable Norman Scott, for as far as I am concerned, no proof has been provided either way. But proof or no, I do not – and did not, that day in January – think it mattered one way or another. I am sure the vast majority of the British people agreed with me then, and still do, for – thank God – they are a forgiving race. Until the minute I walked back into my office, I thought the British press reflected the compassion of its readers. I was wrong!

I now know, although I didn't then, that Scott had been

hawking his story round Fleet Street for months, if not years, and that almost every newspaper in London had photostat copies of various letters which were to leak out in the coming weeks. Some newspapers have claimed, since, that they didn't use this material in print because they were not satisfied that Scott was telling the truth. With my newfound cynicism towards the press and its motives, I do not accept that explanation. What stopped them printing, I believe, was the law of libel. Scott, they knew, would make a poor witness in a libel case, with his chequered past and background of psychiatric care. So they had to find some other way to print their scandal.

They found it, as some MPs have done in the past, in the laws of privilege. The courts, like the House of Commons, are protected by privilege, which means anything said within their walls can be published without the threat of civil action for libel or slander. From time to time, MPs have made allegations in the House which they have refused to repeat outside its walls, knowing full well that to do so would bring the lawyers down on their heads. In the Thorpe Affair, the press lowered itself to the same depths. Why else was the tiny court at Barnstaple packed with reporters from the national press? Were they interested in the case of an unknown self-confessed homosexual charged with obtaining the munificent sum of twenty-nine pounds twenty pence by misusing a supplementary benefits book? The answer, of course, is a resounding No! I now know that Scott had tipped off journalists about his carefully rehearsed 'outburst'. They gathered there, like so many vultures, so that they could rip at the flesh of their still living victim, impervious to counter-attack because of the law of privilege.

I did not know this background as I tried to restore some order in my seething office on 29 January. All I knew was that something had to be done, quickly, and that Jeremy Thorpe was the only man capable of doing it. But where was he? I cleared the office on the promise of a statement later, and began phoning around. I eventually traced him to the office of his solicitor, Lord Goodman, possibly the most influential lawyer in Britain at the time. He had already heard of the news from court. He asked me if I could arrange a meeting with Lord Byers and Lord Wigoder, another Liberal life peer and a prominent

QC. He was to issue a statement, and he wanted the very best legal advice.

Two statements duly followed. Of the London and Counties débâcle, he admitted an error of judgement and said: 'I placed total reliance and faith in quarters where it is now, alas, all too clear that confidence was wholly misplaced.'

To an extent, this satisfied the financial journalists: he had made a mistake, and had admitted it openly, and that, it seemed, was that.

To the pressmen consumed with curiosity over the so-called 'sex scandal', the statement about Scott was far from satisfactory. It said, tersely: 'It is well over twelve years since I last saw or spoke to Mr Scott. There is no truth in Mr Scott's wild allegations.'

With that out of the way, Jeremy returned to Orme Square, locked the door, and told his housekeeper to answer all phone calls by saying that he was not at home. For him to lie low was, I expect, a good idea, but it still left me to fend off the hounds. I must repeat that there are only two officials in the Parliamentary Liberal party – the Leader and the Chief Whip. With the Leader unavailable, I took the brunt of it all. I remember remarking to one of my colleagues: 'I'm glad I had always opposed blood-sports. If I hadn't, I would have been forced to change my views – I now know what the fox feels like.'

All that afternoon, all that night, reporters knocked on my door, or came on the phone, demanding extra information concerning incidents about which I either knew very little or nothing at all. They pursued me that night to the National Liberal Club, where I had a room, and the following day they chased me down to the West Country. I was due to attend a Liberal weekend gathering in Totnes and the press took every available room in the hotel where I was staying. When I answered the phone, which I soon stopped doing, it was the press. When I opened my bedroom door, there was a pressman in the corridor. When I went down for breakfast in the morning, they even joined me at my table.

All I could say, and I kept on saying it, was that the Parliamentary Liberal party thought the whole matter ludicrous and irrelevant.

As that long and desperate weekend progressed, however, it became increasingly obvious that the press had information about the case which – to my knowledge, at least – had never been made available to the Liberal party. The question which began to grow in my mind and, as I learned later, in the minds of my Parliamentary colleagues, was that the situation might be considerably more complex than we first realised. Were we dealing with a simple if sordid matter of sexual aberration – true or false – or had there been something more sinister, like a 'cover-up' operation? The very unpleasant word 'blackmail' was constantly on people's lips. Scott was making even more dramatic claims; that Jeremy had lived with him, had stolen his Insurance Cards, had even threated to have him murdered. We seemed to be losing contact with reality ...

It was at this point that another shadowy figure from the past was dragged out into the limelight in the person of former Liberal MP Peter Bessell, our member for Bodmin from 1964 to 1970. Bessell, one-time party 'whizz-kid' and a close colleague of Jeremy Thorpe, had run into a series of business difficulties on retiring from Parliament and – I had been told – had 'disappeared' across the Atlantic leaving a wife, two children and a welter of debts. I had never met Bessell, nor have I done so since, but I knew that he had made small but regular payments to Scott over a period of two years or more in the late sixties. These payments, proved by photostat letters Scott had given to Liberal MPs, had been the centre of the 1971 party inquiry. The reason for the payments has never been made clear, because attempts to trace Bessell to explain them had failed. Jeremy Thorpe denied they had any connection with him.

Suddenly that weekend, Bessell ceased being the man from the past and became very much the man of the moment although, as yet, no one knew his whereabouts. The *Daily Express* 'broke' the story of the Bessell–Scott payments, and the other papers flocked to follow it up. On 31 January *The Times* reported that I had known about the payments 'but that concerned Mr Bessell's personal affairs and was not related to the Liberal party, nor did it have any connection with Mr Thorpe'. Bessell, said *The Times*, was believed to be in Venezuela.

The confidence with which I made statements on the 'irrelevance' of the situation was to be progressively eroded during the hectic days and weeks that followed.

Other mysteries arose and were dismissed, often in the space of hours. I discovered that Scott had been interviewed by Jeremy Thorpe's Tory opponent in the North Devon constituency, Tim Keigwin, and that a copy of the statement had been sent to Tory head office. I had no idea of the purpose of the interview, or the reason for the keeping of Scott's statement, but it seemed an unusual piece of electoral manœuvring. On 31 January the press made a great play of this information, unaware – as I was – that it was no more than a red herring. Tory head office, however, took it very seriously.

On 1 February the secret of the 1971 party inquiry into Scott's allegations leaked out, when Lord Byers was quoted as having called for a Scotland Yard investigation. 'The Commissioner of Police reported that there was no basis on which action could be taken,' said the party's elder statesman.

On 3 February there was a major development which momentarily seemed to ease the situation. Bessell was tracked down, not to Venezuela, but to California by the *Daily Mail*, which carried a front-page story under the headline: 'MY PART IN THE THORPE AFFAIR.' I read the story eagerly, and with great relief settled on quotes from Bessell which said: 'Payments were not made in connection with any blackmail attempt. It seemed peanuts at the time. The idea that I paid him to keep quiet is rubbish – absolute rubbish. It was purely an act of charity.'

My relief was shortlived. If Bessell had slammed the door closed on one corridor of speculation, another one, wider, longer and more sinister, was opened up. On the very same day, the *Daily Mirror* reported perhaps the strangest twist so far – the payment of two and a half thousand pounds to Scott on election day in February 1974 by a country doctor. I was becoming dazed by the number of almost surreal characters involved as the plot of this weird drama thickened, but a country doctor was one of the most puzzling yet. Why should a doctor give one of his patients such a large sum of money in return, as it was alleged, for a bundle of documents, including letters between Bessell and Scott? Where did the money come from? The *Mirror*'s main headline blared: 'MALE MODEL AND THE £2,500 PRESENT.' But a smaller, secondary headline really said it all: '*Riddle of gift to Thorpe accuser.*'

Riddle was the word, although I would have perhaps used something stronger which, out of simple decency, could never have appeared in public print. By this time, my orderly little world of just five days previously had become a swirling whirlpool of rumour, innuendo, malice and downright slander. There was talk of an affidavit from Bessell, which Bessell was now denying. There was the mystery of Scott's shot dog. Reporters, MPs, members of the Lords were coming to me in a constant stream, reporting the latest gossip. Conservative Head Office had paid the two and a half thousand pounds, said one. Others were even wilder: peerages had been sold, bribes had been demanded, even murder had been contemplated.

Some of the stories were so contradictory that someone, somewhere was not telling the truth. The press were, of course, clamouring for my view on the latest developments, and I told them in my normal forthright manner. The next day, 4 February, I was quoted as saying: 'Somebody is telling bloody lies ... but I don't know who is telling them.' It was a statement that shocked some of my colleagues, and I accept it was not the sort of language normally expected from a Parliamentarian at the centre of a very delicate issue. But I was bewildered by conflicting 'evidence', badgered by hordes of reporters, and my temper gave out. At least I was telling the truth.

What the press did not know about, however, was one of the strangest incidents in the entire saga. On 3 February, Jeremy and I had taken a few minutes off from the drama to discuss Parliamentary business, in the forlorn hope that we should be allowed to get on with the work we had been elected and were being paid to do. A new Speaker, George Thomas, was to be installed in the Commons that day, and we were discussing Jeremy's speech of welcome. There came a knock at the door and, to my vast surprise, in walked the Prime Minister.

'I want to have a word with you, Jeremy,' said Mr Wilson.

I asked if he wanted me to leave, but he shook his head and went on: 'Have you finished your speech for George Thomas yet?'

Jeremy smiled ironically. 'I've been trying to get on with it, but one or two problems have cropped up.'

'I am aware of that,' said Harold. 'But I don't necessarily believe all I read in the press.'

I again offered to leave but the Prime Minister replied that this was not necessary. He turned to Jeremy. 'There will be an interlude this afternoon at about four pm – perhaps I could see you then behind the Chair for a few minutes.'

The Prime Minister has a private office off the Commons chamber, literally 'behind the Speaker's Chair'. In a break during the installation ceremony later that afternoon, Jeremy left our bench and strolled across the floor. He was gone about thirty minutes.

As he plumped himself down beside me, an enigmatic expression on his face, I expected him to say something. He remained silent.

Impatiently, I asked: 'Have you met the PM, then?'

'Yes,' he answered tersely.

'Well?' I queried.

'Well, what?'

'Well – what happened?'

My curiosity was obviously unwelcome but, apart from my personal and I think understandable interest in this strange encounter, I felt I had an official interest, as Chief Whip, in anything which affected the position of my party leader.

'We were talking on Privy Council terms,' said Jeremy, trying to draw the veil of secrecy by invoking the tradition that as both he and the Prime Minister were Privy Councillors, anything that passed between them could remain a matter of total confidence.

'Come on – is it good or is it bad?' I pursued the point, emphasising that, as Chief Whip, I too ought to share his confidence.

Eventually, and with reluctance, he confessed, 'It's good. It will be pushed on to South Africa.'

The total and utter mystery of this remark brought my train of thought to a dead halt. Bewilderment, which, until a week previously, had been a rare state in my life, was becoming an everyday thing.

'What the hell does that mean?' I demanded.

'The PM believes that there are South African influences at work,' snapped Jeremy, and it was obvious from his tone that no further information would be forthcoming.

That evening, I sat on the bench of the House of Commons totally oblivious of the speeches going on around me. What sort of a world have I come into? I kept asking myself. I didn't think it would be like this when I 'left' Rochdale for the big outside world. I wasn't accustomed to feeling bewildered. I wasn't accustomed to feeling out of my depth. But here, obviously, were machinations totally beyond the compass of my experience.

There was no time to brood. The following day, the Parliamentary Liberal party was due to hold its normal weekly meeting in committee room seven of the Palace of Westminster. Normally, these meetings were a pleasant, often amusing 'think-tank' session where future plans and policies were discussed to a background of gentle banter. As Chief Whip, I knew that meeting on 4 February would be no picnic. Already, several members had approached me, expressing grave doubts about the background to the Thorpe Affair. Concern was deepening, not just for the leadership, but for the future of the party as a whole.

Jeremy took the chair on a raised bench overlooking the rest of the room. As Chief Whip, I sat to his left. The looks on the faces of my colleagues demonstrated without doubt that some serious talking was to be done.

It was Emlyn Hooson, with his incisive mind, who began. It was time, he said, for Jeremy to answer some of the allegations that had been made against him. Jeremy protested, but I advised him that it was in the interests of the party to answer the questions. He was obviously under great stress, touchy and nervous, but Emlyn interrogated him gently and firmly, referring always to Norman Scott – which was, in fact, an alias – by his real name of Norman Josiffe. One by one, Jeremy answered the questions refuting totally any of the allegations against him. It was a superb, convincing performance by a man obviously under strain, and you could sense the growing pleasure in the room as our doubts began to fade.

That night, I issued a press statement which received wide coverage the following day. Jeremy Thorpe would stay on as

Leader of the Liberal party, the headlines proclaimed. Members of the party had reaffirmed their support. The report which gave me the greatest pleasure was, in fact, contained in one word from me in the *Daily Telegraph*: 'Afterwards, Mr Cyril Smith, the party's Chief Whip, when asked whether this closed the matter so far as the Liberal party was concerned, replied "Yes".'

I did truly hope that it was all over. The press, however, thought differently. They went through one of their incredible U-turns and decided that it was the Parliamentary Liberals who had been persecuting Jeremy Thorpe! How they justified that incredible 'double-think' I do not know, after the behaviour of the newspapers during the previous eight days. Nevertheless, the *Daily Express* chose to rerun the story on our meeting on 6 February – thirty-six hours later – under the headline: 'THE AMAZING TRIAL OF JEREMY THORPE'. Our meeting, said the report, had turned into a 'star chamber or a kangaroo court'. This was so hurtful to other Liberal MPs and myself – after all weren't we investigating matters raised by the press? – I include here a document handed out at the meeting by Emlyn Hooson. It shows, I think, our true feelings:

> *I think we all share the deepest sympathy with Jeremy Thorpe and his family over the appalling way the allegations against him have been made and the way in which he has been hounded.*
>
> *However, it is high time that the Liberal party generally, and the Liberal Parliamentary party in particular, tried to take a firm grip on the now deteriorating situation arising from Norman Josiffe's (alias Scott) allegations against Jeremy Thorpe. We owe it to ourselves and to the country to do this and to try to bring the matter to a speedy and proper conclusion. Unless we do this, then there is a real danger of allowing the conditions to build up to a major tragedy for both the party and for Jeremy and his family, out of all proportion to the nature of the allegations made against him originally – even if they were true. Jeremy Thorpe has vehemently denied the allegations now, as he did in 1971 when I first put them to him.*
>
> *They must be kept in the right perspective. They are allegations concerning Jeremy Thorpe's private life at a time which is now, on any view, at least twelve years ago and before he was ever leader of the party. In a democratic society a man's private life is properly*

regarded as his own and whereas it may be the subject of public inquisitiveness it is not properly a matter of party concern, unless it is criminal or scandalous in relation to his position. What is important to the party and to the public at large, in the ultimate, is that the party Leader has good judgement and the discretion to be entrusted with high responsibilities. It is entirely on this basis that the Parliamentary Liberal party must, as must the party in the country, review the situation in relation to their Leader.

It would be an appalling injustice and a condemnation of our democratic society if Jeremy were to resign merely because the party is embarrassed by allegations which were untrue. The Parliamentary party at least have a broader back than to tolerate that situation. On the other hand, if there is a sound basis of truth in the allegations, Jeremy Thorpe owes it to the party, which he has led so well and so ably, not to lumber us with the stark choice between apparent disloyalty and engagement in a kind of cover-up, which I do not believe the party would indulge in, in any event.

No one would doubt that Scott, who I met in 1971 when the complaint was first made to me, has, as his former wife has said, a fixation about Jeremy Thorpe and is emotionally unbalanced. No reasonable or detached person would accept his word, without corroboration, as against that of any eminent public man. This is not to say that his evidence is to be dismissed lightly; it must be carefully assessed. In 1971, I pressed him to produce to me letters he claimed were written to him by Jeremy Thorpe. These clearly could have been good corroboration but he either could not or would not produce them. Clearly, he was a person who could easily be used, even unwittingly, by persons who wish to do an ill-service to either Jeremy Thorpe or to the Liberal party.

However, the matter does not end there, as it did not in 1971. The man who holds the key to the truth of the situation is Peter Bessell. He never came in 1971 to face Frank Byers, David Steel and myself in an interview to answer questions about the letters which he undoubtedly sent and the money he undoubtedly paid to Scott. Jeremy Thorpe has always completely denied that any of these payments was made with his consent or knowledge. Bessell never made himself available to be questioned by the three of us on the matter. I have now heard of the statements he is alleged to have made, both in the newspapers and on television and radio, and I think that he owes it to the party, which was so good to him, and to Jeremy Thorpe himself to come back to this country immediately to explain the situation.

In the ultimate, I come back to the position of the Liberal party. It cherishes the tradition and achievements of generations of people who believed in Liberal ideals and it is now the repository of the hopes of millions of people in this country for the further achievement of Liberal ideas. It is bigger and more important than any one or more persons within it. It would be untrue to itself if it for one moment allowed its Leader to become a sacrificial lamb in the face of highly embarrassing but untrue allegations. On the other hand, we owe it to ourself, to our traditions and to our hopes for the future to act swiftly if, in our judgement, the allegations have any sound foundations of truth.

I trust, therefore, that the Parliamentary party will find it possible to resolve this matter within days on a proper and Liberal basis, so that we can get down to the more rewarding task of developing our future policies and programmes.

I think Emlyn's document magnificently summed-up the feelings of the people in committee room seven. I think the fears and anxieties it expressed were justified, and the sympathy for Jeremy and his wife genuinely heartfelt. What the press did not know, and no one outside that room really knows till this day, is the generosity which was shown that night. There were still too many unanswered questions, but the meeting decided unanimously to accept Jeremy's word. The motion that he should be reaffirmed as Leader was put by Emlyn Hooson himself, although the lawyer in him was still obviously far from satisfied.

That became apparent over dinner after the meeting, when Emlyn, with great seriousness, proposed a toast: 'I will drink to your health, Jeremy, but I'm afraid I fear for your future.'

The *Daily Express* painted a picture of a star chamber in which we, the Liberal MPs, were supposed to be baying for our Leader's blood. In fact, we accepted his word as the word of a gentleman. In view of the hysterical press campaign which, in all honesty, had made the meeting inevitable, I think the *Express*'s remarks about a 'kangaroo court' were hypocrisy on a monumental scale.

I returned home to Rochdale that weekend hoping that the incident could be forgotten as, almost exactly, a seven-day wonder. The *Daily Mail* came to see me, and on the Saturday carried a feature under the headline: 'IT'S THE WORST WEEK OF MY LIFE, SAYS CYRIL SMITH.' The article observed, with some accuracy, that a new Cyril Smith had emerged, 'angry and sharp'. I spoke with obvious cynicism, it said, when I told the reporter: 'I have learned things I did not know about the way the system works.'

Were they really surprised?

We were allowed a month of comparative peace, and hopes began to rise that the affair really was over. There was still speculation over the source of the two and a half thousand pounds gift to Scott, but throughout the country, support was rallying to Jeremy's side. Letters poured in by the hundred, a few critical, but the vast majority expressing support. We kept a file of these pro and anti letters, and the 'pros' eventually stacked up a fantastic nine hundred and eighty. March came and we were involved in campaigning again in the Coventry South and Wirral by-elections. By-elections had always inspired Jeremy and some of his old sparkle returned. On the day before the poll, sitting on the bench in the Commons, he turned to me and said: 'A pressman has told me that the two and a half thousand pounds came from someone close to me. I'd love to know who it was.'

The following day, the *Daily Mirror* telephoned and asked: 'Do you know who David Holmes is?'

'No,' I said, 'who is he?'

'He was Jeremy's best man. He paid two thousand five hundred pounds.'

Of all the thousands, perhaps millions, of words written or spoken during the Thorpe Affair, these two short sentences came as the biggest blow. Whether or not Jeremy knew of the payment, the relationship was too close to pass a test of public credibility. A politician without credibility is as effective as a jockey without a horse. The electorate, to our great misfortune, are willing to vote for the most unlikely policies as long as they are proposed by a leader they find credible. When that credibility is destroyed, the finest of policies face destruction too.

Jeremy was electioneering in the North-West, and I could not contact him. The second, and greatest explosion of the affair was at trigger-point and I was unable to warn the victim. Eventually, he telephoned me on Friday.

'Do you know who David Holmes is?' I asked.

'Of course I bloody well do,' he snapped angrily. 'He's Rupert's godfather' – referring to his son, Rupert, by his first wife, Caroline.

I told him of my conversation with the *Daily Mirror*. There was a long pause.

'Where does that leave me?' he asked finally.

It was not a time for mincing words.

'In a bloody mess,' I replied.

The story broke that evening. David Holmes, a wealthy Manchester merchant banker, and a former Deputy Treasurer of the Liberal party, issued a statement through his solicitors admitting that he had paid the two thousand five hundred pounds for letters written to Scott by Bessell. The payments, said the solicitors, were made 'entirely on his own initiative and in particular without the knowledge of Mr Thorpe'.

All hell broke loose once again: the phones, the reporters at the door, the anxious queries from MPs and Liberal peers: 'Is it true? Is it true? Is it true?' Jeremy was on a train from Liverpool to London, and Alistair Mickie, an assistant in the Whip's Office, was despatched to join the train at Watford to warn Jeremy that the press were waiting at King's Cross. When he heard the news, Jeremy insisted he must make an urgent and important phone call the minute he arrived at Euston. Whatever the call was, it wasn't to me, although I was waiting with the greatest anxiety to speak to him.

Quite naturally, the papers on the Saturday ran riot with Holmes's statement. There was great play on Holmes's relationship with the Thorpe family. 'I PAID £2,500 TO NORMAN SCOTT, SAYS THE GODFATHER,' said the *Daily Mirror*. The 'Godfather' title, quite legitimate, took on a sinister ring because of its association with the popular book and film about the Mafia. It gave the tabloids a natural headline, just another of the tiny splinters of ill-fate which seemed destined to stick in the skin of the Liberal party.

For me, as Chief Whip, the crisis was compounded by other things I read in the newspapers that weekend, or from unofficial 'tip-offs' on the telephone. I read that Jo Grimond, commenting on our disastrous show in the Coventry by-election – we dropped thousands of votes and lost our deposit – was saying that the Thorpe Affair was harming the Liberal poll. It was a remark that would have been better not made. I read that my friend and neighbouring MP Richard Wainwright, was seeking a meeting with Thorpe. Richard, a lay preacher and a man of the most rigid principles, had suffered more anguish than any of us as the Thorpe Affair revelations unfolded one by one. But he should not have announced the meeting with Thorpe without at least advising the Chief Whip. Then I was tipped off that David Steel had been offered the Chairmanship of the Race Relations Board, a matter he had never discussed with the Chief Whip.

The fact that Cyril Smith was the Chief Whip is not the point I am trying to make. I had no desire to be at the centre of a continuing round of scandal and internecine party warfare. The strain was already beginning to show physically, and mentally I was tied in a thousand knots. The Liberal party was falling apart at the seams. Liberals who ought to have known better, were sending ridiculous letters by the score. Anarchy seemed the order of the day. I doubt whether there has ever been a case in recent history when a political party needed more desperately to demonstrate a carefully reasoned public solidarity. To do so would have needed long and soul-searching deliberation, and those deliberations could only have been conducted through the Chief Whip's office. Yet it just wasn't happening. The office I had tried so hard to make a centre of co-ordinated and united action was being totally ignored.

And still the press were surrounding me like Apaches round a circle of wagons. The phone never stopped, driving not only me, but in particular my mother, to the verge of screams. Outside in Emma Street, journalists camped out in their cars taking it in turns, every now and then, to hammer on the front door.

Saturday passed in this jangling nightmare, and still I had been unable to speak to Jeremy. Finally, on Sunday, he telephoned and casually delivered the *coup de grâce*. He had spoken to the Liberal party President, Margaret Wingfield, and it had been agreed that he would resign at the party assembly in Llandudno in September, and immediately seek re-election under new rules, to be formulated, which gave the rank-and-file Liberal members the right to elect a new leader.

In this momentous piece of wheeling and dealing, the Chief Whip's views were considered unnecessary. There was no point in releasing it to the press, for Jeremy had already done so – and, indeed, I saw the news on television within thirty minutes. It was obviously time for a decision. What was the point of undergoing the crippling battering to which I was being subjected in the hope of keeping the party together, if the party thought my office unnecessary? That evening I discussed the possibility of my resignation as Whip. My mother, my sister Eunice and my brother Norman all urged me to quit. Perhaps they could see something in my physical appearance I was unaware of. That night I went to bed, exhausted, demoralised and – bluntly – sickened by the whole business of politics.

I began vomiting uncontrollably at about four am the following morning. At first, I thought it was a nervous reaction to the stress of the weekend. After two hours, when I was feeling pitifully weak, my mother telephoned the doctor. Immediately, I was rushed to Birch Hill Hospital – to a public ward, I might add. Gallstones were diagnosed, and I was put under heavy sedation. Unbeknown to me, the press and TV crews were, by mid-morning, already besieging the hospital. The medical staff kept them at bay, but an enterprising *Daily Mail* reporter discovered my ward had a mobile telephone – a coin-box on a trolley – which could be pushed to my bedside. He put in a call.

I was as honest as I could be, perhaps too honest, but I was at the depths of a physical and mental slump and I was heavily sedated. The following day, the *Daily Mail* read: 'Cyril Smith plunged the Liberal party into a fresh crisis last night by revealing his desire to quit as Chief Whip.

'Sick and disillusioned, he largely blamed his intention on the troubles that have engulfed his party leader, Jeremy Thorpe.'

I was quoted as saying: 'I am rather frightened of what may yet come out ... I have not been told everything known about the affair, even by members of my own party. There are things going on I know nothing about. I am being made to almost carry the can for something that's nothing to do with me.'

These comments, which I have never denied although I

might not have given them had I been in a better state of health, were to be widely interpreted as a personal attack on Jeremy Thorpe. Leaders were to appear in the newspapers urging me to 'belt-up', that I was harming my own party by speaking my mind. This, of course, was another example of press hypocrisy at its worst. They hound a man until he says something, and then turn round and pillory him for saying it. If he says nothing, however, he is accused of denying the public its right to the truth. It's a battle you can't win.

I was not alone, that first day in hospital, in showing signs of cracking under the strain. In London Jeremy Thorpe was apparently reaching the end of his self-control. During the day, my mother had been complaining to newspapermen that I should resign because the pressures had become intolerable. At about midnight, after the first editions of the newspapers were leaving the presses, news reached Jeremy that the *Daily Mail* was saying I might resign, and that other papers were quoting my mother's remarks.

Sometime after midnight, my mother was roused from her bed by the telephone. It was Jeremy, obviously in a blinding temper. He told her, bluntly, to keep her mouth shut, and demanded the number of the phone in my ward. So at one am I was shaken from a drugged sleep and a furious Sister pushed the squeaking telephone trolley the entire length of the ward. I took the call to a background of angry mutterings from rudely awakened fellow patients.

'Is it true you are going to resign?' he demanded.

'No,' I replied drowsily, 'but I'm thinking about it.'

He paused, and said 'We'll ask Alan Beith to stand in for you while you are ill. You can have the job back as soon as you are fit – if you want it.'

While my own little drama was being acted out in Birch Hill Hospital, another, infinitely more mysterious, was taking place in the Chamber of the House of Commons. Harold Wilson got to his feet and told the House that the South Africans were behind attempts to smear Jeremy Thorpe. It was out at last!

He said: 'I have no doubt at all there is a strong South African participation in the recent activities relating to the Leader of the Liberal party.' Hedging his bets, however, he placed no blame on the South African government, but hinted that the smear was the work of private agents representing big business. The statement, coming out of the blue at a routine Question Time, threw the House into a state of confusion. As the *Daily Express* was to say the following day, 'MPs were baffled.'

I was certainly baffled when I read the papers, and remain baffled to this day. Of all the enigmas attached to the Thorpe Affair, Harold Wilson's intervention is the most mystifying. I was one of only three people, I believe, who knew of the meeting between Harold and Jeremy five weeks previously, and our conversation on the bench still remains for me a matter of intense speculation.

If the Prime Minister had concrete evidence to justify his remarks in the House, why was his statement so vague? Why, anyway, should he wish to rush to the aid of the Leader of an opposition party? Without being too derogatory, Harold Wilson never built a reputation as a political Good Samaritan, particularly towards members of other parties. If the South African allegations were a calculated red herring, one can only assume that Harold was eager for the Liberal party to hold on to its vote-catching Leader. It was, of course, the Liberals who had given Labour power in the previous two elections, by luring votes from the Tories. So was this intervention at least as helpful to Harold as it was for Jeremy? Or were there other considerations?

I doubt we will ever know the answer, unless Harold 'tells all' in his memoirs. Whatever the reason, it needs to be good. The South African Connection was never taken very seriously, not even by the press, to whom it was surely a source of much sensational material. As Robert Carvel wrote in the *Evening Standard* on 10 March: 'Jeremy Thorpe had still to struggle to keep afloat today, even with the lifebelt kindly tossed to him by the Prime Minister.'

Other headlines on 10 March had more import for me. 'EVA'S SHOCK AT MIDNIGHT' – 'A PHONE CALL FROM JEREMY UPSETS MUM,' said the *Daily Mirror*. My mother, never one to back down without a fight, had related the story of Jeremy's phone call. 'He just started attacking me without warning,' she was quoted as saying. 'I was flabbergasted and terribly upset. I just couldn't say a word to defend myself. I just broke down and cried like a baby.'

The *Daily Telegraph*, under the headline 'SMITH ADVISED TO QUIT BY RELATIVES', reported more soberly: 'Family and local party pressures may force Mr Cyril Smith, the Rochdale MP, to resign as Liberal Chief Whip, despite his protestations that he has not finally made up his mind. Close relatives were yesterday confiding their concern that the Thorpe Affair could undermine Mr Smith's health.'

The writing, for me at least, was not on the wall but throughout the national press, although it was not solely my health that was causing concern. Liberal MPs, even the most loyal supporters, were beginning to worry about the effect of the strain on Jeremy. David Steel telephoned to warn me that Jeremy's behaviour was getting stranger. The warning was reinforced during a visit to my home by John Pardoe. Eventually, Alan Beith, as Acting Chief Whip, came to see me, saying he was conducting a poll to establish if the MPs thought that Jeremy should resign.

I considered my reply very carefully, and spoke with profound regret when I told him: 'Yes, I am afraid so. I accept that nothing has been *proved* against him, but the credibility of the party is being eroded so fast that unless he goes, we will be ground down to dust.'

I came out of hospital after a week with strict orders to give up smoking – which I have done – and to lose ten stones in weight – I shed six of those ten within six months. My doctors warned me to slow down, my mother, brother and sister were urging me to resign, and my relationship with Jeremy had become all but impossible.

When I returned to Westminster, I found that moves were under way to sack me – moves which began to leak into the newspapers. I was furious, and it led to a serious exchange between myself and Alan Beith. Was I to be used as some sort of public scapegoat for the party's problems? Was I to be blamed for the Thorpe Affair? I insisted that I must be allowed to resign in my own time, and not before I had had a long talk with Jeremy.

On 24 March, I saw him in his office, when, despite the rumours of the 'sack', he urged me to stay on. I asked if he intended to resign.

'Certainly not,' he replied. 'I'm bound to win. I have the

three most important people in Britain on my side – Harold Wilson, Lord Goodman, and MI5.'

It was yet another of those unreal remarks. What did it mean? By this time I was too jaded, too disinterested, in the towering ramifications of the affair. I tendered my resignation, knowing that Jeremy had only postponed the fateful day.

The state of my health was given as the reason for my resignation, and this was a major part of the truth. My illness, the warnings from doctors and family, the rigidity of my new diet, left me without the mental or physical strength needed to see the affair through, and I was by then convinced that worse was to come. I resigned, not without a little bitterness, for Chief Whip had been my first and only important job in Parliament. To lose it in a flurry of rumour, spite and downright smear, was an unfitting end to the ambitions I had held for the job. At the same time, I underwent a soaring, spinning sense of relief that no longer would I be even a secondary target for the mudslingers. I was a victim of the Thorpe Affair, as were many others and, indeed, as was the Liberal party itself. Yet in some ways I went, a willing lamb to the sacrificial altar. I was the innocent party who had paid the price, but I regained my freedom.

I became, once again, an ordinary back-bencher, surrounded on the Liberal benches with others who were as demoralised and dispirited as myself. All the zip, all the bright ideas, had gone. Jeremy's decision to stay on as Leader until September, and seek re-election, had, on the surface, been accepted by a majority of the party, but even those who had voted 'Yes' were far from certain in their decision. April passed in a mood of desultory moping and moaning. Depression began to seep into my very bones.

The axe finally fell on 6 May, Polling Day in the Municipal Elections. The executioner was the *Daily Mail*, which had for so long and so assiduously probed every angle, upturned every stone, in the Thorpe Affair. That day, its banner headline proclaimed: 'I TOLD LIES TO PROTECT THORPE.'

Peter Bessell had also found the strain too great. He stated that he had made the payments to Norman Scott as part of a cover-up operation, in the hope it would prevent the loathesome male model standing up in court to make allegations against Jeremy. The final act of the great witch-hunt was under way. Newspapers, television, radio went off once again at full cry. On 8 May, the *Guardian* carried the headline: 'BESSELL TO TELL ALL ON THE THORPE–SCOTT LINK.' The story carried quotes from Bessell saying, 'I am sick of carrying the can. I am at the disposal of the party for any further investigations they wish to make into this matter. I did my best to help the poor kid at Jeremy's request, and every penny came from my own pocket.'

On 9 May, the *Sunday Times* carried a six-point categorical denial from Jeremy of all Scott's allegations. I think it is necessary to publish it here:

When Norman Scott made his outburst in Court, I issued a brief statement that I had not seen him for twelve years and that the allegations were baseless. I would have hoped that the assurance would have sufficed, but I am advised that a further refutation in the most categorical and unqualified terms is necessary.

Mr Scott has made the following allegations against me:

(a) The existence of a homosexual relationship with me.
(b) That I stole his National Insurance card.
(c) That the Liberal party, Lord Byers and others have made him from time to time subventions to keep him quiet.
(d) This referred to an allegation that Mr Thorpe or his wife 'had hired a gunman at a five-figure sum'.
(e) That the identity of the gunman was, variously, my helicopter pilot, or a Liberal worker in the Devon and Cornwall region.
(f) In addition it is alleged that I was acquainted with, or involved in a correspondence between Scott and Bessell and that I knew or was involved in the purchase of the Bessell letters from Scott for a sum of £2,500.

All these allegations are totally false.

At the same time, the *Sunday Times* carried photographs of letters written by Jeremy to Scott in February 1961, and September 1962. These letters, which had been in the hands of Scotland Yard, were written in friendly terms and for the most part, seemed innocuous enough. They discussed Scott's various difficulties, and photographs: one which Jeremy wanted returned in 1961, and another – or perhaps the same one – which Jeremy was unable to send to Scott in 1962.

The phrase which seemed to puzzle everyone, the press in particular, was the final line of the first note: 'In haste, Bunnies can (and will) go to France.'

The combination of effects of Bessell's admission about a cover-up, and the apparent affection expressed in the letters, was electric. Throughout the country, politicians, pressmen and the general public were avid with gossip and doubts.

On the Saturday night, as the *Sunday Times* was coming off the presses, Richard Wainwright went on radio to discuss the latest situation. Jeremy's six-point denial had already gone out over the Press Association wires to every newspaper and broadcasting station in the country.

Richard, as I have already said, had taken each successive revelation of the affair with increasing despair. He found the rumours, the smears, the half-truths and the out-and-out lies deeply repugnant, personally, and of the gravest public concern, politically.

On the radio that night, he asked calmly when Jeremy Thorpe was going to issue a writ against Scott to have his name cleared in a public court.

Jeremy chose to make this broadcast the last straw, which I think was grossly unfair to Richard who, in all honesty, was only expressing views which were the gossip of virtually every tap-room, bus-queue and political committee room in the land.

On 10 May Jeremy resigned. As Alan Beith, the new Chief Whip, was out of the country, he sent his letter of resignation to David Steel. It accused the press of a sustained witch-hunt, and complained: 'A parliamentary colleague has now taken to the air publicly to challenge my credibility.'

He added: 'No man can effectively lead a party if the greater part of his time has to be devoted to answering allegations that arise and countering continuing plots and intrigue.'

Whether that barb about 'plots and intrigue' was aimed at his fellow MPs I do not know, but if so he misjudged our feelings. We all agreed with Steel's letter of reply which said: 'Your personal qualities of leadership, charisma and sheer perseverance, and your triumph over adversity, are held in the highest regard.'

My own feelings were of deep compassion, of numbing sadness, and a burning anger that such an outstanding man should have been brought down in such a shabby manner. Nevertheless, my political judgement told me that the resignation was necessary – in fact, that it had been delayed too long. Jeremy, I think, did much harm to the Liberal party by obstinately clinging on to the leadership. I also think he did himself much damage. The more the affair continued, the more the public began to question. No right-thinking person in this day and age would give two hoots about the allegations of a homosexual affair twelve years or more previously. Whether it happened or did not happen is a matter of no importance. What did matter was the public disquiet raised by the continuing, sickening revelations which, again true or false, nevertheless exposed some undeniably damning machinations by members of the Liberal party, from its very centre to its ultimate lunatic fringe.

We sat back and thought, once again, 'Well that's that.' Once again, we were wrong ...

The press, which had shown merciless determination to ferret out the rotting of a scandal a decade and more old, went into its ultimate *volte-face*. Suddenly, it wasn't Fleet Street which had hounded Jeremy Thorpe over the precipice – it was us, his fellow Liberal MPs.

On 11 May *The Sun*, taking on an unaccustomed role as keeper of the nation's political (rather than moral) conscience, carried one of the most vitriolic pieces of journalism I have ever read under the headline: 'THE ASSASSINS'.

In it Walter Terry, a commentator with close contacts within Harold Wilson's inner circus, wrote: 'In the end, Liberal leader Jeremy Thorpe was reduced to nothing but a shadow.

'He has become a broken man, destroyed by innuendo, the contempt of colleagues he should have been able to trust, and by the assassin's knife.

'Never before has the leader of a political party in Britain been driven out of office by such an evil concoction of smear, scandal and confused allegations.

'The Liberal party will pay dearly for this. Rightly so. When it comes to the dirty work, they are pure Chicago.

'Day by day, inch by inch, the Liberals whittled down their

chirpy, ebullient leader to the level of a sordid backstreet intrigue.'

The *Liberals* whittled down Jeremy Thorpe inch by inch? Was it members of the Liberal party who sat in that magistrates' court in Devon, hoping to catch a carefully rehearsed 'outburst' under the cloak of the laws of privilege? Was it the Liberals who offered Scott's first wife money for her story? Was it the Liberals who invested huge sums of money and time to track down Peter Bessell in California? Was it the Liberals who pressured David Holmes into admitting that he had paid Scott two thousand five hundred pounds? Was it the Liberals who telephoned me in hospital when I was drugged half-conscious, or who crowded round my stretcher as I was pushed from ward to X-ray room?

Was it the Liberal party which was paying the salaries of two freelance journalists who, as late as 7 August, were still working for the BBC investigating wild rumours of South African agents, Mafia-style negotiations for planned 'contract' killings, the sale of honours etc., etc., etc. . . .

Of course it was not!

It was the press and, on occasion, the broadcasters, who launched, sustained and eventually brought to grisly fruition the campaign that destroyed Jeremy Thorpe's career. If an assassin's knife were ever wielded, it flashed in Fleet Street, not Westminster. Members of the Parliamentary Liberal party were unhappily forced into a corner from which there was no escape by the pitiless weight of disclosure upon disclosure. Our party rank and file turned on us, too, demanding that we make a stronger defence of Jeremy. They did not know we were powerless – we dared not issue denials which may be proved untrue the following day . . .

But it is all over now, I dearly hope. One man's life has been irredeemably broken, and others will bear scars to the end of their days. The only reason I have gone into the affair in such detail is to pose my final question: What were the motives that inspired the press campaign?

Like every politician in the world, I was totally mesmerised by the American press's handling of Watergate, how great reporters brought down a man who was subverting the apparatus of the most powerful state in the world to his own ends. Watergate, I imagine, will never be paralleled as an example of the role of a free press in a democratic society.

Very early on in the Thorpe Affair, a gloating reporter told me that this was to be Britain's Watergate and, it is true, a sort of Watergate fever seemed to grip Fleet Street as rival newspapers battled to outdo each other in sensational revelations. But Watergate? Can Jeremy Thorpe, a man of real talent and sincerely held opinions, be compared with Richard Nixon? Was the bringing down of the leader of a popular minority party in any way comparable with the toppling of a paranoid American President?

The comparison is absurd.

The motives of Fleet Street in this affair can only have been one of three. None of them, in my opinion, can do anything but stain the reputation of a free press.

Was it, firstly, just the need to get in on the act? Once the ball was rolling, did the entire industry feel it had no choice but to kick out with the rest? If this is so, my heart is heavy with the thought that there was not an editor in Fleet Street with the strength of character to say: 'I will have nothing of this sordid affair.'

Was it, secondly, merely the need to sell newspapers, the compulsion to serve up ever more spicy courses of sensationalism to keep the money rolling in? If this is so, I hope there are men of conscience in the newspaper industry today who feel a genuine remorse that the reputation of a good man was butchered for the benefit of such jaded palates. Even the Romans tired of feeding Christians to the lions to keep the mob happy.

Or was it, thirdly and much more sinisterly, the action of a politically motivated Fleet Street, aware and afraid that Jeremy Thorpe was leading a party which was threatening the cosy, if ineffectual, two-party system? Furthermore, had they realised that the success of the Tory party could be achieved by destroying the Liberal party – a cause for which a few newspaper proprietors would prostitute the British press. If this is so, there will be journalists, editors, or proprietors who, one day in the not too distant future, will regret the destruction of one of the few truly able men on the desolate British political scene and the demise of a third party in British politics believing in freedom.

The press often boasts of its duty towards the public, and it is by the public that it will eventually be judged. The newspapers thought they were doing a praiseworthy job by hounding Jeremy Thorpe, but I have yet to meet one single member of the public, and I make it my business to talk to ordinary people everywhere I go, who has not expressed loathing of the press treatment of the affair.

At a time when Britain is crying out in desperation for leaders of vision, the extinction of a small but inspirational flame was a grave disservice, not just to the Liberal party, not just to Parliament, but to every man, woman and child who lives in this nation!

CHAPTER TWELVE

Where Now, Land Without Leaders?

If we would not give power to Ted Heath in 1974, why prop up Jim Callaghan's creaking administration in 1977? David Steel's decision to lead the Liberals into an arrangement of support for Callaghan was subject to several grotesque misunderstandings helped along by an incredible campaign of vituperation by large sections of the national press. Most newspapers decided, without too much thought, that it was an attack on Margaret Thatcher and her Tories. In some ways, of course, it was. Certainly we robbed her of the prize of her personal desire – indeed it was even rumoured that she had started measuring curtains for No. 10. But to me, and to some of my Liberal colleagues, the major target was the far end of the political spectrum, the extreme Left of the Labour party.

First, consider the differences in the political situation between February 1974 and spring of 1976. Ted Heath had just LOST a General Election, largely because many millions of likely Tory voters had supported the Liberal cause. Was our party then supposed to turn round and say, 'You helped keep Heath out, but we disagree. We are going to put him *in*.' That would have been a major break of faith which Jeremy Thorpe decided, after lengthy consultations within the party, would have been totally unacceptable to our electorate.

When Jim Callaghan lost his tiny working majority through a handful of by-election defeats and deaths of sitting members, an elected government was facing the crucial 'crunch' in its attempt to tackle the country's worst economic crisis since the 1930s. Not only the Liberals thought it was necessary for Labour, however unpopular – and I agree, they were probably the most unpopular government since the war – to be nevertheless allowed to get on with the job; rumours of an election wiped more than a billion pounds off the value of shares overnight as the stock market tottered on the edge of hysteria. An unusual area of support for Callaghan, proved that the professional money-men, too, wanted at least a stay of execution and did not want a General Election.

Stage Three of the Social Contract was, of course, the crucial anxiety for the money-men, the Liberal party and for millions of sensible people throughout the country. An *orderly* return to collective bargaining was an absolute necessity for the country's economic survival. Ultimately, the demands of the managers and the skilled workers whose pay differentials have been totally eroded must eventually receive the financial recognition for the skills on which the very future of Britain depends. But were we going to reach that happy situation in an orderly manner – or in a stampede by the big battalions of the unions, with the weak and unrepresented being trampled underfoot once again?

Only a government capable of dealing with the unions in an atmosphere of mutual confidence could achieve a reasonably stable solution. Who was more fitted to lead that government: Jim Callaghan or Maggie Thatcher? The answer was so obvious that the question was hardly worth asking in the first place. Largely because of its own pathetic economic policies, the Labour government had worked itself into a position where, having led the country into the sinking sands, it was nevertheless the only one with a lifeline with which to pull us out again.

I do not pretend that it was a pleasant choice; I do not like the Flash Gordon style of politics, when our poor hero, having landed himself in some appalling predicament, can write in the next exciting episode, 'with one bound, he was free ...' Sadly, it was the *only* decision. We Liberals felt that we had to bite on the bullet and endure it.

The position within our party had also undergone a fundamental change. David Steel had announced to the world that he wanted a realignment of power, a place at the centre of influence. 'We must stop being a debating society', he had told our Annual Conference the previous autumn, and despite protests from a highly vocal minority, had carried the vast majority of our supporters with him. Having decided this course of action, it was only a matter of time before it was put into practice.

WHERE NOW, LAND WITHOUT LEADERS?

A series of disastrous by-elections for Labour during the winter of 1976 and spring of 1977 set the scene.

The trouble was, with thirteen Liberal MPs we could only act if the Conservative party flexed its flabby muscles in unison – and for several months Mrs Thatcher seemed happy to sit this one out!

Jim Callaghan was well aware of this situation. Early in the year, David Steel and I discussed our campaign to win a position of being able to win real influence over the government, and it was decided that I should try to meet the Prime Minister: I did, after all, know him quite well from my days in the Labour party – he had once sat down and had tea at my home in Emma Street, Rochdale. Jim, however, was not going to play this game unless he had to. Number Ten sent a 'brush-off' message, asking if I, instead, would meet Cledwyn Hughes, Chairman of the Parliamentary Labour party. That may sound an imposing title, but to me it carries very little weight: Cledwyn is a backbencher like the rest of us. He is a man I deeply respect but still a back-bencher in real terms, I therefore rejected the offer, and looked round for another angle of attack.

It came by chance on 11 March, when at a dinner in Manchester I found myself sitting close to Michael Heseltine, one of the heavyweights in Mrs Thatcher's Shadow Cabinet.

'Why don't you put a censure motion down?' I asked. 'You might get Liberal support.'

'Are you serious?' he asked, and I nodded.

The Great Censure Motion drama was under way. The motion was ended, as everyone is aware, by the Liberal party being given consultation rights on government policy for a period of *six months* approximately, on condition that we would support them in censure motions. For the first time for half a century or more, the Liberal party had an effective say in *policymaking* by the government of Britain.

The Tories cried 'Foul' and the press clamped the Liberals into the pillory once again. It has long been a Socialist cry that most of Fleet Street is the tool of the Tory press barons. I have never believed it fully, not even during the worst excesses of the Thorpe Affair. Now, I am afraid, I believe it is true: there are newspapers who will slant news for the political whims of their owners. There is no other conclusion I can draw. The press barons of this country, nurtured on class and privilege, seek to destroy the Liberal party in order to strengthen the Tory party.

The Liberals were attacked for 'playing politics', as though we had no right to engage in the game which Labour, Conservative and Nationalists have turned into a blood-sport. For once, we had bared our teeth and, in no small way, had won. We had learned a little from our political opponents!

I have no hesitation in admitting that, as things turned out, the March censure debate was 'engineered' by the Liberals. It gave us a real say, a real influence, which, since the election of David Steel as our leader, had been our stated policy. Our motives, however, were widely misunderstood, leading, as it did, to the bad result of the Stetchford by-election, when we lost our deposit and suffered the humiliation of finishing behind the National Front – a party I loathe!

We were condemned for seeking power for party political reasons, a trait we have so roundly condemned in our opponents. This, I am glad to say, is NOT true, for had it been so, I could not have supported the action.

Firstly, let me emphasise that had Mr Callaghan refused the Liberals our consultative arrangement, he would have fallen. No worry about the Liberal performance at the election which would have followed would have stopped us trooping into the lobbies with the Tories. This was the unanimous decision of the Liberal Parliamentary party at a secret meeting forty-eight hours before the censure debate. Let there be no doubt about that – no deal, no support – we were quite determined and quite unanimous.

My reason for supporting the Prime Minister, shared by several of my colleagues, was not to attack Mrs Thatcher, although I bear her no great love, but to wound the single sectional interest which, to me, represents the greatest single threat to the future stability of this country, the Labour Left wing.

The attacks of the Tories following the censure debate were no more than the expected election-hoarding sneers, the obvious spoilt-child retorts we readily anticipated. They stole our seats in the Commons just like overgrown schoolgirls, but that is what I expect of them. Our real satisfaction, however, came from the deep snarl of pain from the Labour Left wing which suddenly awoke to the astonishing truth that they no longer controlled the government; no longer could they foist extremist measures on a reluctant country through the art of political blackmail practised against their own party.

The regrets I had and still have were that we had not been in a position to combat the Left earlier. Had we done so, the shipbuilding and aircraft industries would not have been nationalised. The Community Land Act would not have reached the Statute Book; the dockers would not have been given the right to pose an even greater threat to the country's lifelines at the whim of politically orientated leaders. If only we could have had that influence earlier and in greater strength.

As it was, Mr Callaghan agreed to drop a Bill to increase the scope of direct labour forces in local government – too often proved hopelessly costly and inefficient – which was the only Left wing measure still to be enacted during that term. It was a small but significant victory. We also had a commitment to direct elections to a European Parliament, and a return to the Devolution debate.

If Britain as a country is to benefit in the short term from the working relationship between Labour and Liberals, it will be from this cause: our balancing effect against the doctrinaire demands of the fringes of the Labour party. If we are to benefit in the long term, our alliance, so heavily criticised, could one day be seen to have been a turning point.

What Britain desperately needs is a realignment of the moderate centre of our politics, the area representative of the will of the vast majority of people which, because of the rigidity of the two-party system, has become important. The test will come when Mr Callaghan decides if he wishes to continue to another year in office, which he can do only with continued Liberal support. That means that his next Queen's Speech will have to be written in consultation with David Steel, and I can assure you will contain no further stepping stones on the way to an Iron Curtain style Socialist state.

How will the Labour Left react to that? My bet is that they will choke on their own gall. They will be left with two *stark* decisions: to allow a 'liberal' – with a small 'l' – government, or to bring their own party down (and, incidentally, lose many of their own seats in the process!). If that happens, the disintegration of the Labour party as it now stands will begin – and the Age of Realignment will be on us. What a pity it is that the tool of the Tory party – the British press – fails and failed to see this truth.

Perhaps I am being over-optimistic. The next year or so will tell. If realignment does not come, I fear for the future, but I wish to discuss that at the end of this book.

In the meantime, I would be wrong not to discuss some of the people I have met in a lifetime of politics, some of whom have given me great pleasure, others some pain...

The only contribution I made towards the election of David Steel as Leader of the Liberal party was to devise the system by which he was elected.

He was not my choice for the job, as the media, quite fairly, made clear during the contest, but he was elected fair and square by a large majority of the Liberal rank and file and, because of that, no one can question his right to the job. In a contradictory sort of way, that was probably my greatest contribution to the party, one of the few concrete achievements of my brief if climactic office as Chief Whip.

Immediately on taking that job, I became aware there was a growing rift between the Parliamentary Liberals and the card-holding members throughout the country. The regular complaint from the regions was that they had too little influence on their MPs' thinking, that their views were too often treated with disdain. If there was any single grievance which justified these criticisms, it was the party's method of choosing its Leader which, by tradition, had been the sole prerogative of the Parliamentary party. Certainly, the Liberal Lords were consulted and, as I believe, probably carried too much influence in the decision. But the workers, the canvassers, the stickers-on of stamps, the local Councillors and the fund-raisers, believed they were totally ignored. MPs were *supposed* to consult the constituency parties and were *supposed* to base their individual vote on constituency advice, but all the evidence suggested that these were suppositions that rarely became realities.

Even before the Thorpe Affair exploded, a groundswell of opinion was growing which questioned the right of the MPs to make this all-important decision. A committee was looking into the constitution of the party, which in itself pointed to changes in the leadership process. Anxious to avoid a head-on confrontation between the Parliamentary party and the grass-roots, I began to look for a mutually acceptable method of election.

The opposition I received inside Westminster came as a shock. Several MPs, including David Steel and Emlyn Hooson, were opposed to permitting the Party members to vote in the leadership. Our members in the Lords acted very much as I expected: 'By all means get more democracy in the party, old boy, but let's not allow it to run rampant!'

As the Thorpe Affair progressed, and it became obvious that we might have to actually elect a new leader, rather than merely argue about the rules for his election, a decision had to be made. My major concern, as I judged the mood of the regional parties, was that an election open to all members might in fact come up with a leader unacceptable to the Parliamentary party – there was even an outside possibility that he might not be an MP at all. So I drew up a compromise procedure, which gave the MPs the right to nominate the candidates, and the entire membership to vote for their favoured nominees. This scheme was eventually adopted by a special conference in Manchester, and only slightly watered down: I had wanted nominations backed by a third of the Parliamentary party – meaning a maximum of three candidates – whereas the conference accepted nominations from a fifth of the MPs.

As it happened, only two candidates went forward, David Steel and John Pardoe. I threw my weight behind John who was well beaten in the poll.

My reasons for backing John Pardoe, and opposing David Steel, have been widely misunderstood. So, strangely enough, have my reasons for not standing for election myself, although I set them out very specifically at the time. Perhaps I was too specific, for it is possible to make a very good case for the argument that the cynical media and public of this country suspect politicians who say things directly and honestly.

In my case, the cynicism came into the open when I declared that I had no personal interest in the leadership of the Liberal party. Why not? asked the incredulous press. Because, I said, I did not think I was intellectually suited for the job. I didn't have the sort of mind to mull over problems at length before coming to a considered decision. I didn't have the diplomacy to listen to conflicting wings of party thought and then reconcile the differences. I don't think I could have been more open, but so few politicians admit to weaknesses in private – much less voice them in public – that some sections of the press refused to drop the idea that this was part of some devious campaign to attack the leadership by stealth.

My attitude towards David Steel was equally misunderstood. In a world where everything must be black or white, it was widely assumed that I had a deep, personal grievance against David. Nothing could be further from the truth, because I have always found him an exceptionally agreeable man – indeed, a man in many ways far more likeable than John Pardoe, whose abrasiveness can sometimes turn into stinging rudeness.

My arguments over the merits of these two men had nothing to do with their personalities – they are both magnificent companions – or their abilities – they both possess talents head and shoulders above the normal Commons herd – but about their *style*.

David, like Jeremy Thorpe, is a drawing room politician, a smoother-down of ruffled feathers, a man who leads with gentle pressure from behind. I think he lacks the killer instinct which I believe to be necessary if the Liberal party is ever to drag itself out of its gentle minority status to become a full-blooded and effective political force in this country.

It would be difficult to invent a more opposite character than John Pardoe, a rough-and-tumble protagonist who insists on saying what he means however hurtful that may be to the recipient of his invective. John, who accepted the tag of being a 'bit of a bastard' during the contest, is as tough as a diamond, both physically and intellectually. He is the sort of man I believed necessary to take the Liberals 'over the top' like a Great War infantry commander. He could well lead the party into the very muzzles of the machine guns, and there would no doubt be many casualties, but I would much prefer to go down on the attack rather than under the remorseless attrition of static political warfare.

Make no mistake, I was very disappointed when David Steel defeated John Pardoe so decisively. I refused to serve in any office under him until he proved he could pull the party back together, and I also refused to go electioneering in any of the Liberal constituencies which had voted against John Pardoe. I would, I agree, have been wise not to communicate these views to the press, who, having used them avidly, then turned on me once again to accuse me of 'petulance' and 'sour grapes'.

I have, however, stuck to my guns. I accepted a minor post as party spokesman on social services because David has proved that he can hold the party together – his magnificent speech at the Llandudno Assembly in September 1976 amply demonstrated that. I do not intend to go electioneering in constituencies which rejected John Pardoe's brand of politics – and therefore mine – because I consider that their votes were a vote of 'no-confidence' in our methods. Campaigning is a hard and harrowing business, making great demands both physically and mentally which I can no longer readily spare. I most certainly cannot squander them in areas which prefer a different sort of campaigning to mine.

If these remarks are to be construed as 'petulance' and 'sour grapes', then let it be so. I would like to point out for the record, however, that I have never questioned the Liberal party's right to make its democratic choice – after all, did not I play a major part in giving it that choice?

With the leadership settled, and some of the scars of the Thorpe Affair beginning to heal, there came a time for re-assessment, for the re-establishment of political policies, of personal relationships. It was a time for me to reflect on my achievements in a lifetime of public service both local and national – a time to count memories. I realised that the milestones of my life were measured out by the people I had met, rather than ambitions conquered, and it will probably come as no shock to my readers that few of the really outstanding people I have met have been politicians.

Even before I was an MP I had come into contact with members of the Royal Family. The Queen, such a diminutive figure, had been forced almost on tip-toes, despite the podium on which she was standing, as she pinned my MBE on my lapel in 1966. A twinkle in her eye suggested she wanted to make a joke; her strong feelings of correctness no doubt stopped her. She probably thought a joke about my size would be offensive, so she merely wished me a happy year of office as Mayor of Rochdale.

Her husband, Prince Philip, is less concerned about the correctness of things. In fact, I am tempted to believe that he deliberately stirs tranquil waters for the sheer mischief of it. I have met him on more than one occasion, but I remember one elegant luncheon party in Manchester City Hall for organisers of the Duke of Edinburgh Award Scheme. The drinks table was groaning under bottles of every wine and spirit known to man, as far as I could see. There was whisky, gin, vodka, brandy, martinis, sherry, port, the lot.

'Would you like a drink, Sir?' someone asked.

The Prince surveyed the serried ranks of bottles with grave introspection.

'Can I have a pint of ale?' he asked finally.

There was a flurry of panic in the room. Councillors whispered to clerks, clerks whispered to deputy clerks, deputy clerks whispered instructions behind raised hands to uniformed flunkies. After five or ten embarrassing minutes, a gold-braided servant came into the room, carrying a red barrel over his shoulder. Behind him, more men carried gas cylinders and plastic pipes.

More silent minutes passed, as the men struggled to erect the equipment. Finally, with much spluttering and fizzing, a pint pot was filled and handed to the Prince.

'Thank you, gentlemen,' he said. 'I hope it will be worth the wait.'

All around him, men and women who had been standing with full, but untouched gins-and-tonics, sherries and brandies – they could not drink before their royal guest, could they? – tossed back their glasses with relief.

The Prince surveyed the room over the top of his pot, the laughter lighting up his eyes. You could almost hear him thinking: 'Well, that's unstuffed a few shirts ...'

It is unfashionable, now, to be a vocal supporter of the Monarchy, but fashions have never given me much cause for concern. I think this country has a truly magnificent Royal Family, and our debt to them is too rarely expressed. As our constitutional head, the Queen allows us to preserve our national feeling while, quite rightly, we observe and criticise our political leaders without qualm. No President can happily fill this role: America's suffering over Watergate was grossly magnified because Nixon was not only the nation's political leader, but he was also the symbolic First American. Watergate sank the knife into a dubious politician, but also wounded Americanism itself. As for the many people in Britain, and not a few MPs, who constantly carp on the cost of maintaining the Royal Family, I say we get a sensational bargain. On the public relations front alone, the Queen, by her foreign visits and the entertainment at home of foreign visitors, can do more in a few hours than all the slickest public relations men from all the most expensive advertising agencies in the Western world could do in their entire careers!

I have not yet met Prince Charles – if he cares to invite me to dinner, I will gladly go! – but I suspect he will make a fine monarch. He seems to have inherited some of his father's *steel*, and if he can combine that with his mother's *charm*, the Throne will be in good hands – and good hands may be needed, if some of the subversive elements in our society continue to gain power at the present rate. And talking about 'steel', I cannot let this passage go without mention of my favourite 'Royal', Princess Anne.

By agreeing, at a few days' notice, to visit Rochdale in 1975, she helped me save an event I hold very dear, the Rochdale Youth Music Festival, which my former Labour colleagues on the town council were trying to axe as an economy measure. I managed to raise the three thousand pounds needed to save the festival – which has done sterling work in creating musical interest in the town – and Princess Anne's presence gave the occasion the final touch of gilt.

Anne is very much my sort of person: tough, knows what she wants, and – within the constraints of her position – a rebel. When she arrived that day, I found it totally impossible to call her 'Your Highness'. Instead, I merely said, 'Hello, Anne, nice of you to come,' as if I were addressing any other attractive young woman. Aware of her reputation for having a sharp tongue, I waited for the rubuke, but none came.

We chatted for several hours on the Anne and Mr Smith level – she didn't call me Cyril, unlike everyone else I have ever met – and she revealed a considerable knowledge of music. She told me, having found learning the piano difficult, she had taken up the kettle-drum, which she still enjoyed playing!

That evening, after what had been, for me, the most delightfully informal formal occasion I had ever attended, I thanked her with real sincerity and she said: 'That's all right, I enjoyed it. Next time, you must ask my mother.'

Suspecting a leg-pull, I laughed and replied, 'Go on, lass – the Queen would never come here.'

'Don't be so sure,' she replied, tantalisingly. 'She often sends me out on pioneering missions. If I report back that it had been a good day, she might well consider it next time.'

When I set out on my career twenty-five years ago, I never dreamed that I would end up on first-name terms with a Princess. I never dreamed, either, that I would become some sort of a 'personality' in my own right, and that television studios would become a second home. Unlike many politicians, I thoroughly enjoy appearing on TV because, again unlike the many others, I do not mind saying what I feel to be the truth. The men and women who face difficulties during interviews, particularly on live television, are the ones who, constrained by party dictates, cannot say what they really mean. Evasiveness not only gives a good interviewer the chance to go for the throat, figuratively speaking, but it also *shows* that cameras don't lie, only politicians. The hesitant stutter, the bead of perspiration on the forehead, the nervous fluttering of an Adam's apple, tell an audience far more about a politician than a million words.

Robin Day, is undoubtedly, the doyen of the TV interrogators. He is held in awe, if not in terror, by many of my colleagues at Westminster and many of the ill-disguised attempts to 'gag' the BBC which have emanated from Westminster in recent years have been sparked off by a barbed question from Mr Day. Despite this, I find him an extremely likeable man who, off camera, exhibits a remarkable shyness. Not for him the back-slapping bonhomie in the 'hospitality room' before the broadcast, where interviewees are given a couple of quiet drinks to calm their nerves. Robin, instead, sits quietly in a corner, studying the script. He has done his homework: he has read up all the press cuttings on the subject at hand, and has studied the careers of the people he is to interview. That's why he is an impossible man to 'flannel'. That's why I enjoy my appearances with him.

There are others, mainly youngsters, who see themselves as the Robin Days of the future, who can be rude and boorish. They are not incisive, merely impudent. They are the ones who need to be slapped down – I do it with relish – but, sadly, too many of my colleagues allow them to escape.

Other TV appearances I have made, on the strictly entertainment front, have brought more criticism down on my neck. I once attended a medieval banquet at Worsley, Lancashire, along with Jimmy Savile. When I joined in the community singing, Jimmy blurted out: 'You've got a nice voice there, Cyril, you must come on my programme.' That's how I ended up singing *She's a Lassie from Lancashire* on *Clunk-Click*. It led to another invitation, to take part in a comedy routine with Les Dawson. I went, and enjoyed that too. There was no applause from the Liberal party.

'Knock it off, Cyril,' they said. 'You say enough funny things as it is, without turning into a professional comedian.'

It's a point of view that I do not accept, and although this particular incident was on a fairly trivial level, it reveals a much more important deep-seated difference over party policy. When I am electioneering, or in fact speaking anywhere, my greatest hatred is addressing rows of empty seats. If you are Prime Minister or Leader of the Oposition, people will come to listen to your meetings because you are a political 'star' in your own right. If you are a humble back-bencher, from a minority party at that, your chances of filling a political hall are virtually nil. You may have the greatest political message ever handed down to man – except that there will be no one there to receive it.

That's why I took, and still take, any available opportunity to appear before the general public and, in particular, before the non-political general public, for it is *their* votes that we have to win. The politically committed, the ones who attend public meetings, have already decided which way they will vote: however brilliant your oratory, the chances of changing their minds are minuscule. So, copying the American style of mixing show-business with politics, I have done everything I can to become and to remain a *personality*. It has grave disadvantages, like the complete loss of privacy in public places, but I believe it wins votes – and that, as far as the Liberal party is concerned, is my job.

Apart from the political advantages to be gained by walking the peripheral paths of show-business, there are also the very personal ones – like meeting interesting people. As a species, I find the majority of politicians utterly boring: tedium is the normal state of their lives. Show-business people fascinate me and not for the obvious reasons of their wealth and fame. Theirs is, in fact, a very similar type of work, except they have to be much better at it than politicians. They can never be guaranteed comfortable, lobby-fodder lives by benevolent party masters. They have to win every 'election' they fight, for every appearance they make is in fact a demand for the public's vote that they should be allowed to appear again.

I find them kind, thoughtful, stimulating, and funny. Jimmy Savile admits openly that his work as a disc jockey is a joke, but his record of public service and charity must be unequalled. Les Dawson, television's perpetual buffoon, is a man of the deepest political insight. While I was talking to the ballet dancer Rudolf Nureyev at a cocktail party in Number Ten, Downing Street, my mother fell into conversation with Doris Speed, the actress who plays Annie Walker in *Coronation Street*. It was the only party we attended at Number Ten – Harold Wilson had organised it for the visit of Canada's Liberal Prime Minister Pierre Trudeau – but what does my mother remember about the evening? Doris Speed invited her to go down onto the *Coronation Street* set at Granada Television studios in Manchester! She went with the greatest excitement, and although she didn't have a drink in the Rovers Return, she did have a cup of tea with most of the cast.

And, as I said, these people are funny, and political life today is very short on humour. Harry Secombe, on a visit to Rochdale to sing in a concert, did his best to keep me in his dressing-room drinking during the whole of the first act. When I protested I must see the show, he said: 'Don't worry man, you're missing nothing – I'm not on until the second half.' Ronnie Corbett, when he was appearing at a Manchester theatre, gave me one of the more hilarious evenings of my life when he came to a Liberal party Burns' Night Supper in Rochdale. I was wearing a kilt (a local businessman had agreed to buy ten tickets for the supper if I would don the tartan: he paid up!) and it is not difficult to imagine the incongruity of the tiny Ronnie next to me and my multi-coloured tent. He limped into the hall and would only explain: 'I fell off a ladder decorating the skirting board.' The photographers loved it: I had to spend half an hour trying to prevent Ronnie filling my sporran with whisky.

I have learned to grab evenings like that by the shoulders and shake every last drop of pleasure from them, for of all the things that I have suffered during my stay in the House of Commons, my sense of humour seems to have fared the worst. It is not just the fact that the Commons, with all its distinguished history for drollery, now believes that witticism can be adequately replaced by the shouted insult, just as football crowds have replaced marvellous shafts of sarcasm with chanted obscenities. It is not humour alone that is dead. This priceless commodity is just one of the casualties of recent years, along with individual brilliance, rhetoric, passion and compassion.

All of these five things, which from time to time should shine a brilliant light into the cold grey corners of Westminster, have gone. That makes the House of Commons a much poorer place to work in and causes me a terrible personal loss. From the point of view of this nation as a whole, there is the serious loss of a quality which, above all else, that Chamber should provide ... the quality of leadership.

When I look round the House of Commons, when I listen to the speeches of its so-called 'stars', my heart bleeds for Britain.

At a time when the country cries out for leadership, what do we have to offer? The prospects look grim.

James Callaghan, the Prime Minister, got the top job after a series of ministerial disasters, particularly as one of the most damaging Chancellors of the Exchequer in history. He is a sincere man and, on a personal level, a very likeable and honest man. He is a trier but, I suspect, not a succeeder. He lacks, in my opinion, the intellectual ability for the job, but he cannot acknowledge it. His abilities are largely irrelevant anyway because he is rapidly losing control of the Labour party to his own Left wing. Callaghan's power to act can only shrink in inverse proportion to the irreversible growth of the Left.

There is Margaret Thatcher, the iceberg, tough as nails, who will be, in my opinion, a total disaster for the Conservative party. I have little doubt she will be Prime Minister after the next General Election but her disdain of minority interests prophesies disaster. Her lack of warmth and her very approach even before negotiations start, will lead the Conservatives inevitably into yet another, much more damaging, confrontation with the trade unions.

Michael Foot, the best orator in the House, is nevertheless past his best. He holds his beliefs with great sincerity, but his beliefs come from doubtful sources. He will continue to take the word of the TUC as his unquestioned gospel, despite the fact that a mere fifth of the British people are members of unions, and those who are members are no longer represented in any democratic sense by the TUC leadership.

William Whitelaw is an able man but, for my liking, too smooth and too soft. He is an exceptional negotiator, a supreme mediator, but not a leader. He makes an ideal Number Two or Number Three – *but to whom?*

Roy Jenkins, of course, can no longer be considered, because he threw in the towel by taking one of the Common Market's top jobs. Intelligent, efficient, but rather self-opinionated, he may have saved the Labour party from its Left wing extremists. In the end, he gave up the fight.

Michael Heseltine is possibly a future leader of the Conservatives, but only if he can live down his reputation for erratic behaviour. In many ways he is a man after my own heart; tough, emotional, spontaneous. But when he picked up the Mace and swung it round his head in that notorious Parliamentary fracas over the ship and aircraft nationalisation Bill, he shocked the old-style Tories to the core. Will they ever let him forget?

Shirley Williams is a clear thinker, an exceptional debater, and a fine administrator. Because Parliament is such a cynical place, her greatest attribute is her greatest failing: she is too *nice*. Nice people, much less nice *ladies* rarely reach the very top in our present politics. She lacks the killer instinct to trample down opposition, friends and foes alike.

And finally, Wedgie Benn, who can do more harm to British

industry in one speech than the combined efforts of the Luftwaffe and the U-boats did in the whole of the last war. Many men are made by their backgrounds – I most certainly was – but he has been *destroyed* by his. In his frenzied attempts to discard his silverspoon and his inherited title, he has also discarded much political commonsense. I suspect that he will one day be leader of the Labour party which would mean the destruction of the party for a generation or more as a credible political force.

The list makes dismal reading as Britain faces greater pressures on its social fabric than it has ever known in peacetime. With politicians discredited, at best, and generally despised, at worst, where else are we going to find the strength to keep our society together in the tortuous years ahead?

The Churches? Sadly, their influence is now negligible. The middle classes? They, too, have been destroyed and demoralised by taxation and inflation. The trade unions? To put them forward, with their totalitarian attitudes, would be to make a sick joke. The High Court? The House of Lords? Both bodies are now under attack from the Left for daring to question the absolute power of a Labour government, and, significantly, I have heard no suggestions from the Left of how they should be replaced with bodies of real Constitutional power.

Can we fall back, then, on the traditional British virtues – tolerance, self-sacrifice, simple good sense? These undoubtedly exist still in large sections of the community, but can only be effective within a framework that allows them expression. The framework is being dismantled, day by day, by the refusal of Parliament to heed the will of ordinary folk. The little man is being stifled. Big Brother – in the guise of Big Business, Big Trade Unions, Big Party Machines – is taking over.

The ultimate result of these trends, unless someone, somewhere, halts them very soon, can only be revolution followed by dictatorship. Whether it is a revolt by the Left or Right, whether we face living under the Left or the Right, is of little importance. What we must do, in the next ten years, is to recognise that this threat exists and must be faced. It can only be beaten by a massive show of strength from the ordinary, middle-of-the-road men and women of this country.

There will no doubt be politicians who attack this dismal

view of the future as 'scare-mongering'. There are journalists who will write much the same thing. But I wonder if those who attack the idea publicly will be among those who have discussed it, privately, and have come up with similar conclusions. For the last three years, ever since the miners brought down Ted Heath, there have been long and passionate discussions in all the rooms of Westminster except the Chamber of the House of Commons, in the bars, in the restaurants, even in the splendid marble halls of the toilets, about the possibility of revolution in this country. I am by no means the only MP who thinks that it is not only possible, but, in fact, quite likely *if* the present situation is allowed to drift.

No one will say it publicly, of course. The party Whips wouldn't like that, and the Whips, like the Ministry of Truth in George Orwell's *1984*, control political thought – or at least, publicly expressed political thought. So Members of Parliament happily don their muzzles and do nothing about the direct threat to our freedom since the days before the signing of the Magna Carta.

Why is revolution impossible? Because of our historic traditions? Yet our traditional freedoms are being whittled away, day by day, with hardly a word of united protest. Because of the country's inherent financial stability? What stability? I ask. But for the IMF and the Arabs who keep their sterling here out of risky sentiment, this country would have become bankrupt in the autumn of 1976. How long will the EEC, America and the rest of the free world be prepared to go on supporting this industrial cripple? As long, I suggest, as we are not a threat to their own stability and, judging by our recent operations in the Common Market, that might not be too long. If the rest of the world decided to kick away our crutch, the pound would immediately collapse. Who can forget what happened in Germany in the 1930s, when a wheelbarrow full of Deutschmarks would not buy a loaf of bread?

I have spent a lot of time in Germany, and have talked at length with politicians, trade unionists and ordinary, sensible men and women, and asked what caused the rise of Nazism. The only force that could have kept Hitler out of power, I have been told time and time again, was the trade union movement. But the unions were divided among themselves, Christians fighting Communists, tradesmen of one industry fighting those from another. Hitler had moved in and established his reign of terror before they recognised the threat.

I believe the situation in Britain today is not dissimilar to that of Germany in the 1930s, except the enemies are different. Germany had suffered the enormous blow to national pride by losing the Great War. In Britain, we have lost another sort of war, on the economic front, and our national pride has similarly been crushed. There is an enemy growing in our midst, stretching the fabric of our society to its very limits, but the men and women of goodwill who should be fighting it are too busy bickering amongst themselves, that they too fail to recognise the threat.

The enemy we face is the cold-blooded takeover of our national institutions by the Extreme Left. Large slices of our industry are already in their hands, won over bloodlessly by a few tireless militants in key trade union posts. Our political structure is now under attack, and some of its bastions are being surrendered without a fight.

The takeover of the Labour party by the extremists suddenly became big news in 1976, as though it had just begun. Scottish Tory Ian Sproat put up a 'Reds-under-the-Bed' scare by naming Labour MPs he said were crypto-Communists. I think he missed the major targets. The danger to the Labour party comes, not from within Parliament, but from its constituency parties, where extremists are one by one taking over Labour's safe seats. The Parliamentary Labour party is not yet a subversive organisation, but it will be within a matter of a few years – perhaps after the next General Election – if the extremists are not fought at grass-roots level.

Even Sir Harold Wilson now sees the danger, but he chose to make his attack on Communist infiltrators within his own party after he had retired from a position which allowed him the power to fight the trend. He chose to grasp the nettle when the sting was embedded in someone else's hand. As one of his own colleagues, Mr Frank Tomney, the Labour member for Hammersmith North, chose to remark acidly: 'Sir Harold is ten years too late. Successive leaderships have failed to move.'

If the Trotskyists, the Maoists, the International Socialists or whatever they wish to call themselves ever do take control of the Labour party, revolution will only be a step away. If they ever won an election, international confidence would collapse, and along with it the pound. There would be mass unemployment, the return of the bread queue and the soup kitchen.

Tragically, the election of an Extreme Right Conservative government could lead to the same thing: confrontation with the unions, a general strike and a similar collapse of the economy.

Under whichever guise the final collapse came, the result would be the same: food supplies and transport paralysed, mob violence and the inevitable confrontation between the two wings of our society who have been pushed inexorably apart as an act of deliberate policy by guileful politicians.

Britain would become the land of the political prisoner, the censored press, the puppet Parliament, and the political police.

These are big alarm bells that I ring. I hope they will be heard, but I have grave doubts. I only wish there were someone, somewhere, in this country with greater political authority than mine who would be prepared to express these fears in a way that would make them more real through the blanket of apathy which lies over the land.

No one will argue, I should think, with the proposition that political views are more polarised today than they have ever been in living memory. Class hatreds, which I hoped the Welfare State would destroy, have in fact been exploited to cynical political ends so that they now carry the seeds of our self-destruction.

The vast majority of people in the United Kingdom, the moderates who merely demand the right to work and to spend the money they earn in the ways in which they think fit, are virtually unrepresented by our existing political system. Their votes are blankly ignored by the demands of party politics under the two-party system which seems obsessed only with its own self-perpetuation.

I had hoped that in 1974, the Liberal party would break through to become the main proponent of the voter whose views are unrepresented by the Marxist on the shop-floor or the property speculator on his expense account yacht. To the immeasurable loss of this great country, the breakthrough did not happen. I have now concluded that without major electoral reform the Liberals are on a sticky wicket. Reform is not likely within the next decade . . . and by that time it could be too late.

I was not betraying liberalism – with a small 'l' – when in November 1976 I called for the foundation of a new party of the centre to be joined, I hoped, by such political heavyweights as Edward Heath, Peter Walker, Shirley Williams, Reg Prentice, David Steel and John Pardoe.

I believe that liberalism, the respect for the individual and his point of view, his right to live his life in the way he sees fit, for social justice for the poor and the un-organised, as well as the rich and the trade-unionised, could be embodied in such a new party. Liberalism is more important to the nation than the Liberal party. If it needs a new alliance of Social Democrats with the power to force it through the extremists in Parliament, then the Liberal party must be sacrificed for the sake of its ideals. Liberalism under a new name is more important than a political party.

There is so much that must be done, but I earnestly believe only a new grouping of influence can escape the 'party badge' image to carry it out. Neither Labour nor Tories can escape the chains of their past to introduce the sweeping legislation necessary to heal our society's wounds. They are prisoners of their own power 'blocs', unable to act for fear of offending their support!

Britain must become a Federal State, with Parliaments, not only in Scotland, Wales and – if they wish, Northern Ireland – but also in the readily defined regions of England. These 'mini-Parliaments' would have almost complete autonomy over local affairs: only foreign policy, economic policy and defence would remain in the hands of a Westminster drastically reduced in size.

The present county councils would be scrapped, and the amount of government in the regions reduced to the bare minimum. The stranglehold of power in the hands of senior civil servants would be broken.

True democracy must be brought to industry, with profit-sharing schemes and workers participating in the policy decision of their factories.

Social and welfare needs must be given a fair share of regional income, and the rights of the poor and the infirm watched over by a series of Ombudsmen.

But most important of all, ordinary men and women must be allowed to pursue their lives, their work, their leisure, with the minimum of interference from State, local authority or shop-steward.

Sweeping changes in our way of life are, to me, the only alternative to the steady decline towards poverty and dictatorship. They cannot be achieved without fundamental changes in our attitudes, and can only be hastened by men and women of moderation and determination pooling their talents.

I stress, I do *not* want a moderate government – I want a *strong* government of men and women of moderate persuasion.

Where do I fit in with this grandiose scheme? In a very minor way, I am pleased to say. My five years in national politics have been long years: I seem to have packed more pain, disillusionment and personal stress into that short time than many others suffer in a lifetime. I would be happy to quit now, to settle down in my slippers in front of the television set, surrounded by my family and friends. I will not do that, for a little while at least, if I can see any hope of bringing about any realignment in British politics.

I do not flatter myself that I have the political stature to bring about major changes on my own. I could not form a new political party which would win an overall majority in the House of Commons or at least a substantial number of seats. Yet I hope I am not a single voice crying out in the wilderness.

If, however, I could persuade a few men and women of real political weight to consider these plans, to form some sort of grouping to give battle to the extremists in our society, I would pledge them all my support. If I have any single talent, it is that of being able to communicate with ordinary people. The fears which I have expressed in these last few paragraphs are, I can assure politicians of all parties, very much the fears of ordinary folk. They are anxious, confused and frightened at the direction in which this country is heading.

We owe them leadership. Is there no one at hand to give it?

WHERE NOW, LAND WITHOUT LEADERS?

Or are we to sit back and slide at best into abject poverty, at worst into totalitarianism?

People who speak their minds are always the first victims of dictatorship. I do not wish to spend my sixtieth birthday in jail!

Index

Adamson, Sir Campbell, 153–4
Adjournment Debates in House of Commons, 132, 139
Anne, HRH Princess, 223; meeting with Cyril Smith, 223–4
Asquith, Herbert Henry, 1st Earl of Oxford and, 38
Attlee, Clement Richard, 1st Earl, 10, 47, 103–4; views on proposed Egyptian move on Sudan, 103
Austick, David, 147, 151; wins Ripon by-election, 147

Barber, Anthony, 169
Beaconsfield, Benjamin Disraeli, Earl of, 143
Beaumont, Lord 'Tim', 145; finances opinion poll in Sutton and Cheam constituency, 145
Beith, Alan, 129, 149, 203, 205; conducts poll among Liberal MPs regarding resignation of Jeremy Thorpe, 205
Benn, Anthony Wedgwood, 150, 169, 228–9
Berwick-on-Tweed by-election, 148–9
Bessell, Peter, involvement in Thorpe Affair, 191–2, 197, 206–8, 210
Birch Hill Hospital, 92–3, 202–3; Bateman Centre of, 92–3
Bright, John, 10, 15–16, 38
Byers, Lord, 182, 189, 192, 197

Cabinet, decision of majority of Parliamentary programme by, 135
Callaghan, James, 133, 171, 213–17, 227; Docks Bill, 137
Campbell-Bannerman, Sir Henry, 38

Canvasser(ing), 47, 68–70, 145
Carvel, Robert, 187–8, 204
Charles, HRH Prince, 223
Chester-le-Street by-election, 148–9
Chorlton, Alderman Harold, 43, 90; proposes Alderman Smith as Mayor of Rochdale, 90; death of, 94
Churchill, Sir Winston, 47, 58, 137, 143
Coalitions, public opposition to, 175–6
Confederation of British Industry, 112, 134, 153–4
Conservative Party: undesirous of another General Election, 1974, 172; remarks concerning Liberal party's non-attendance at divisions, 181; attacks on Liberal party following Censure Debate, 1976, 216
Co-operative movement, 15–16
Corbett, Ronnie, 226–7
Corn Laws, repeal of, 1846, 15
Corruption trials, 97; involvement of Labour Councillors in, 97
Cotton industry, decline of, 16–17
Council house: society revolutionised by, 78; building programme not qualified success, 78–9; failure of programme due to inability of planning departments to visualise, 79
Councillors: role of, 67; allegations of corruption among Labour, 97, 148
Councils, need to revise basic structure of planning of houses, 79–80
Cousins, Frank, 96
Crossland, W. H., 15, 16

237

INDEX

Crossman, Richard, 100

Daily Express, 100, 121, 191, 196, 198, 204, 207
Daily Mail, 192, 199, 202–3
Daily Mirror, 120, 184, 192–3, 199, 204
Daily Telegraph, 196, 205
Daly, Len, 153
Dawson, Les, 225–6
Day, Robin, 224; character of, 224–5
Disraeli, Benjamin, *see* Beaconsfield, Benjamin Disraeli, Earl of
Divisions in House of Commons, procedure for, 128

Early Day Motion, 135
Electoral system, 'rigging' of British, 159
Elizabeth II, Queen, 221–2; important constitutional functions of, 170–1
Evening Standard, 187, 204

Fields, Gracie, 84, 95
Fields, Squadron Leader Sidney, 111
Foot, Michael, 169, 228
Fothergill & Harvey, Messrs, 49–51
Freud, Clement, 129, 147, 179; wins Isle of Ely by-election, 147
Frost, David, 160

Gaitskell, Hugh, 96
Gale, Frank, 106–7
General Elections: 1945, 47; 1950, 61; 1974, 154, 158, 177, 178
George-Brown, Lord, 137–8; criticism of Whips, 137
Gill, Frank, 58–9
Gladstone, William Ewart, 10, 38, 55, 143
Goodman, Lord, 189, 206
Gormley, Joe, 153–4
Great Censure Motion, 215; engineered by Liberal party, 215–16
'Great Debates', 132, 134; example of, 134

Grimond, Jo, 8, 146, 200–1: supports all-out coalition, 163; remarks concerning Thorpe Affair, 200–1
Guardian, The, 101

Hailsham, Douglas Hogg, 1st Viscount, 137; criticism of Whips, 137
Halstead, Mrs, 25–6
Hansard, 134
Harrison, Geoff, 109, 111, 113
Hartnell, Sir Norman, 146
Harvey, Alec, 51
Harvey, Charles, 44, 47, 49
Healey, Denis, 1; Finance Bill, 1976, 1
Heath, Edward, 6, 140, 145, 149, 150, 152, 159–60, 169, 213, 230, 233: industrial crisis during administration, 150–4; opposition to miners' pay claim, 152; calls General Election, 154; shyness of, 160; distrust of compromise, 160; hostility between H. and Sir Harold Wilson, 161; offers Liberal party coalition, 163; letter to Jeremy Thorpe quoted, 164–6; resigns as Prime Minister, 168
Heseltine, Michael, 215, 228
Hewitt, Reg, 63
Holden, John, 7–8
Holmes, David, 199, 210; alleged payment of money to Norman Scott by, 199–200
Hooson, Emlyn, 1–2, 162, 186, 219: requests Jeremy Thorpe to answer allegations in Affair, 195; hands out document concerning Liberal party's position in Thorpe Affair, 196–8
House of Commons, 1: taking seat in, 7–8; Members' Entrance, 123–4; snobbery of, 125; Visitors' Gallery, procedure for tickets for, 127; Divisions in, procedure for, 128; cynical hypocrisy of, 129; impotence of as political force, 134
Hoyle, Sam, butcher, 22–3

INDEX

Hughes, Cledwyn, 215

International Labour Organisation, 63
International Socialists, 231
Isle of Ely by-election, 147

Jenkins, Roy, 171, 186, 228
Johnston, Russell, 162
Jones, Trevor, 144

Kaufman, Alfred, 65
Keigwin, Tim, 192

Labour party: becoming monolith, 96–7, 99; vulnerable to 'safe seat' manipulation, 97; reaction of Left wing to joint Lab–Lib consultations regarding Queen's Speech, 217–18; takeover of by extremists, 231
Lambton, Lord, 148–9; involvement in immoral association, 148–9
Leader of Opposition, 135, 140
Lennox, Rear Admiral Sir Alexander, 127–8
Liberal party: disastrous results for in General Election, 1950, 62–3; leadership involvement in miners' pay claim, 1974, 152–4; 1974 election campaign policy, 156–7; favouring proportional representation, 157; votes polled in 1974 General Election, 158; views of sought regarding offer of coalition made by Edward Heath, 163–6; anti-coalition in, 166–7; puts down amendment to Queen's Speech, 170; amendment not called, 171; conference in Brighton, 174–5; job of Chief Whip in, 178; aim to persuade industrial companies to hold back financial contributions to Tories, 183; situation in Thorpe Affair, 196–8; disintegration of, 201; breakthrough not achieved in 1974, 232–3
Lloyd George, David, 1st Earl, 143

Lloyd of Kilgerran, Lord, 162–3
Lloyd, Selwyn, 9, 127, 171
'Lobby correspondent' tradition, criticism of, 126
London and County Bank: collapse of, 151, 184; Department of Trade report on, 187
Lord, Frank, 43
Lubbock, Eric, 147

Macmillan, Maurice, 173
Maoists, 231
Marshalsea Brothers, 110–11
Mayhew, Christopher, 174–5
Mayor: duties of, 85–6; election of, 86–7
'Mayor Making', 72, 86–7; ceremony, 87, 89–90
McCann, Jack, 4, 6, 8, 10–11, 116, 118; death of, 6, 8, 117
McFadyean, Sir Andrew, 55–6
McGahey, Mike, 153
Member of Parliament: swearing in ceremony of, 9–10; 'lobby-fodder' mentality of, 14; attend Westminster to represent party interests not people, 138
Milne, Eddie, 138, 149
Moore, Kenneth, 86–7

National Executive of the Young Liberals, 54
National Front party, 119, 216
National Union of Mineworkers, 153–4
Nationalisation, 57–8
Nationalism, 166
New Palace Yard, Westminster, origins of, 123
Nimmo, Derek, 146
Nixon, Richard, 211, 223
North, Alf, 44–5
North-West Federation of Young Liberals, 54
Nureyev, Rudolf, 226

Operative Spinners, 20
Orwell, George, 97, 230; works, *Animal Farm*, 97q., *1984*, 230q.

INDEX

Pairing system, 131–2
Pardoe, John, 9, 153, 173, 180, 205, 219–21, 233: as candidate for leadership of Liberal party, 219; character, 220
Parker, Alderman Clifford, 90–1; seconder of motion for election of Alderman Smith as Mayor of Rochdale, 90
Parliament: large part in life of played by tradition, 12; facilities for members and staff at, 128; hypocrisy of procedure in, 129
Parliamentary debates: paucity of members at, 13; a sham, 130
Parsons, Nicholas, 146
Payne, Dr H. F. W. (Docker), Headmaster, 37–8, 83
Philip, HRH Prince, Duke of Edinburgh, 222
Pinney, Aza, 120
Pitt, William, 143
Power, as principle of politics, 64
Prentice, Reg, 138, 233
Prescott, John, 125–6
Press, as destroyer of Jeremy Thorpe's career, 210–11
Press relations, 120; progress made by Liberal party in field of, 183
Private Member's Bill, 139, 141: tragedy of, 141–2; stopping, 142; death of, 142
Privilege, laws of, 189
'Professionalism', growth of in local government work, 76

Queen's Speech, 135, 170, 182, 217; debate on, 11
Questions to Prime Minister, 139–40, 204; procedure in addressing, 139

Racialism, 119
Radicals, the, 175
Ratcliffe, Fred, 106, 108–9
Rates, payers not receiving adequate service in respect of, 74–5
Rhodes, Hervey, 103–4; difference with Prime Minister over question of Egyptian move on Sudan, 103
Ripon by-election, 147
Rochdale, 15; Town Hall, 15–16; Open Air School, 27–8; educational system abolishes eleven-plus examinations, 81–2; schools system third most efficient in England and Wales, 82
Rochdale Childer charity, 12
Rochdale Corporation Club, 72
Rochdale League of Liberals, 54
Rochdale Observer, 5, 17, 65, 66, 70, 73, 90, 102
Rochdale Society of Equitable Pioneers, 16
Rochdale Trades and Labour Council, 68, 99; an unusual organisation, 99
Rochdale Youth Music Festival, 223
Rothwell, Fred, 91; recollections of Cyril Smith's Mayoral term of office, 91–5

'Safe seats', 97
Savile, Jimmy, 225–6
Scarr, Dr, 27, 52–3
Scott, Norman, 185–93, 195, 197, 199, 200, 206–8: alleges homosexual affair with Jeremy Thorpe, 185–6, 188; further claims made against Jeremy Thorpe, 191; alleged payment of money paid to, 192, 199
Secombe, Harry, 226
Shawfield school, Rochdale, 8
Sheard, John, 126
Shore, Peter, 169
Short, Edward, 180–1
Silverman, Sidney, 141
Sinclair, Sir Archibald, *see* Thurso, Archibald Sinclair, Viscount
Smith, Cyril: illegitimacy of, 2, 18; as Mayor of Rochdale, 2, 3, 86; no plans to become MP, 2; owner of engineering factory, 2; beginnings of political career, 3; as executive member of Young Liberals, 3;

INDEX

Smith, Cyril—*contd*
joins Labour party, 3; rejoins Liberal party, 1968, 3–4; agrees to stand as Parliamentary candidate in 1970, 4; Chairman of Rochdale Labour party, 4; first time as loser of election, 1970, 5–6; obesity problem of, 5, 30–2; winner of by-election, 1972, 6; high spots in life, 6–7; religion, 9; makes Maiden Speech in Parliament, 11–12; founder of Rochdale Childer charity, 12; birth, 18; life at Falinge Road, Rochdale, 20–3; conditions in house, 21–2; schooldays, 24; as monitor at school, 24; Christmas at home detailed, 24–5; contracts nephritis, 27; moved to Rochdale Open Air School, 27–8; passes eleven-plus examination, 28; enters Rochdale Municipal High School, 29; life at school, 31; queries 'system', 33–5; involvement with Unitarians, 35–6; chairman of Chapel Trustees, 36; love of singing, and recognition of ability of, 37; joins Debating Society, 37–8; total immersion in modern history, 38; innate distrust of Tory party motives, 39; credits gained in School Certificate, 39; odd jobs carried out, 39–41; holidaying at Cleveleys, 41; motives for leaving school, 42; as clerk in Rochdale Inland Revenue offices, 42; determination to be involved in politics, 42–3; takes active part in first election campaign, 43–4, 46; decides to go into politics, 45; realisations of electioneering campaign, 46–7; unemployed, 48; as office boy in mill, 49; elected as office-staff representative on works council, 50; enters Carrol Levis Discoveries Show, 50; accused of inciting works to rebellion, 51; move of family to Emma Street, Rochdale, 52; as student teacher at training college, 52; fails medical examination for teaching post, 53; reasons for rejection, 53; chairman of Rochdale League of Liberals, 54; forms youth 'Parliament', 54; executive member of North-west Federation of Young Liberals, 54; a member of National Executive of Young Liberals, 54–5; Young Liberals representative of Liberal party's National Council, 54–5; breakfast with Sir Andrew McFadyean, 55–6; possesses emotional belief workers have right to bigger say in running of own industries, 56–7; deep interest in problem of working men, 57; abhorrence of nationalisation, 57–8; helps sway Liberals towards policy of worker-participation, 58; arrival at first Liberal party Annual Conference, 58–9; makes first conference speech, 59; appointed fulltime Liberal agent for Stockport, 59–60; concern post-war Liberals becoming anti-Labour group, 60–1; first introduction to realities of party politics, 61–2; carries great bias favouring worker-participation, 62, 64; resignation from Liberal party accepted, 63; labelled turncoat, 64, 66; speaks at meeting in support of Labour party candidate, 65; seeks membership of Labour party, 65–6; membership of Labour party confirmed, 66; asked to stand for council, 68; realities of canvassing, 68–70; wins municipal election seat for Falinge Ward, 70; as councillor, 71; experiences greatest sense of victory, 71; duties as councillor, 72; complains about Corporation salaries, 73; proposes reduction in senior officials' salaries, 73–4; elected chairman of Rochdale Establishment Committee,

Smith, Cyril—*contd*
74; observations on degree of involvement of Chairman in council matters, 75–6; valuable experience gained in Establishment Committee workings, 77; voted Chairman of Estates Committee, 77; publicly promises to build two thousand council houses in coming two years, 77; education as chief concern in local government career, 80; elected to Education Committee, 80; as chairman of Education Committee, 80; opposition to eleven-plus examination system, 80–1; opposed to grammar schools, 81; in favour of comprehensive schools, 81; initiates programme to discuss implementation of comprehensive schools system, 82; success of comprehensive school efforts, 82–3; ambition to become Mayor, 84; propensity for fund-raising activities, 92, 106; receives MBE, 94; invites voters from Falinge Ward to meet him, 95; high expenditure of finance during mayoral year, 96; chairman of Corporation, 99; prices 'freeze' unacceptable, 100; resigns membership of Labour party, 100; retains many Corporation offices, 101; sackings from Committees, 101; sacked from Boards of Governors of twenty-three schools, 101; great believer in ambition, 102; urgency for security of sound financial foundation, 102; becomes agent to Labour MP, 103; purchases newsagent's shop, 105; interest in Rochdale AFC, 106; offered fulltime job as fund-raiser for Rochdale AFC, 106; introduces wrestling bouts, 107; introduction of bingo to Rochdale, 107; offered job in spring factory, 108; promoted to production controller in spring factory, 108; as commercial traveller in own company, 109–10; speech stating Liberals in favour of trade unions taking responsible place in industry, 112; policy mooted for maintaining high shop-floor morale, 112; belief in profit-sharing philosophy, 113; fringe-benefits offered, 113; rejoins Liberal party, 114; asked to fight 1970 General Election, 115; still Chairman of Rochdale Education Committee, 115; asked to stand in Rochdale by-election, 116; declines offer to fight next election, 116; decides to fight by-election, 118; views on racialism, 119; principles of campaign, 120; wins election, 122; declared MP for Rochdale, 122; asked views on working conditions at Westminster on *Nationwide*, 125; critical of many traditions, 126; considers MPs could do more to earn pay, 131–2; avers Britain governed by Cabinet not Parliament, 133; queries useful purpose of MP, 138; first brush with Jeremy Thorpe, 149–51; enjoys electioneering, 145; intensive electioneering campaign, 155; wins Rochdale election, 1974, 157; opinion of Sir Harold Wilson, 160–1; analysis of Jeremy Thorpe's character, 161; in favour of government of national unity, 161; accusations regarding Sir Harold Wilson's appointment as Prime Minister, 168; accuses Speaker of inexcusable Parliamentary bias, 171; apology rendered to Speaker, 172; accuses Sir Harold Wilson of blatant bribery of British voter, 172, 175; proposes Liberal party should be more abrasive, 172–3; suggests electioneering barn-storming tour, 173; states Labour party fraud, 175–6; becomes Chief Whip of

Smith, Cyril—*contd*
Liberal party, 177, 180; estrangement with Jeremy Thorpe, 177; conditions stated before acceptance of Chief Whip post, 180; finance raised to appoint fulltime liaison officer, 181; meets with resistance from own party regarding lack of impact on voting public, 182; plan to publicise 'Electoral Reform', 182–3; attitude towards Thorpe Affair, 188–96; discusses possibility of resignation as Chief Whip, 202, 205; sudden illness, 202; in hospital, 202; tenders resignation as Chief Whip, 206; feelings after resignation, 206; reactions to Jeremy Thorpe's resignation, 209; queries motives of press in involvement in Thorpe Affair, 210–12; motives for Liberal party's decision to support Government, 213; reasons for supporting Mr Callaghan, 216–17; states Britain must combat Left-wing elements of Labour party, 217; need for realignment of moderate centre of politics, 217; awareness when Chief Whip of split between Parliamentary Liberals and party supporters, 218; seeks mutually acceptable method of selecting Liberal party leader, 219; reasons for supporting John Pardoe's candidature as Liberal leader, 219; attitude towards David Steel, 220; disappointment at defeat of John Pardoe, 220–1; accepts minor post in party, 221; contacts with members of Royal Family, 221; meeting with Queen Elizabeth, 221–2; regard for Royal Family, 222–3; meeting with Princess Anne, 223–4; enjoys appearing on TV, 224; takes every available opportunity to appear before public, 225–6; fascinated by show-business people, 226; views on lowering standards of repartee in House of Commons, 227; opinion of James Callaghan, 227–8; opinion of Margaret Thatcher, 228; opinion of Michael Foot, 228; opinion of William Whitelaw, 228; opinion of Roy Jenkins, 228; opinion of Michael Heseltine, 228; opinion of Shirley Williams, 228; opinion of Anthony Wedgwood Benn, 228–9; fears for future of Britain, 229; asserts probability of revolution in Britain, 229–30; fears enemy in Britain extreme Left, 231; anxiety of extreme Right Conservative government elected and reactions, 232; states class hatreds exploited, 232; majority of public unrepresented by present political system, 232; calls for founding of new centre party, 233; belief liberalism possible embodiment in new party, 233; Britain must become Federal State, 233; scrapping of present county councils, 233; proposes sweeping changes in way of life as alternative to dictatorship, 234; would support groups to oppose extremism, 234

Smith, Eunice, sister of Cyril, 7, 18, 21, 42, 202

Smith, Eva, mother, 7, 18: as housemaid, 18–19; total devotion to family by, 19; ensures plentiful supply of food for family, 22; agrees to become Mayoress, 88

Smith, Norman, brother of Cyril, 7, 18, 21, 110, 202

Smith, Sarah, grandmother, 20–1; industriousness of, 20; death, 52

Smith's Springs company, 7, 89: opening of, 88–9, 109; employment of seventy people, 111

Smith, T. Dan, 98, 148; non-involvement by Cyril Smith in corruption charges concerning, 98

INDEX

Social Contract, Stage Three, 214
South African Connection, 204
Speed, Doris, 226
Spiller, John, 118–20
Spotland Primary School, 24, 28
Sproat, Ian, 231
Standring, James, 20
Steel, David, 8, 9, 116, 128, 129, 141, 162–3, 171, 174, 178, 186, 197, 218–21, 233: resigns as Chief Whip of Liberal party, 178; offered Chairmanship of Race Relations Board, 201; decision to ally with Labour party, 213; desires realignment of power, 214; as leader of Liberal party, 216, 218; character, 220
Stetchford by-election, 216
Stockport Liberal Association, 63
Stonehouse, John, 120, 174–5
Sun, The, 170, 209
Sunday Times, 207–8
Sutcliffe, Mrs, Headmistress, 25
Sutton and Cheam by-election, 145–6

Table Office, House of Commons, 139–40
Taverne, Dick, 138
Telephone talk-in, 146
Ten Minute Rule Bill, 139, 140: First Reading, 140; Second Reading, 140
Terry, Walter, 209–10; states Liberal party cause of Jeremy Thorpe's downfall, 209–10
Thatcher, Mrs Margaret, 132, 160, 213–16, 220
Thomas, George, 192
Thorpe, Jeremy, 2, 6, 8, 12, 116, 117, 118–19, 146, 149–54, 158: 'Affair', 1, 177, 188–212, 215, 218–19, 221; enormous help given to Cyril Smith by, 121; biggest asset, 121; derogatory remarks about Cyril Smith, 151; resigns directorships in companies, 151, 184; becomes figure of national importance, 159; meeting with Edward Heath, 162; letter to Edward Heath, 167; press statement issued, 168; tours by hovercraft in election campaign, 174; opposition to Cyril Smith as Chief Whip of Liberal party, 177; delay in appointing Chief Whip, 178–80; background to career, 184; agrees to resign, 201; annoyance over reports of possible resignation by Cyril Smith, 203–4; resignation, 208
Thurso, Archibald Sinclair, Viscount, 44
Tillotson, Alan, 104–5; advances finances to Cyril Smith, 104
Times, The, 191
Tomney, Frank, 231
Tope, Graham, 145–6; wins Sutton and Cheam by-election, 147
Trade unions: gravity of among rank-and-file of council workers, 76; could have kept Hitler out of power, 230–1
Trades Union Congress, 1, 77, 134, 151
Transport and General Workers' Union, 112
Trotskyists, 231
Trudeau, M. Pierre, 226
Turner Brothers, Messrs, 48, 89; rejects Cyril Smith's application for job, 48
Turner, Sir Samuel, 89
Two-party system, 130, 133, 134, 217; as serious fault, 13

Unitarians, 35, 38; love of singing, 36

Van Straubenzee, William, 181

Wainwright, Richard, 129, 173, 182, 184–5, 201, 208
Walker, Peter, 233
Watergate scandal, 1, 210–11, 223
Weatherill, Bernard, 181–2
Westminster, Palace of, 1, 9, 125
Whip(s), 13: rigidity of system, 14; Party, 130; power wielded by,

INDEX

Whip(s)—*contd*
136; 'three-line', 136–7; 'two-line', 136; 'single-line', 136; advisers of national organisers, 138
Whitelaw, William, 171
Wigoder, Lord, 189–90
Wild, Hilda, 7; Sunday school superintendent, 7
William Rufus, King, 123
Williams, Mrs Shirley, 228, 233
Wilson, Sir Harold, 10, 140, 150, 159–60, 206, 226: personal hostility with Edward Heath, 161; as Prime Minister, 168; announcement of Cabinet, 169; calls General Election, 174–5; forces through amendments to amendments, 178; states outside influences obtaining in Thorpe Affair, 193–5; informs House of Commons South Africa involved in Thorpe Affair, 203–4; recognised danger of Communist infiltration in Labour party, 231
Wingfield, Margaret, 201
Winstanley, Dr Michael, 6, 117
Worker-participation, 58, 61–2

Young Liberals, 3, 175; opposition to coalition among militant, 175